Gary Rosenzweig

SAMS

Teach Yourself Flash™ MX ActionScript in 24 Hours

SAMS
201 West 103rd St., Indianapolis, Indiana, 46290 USA

Sams Teach Yourself Flash™ MX ActionScript in 24 Hours

International Standard Book Number: 0-672-32385-0

Library of Congress Catalog Card Number: 2002100939

Printed in the United States of America

First Printing: May 2002

05 04 03 02 4 3 2 1

Trademarks

All terms mentioned in this book that are known to be trademarks or service marks have been appropriately capitalized. Sams Publishing cannot attest to the accuracy of this information. Use of a term in this book should not be regarded as affecting the validity of any trademark or service mark.

Warning and Disclaimer

Every effort has been made to make this book as complete and as accurate as possible, but no warranty or fitness is implied. The information provided is on an "as is" basis.

Acquisitions Editor
Betsy Brown

Development Editor
Damon E. Jordan

Managing Editor
Charlotte Clapp

Project Editor
George E. Nedeff

Copy Editor
Geneil Breeze

Indexer
Becky Hornyak

Proofreader
Abby VanHuss

Technical Editor
Lynn Baus

Team Coordinator
Amy Patton

Multimedia Developer
Dan Scherf

Interior Designer
Gary Adair

Cover Designer
Aren Howell

Page Layout
Michelle Mitchell
Cheryl Lynch

Contents at a Glance

Contents

About the Author

Gary Rosenzweig started programming in the early '80s on TRS-80 and Apple computers. After getting a degree in computer science from Drexel University, he started using the Flash-like tools Hypercard and Macromedia Director to create multimedia applications.

After getting a degree in journalism and mass communication from the University of North Carolina at Chapel Hill, Rosenzweig began to work with Macromedia Director professionally and eventually wrote six books about Director. His most recent is *Special Edition Using Director 8.5* from Que publishing.

In 1995, Rosenzweig started CleverMedia, a game development company that specializes in Shockwave games. CleverMedia now has four game sites, including `http://clevermedia.com/` and `http://flasharcade.com/`. The latter is a site composed completely of Flash games, some dating back to Flash 2.

Rosenzweig also speaks at Macromedia User Conferences, the Game Developers Conference, and other events. In his spare time, he reads a lot of classic science fiction, watches independent films, and listens to alternative rock music. He lives in Denver, Colorado, with his wife, Debby; dog, Natasha; and daughter, Lucy. You can find out more and contact him through his Web site `http://www.garyrosenzweig.com/`.

Dedication

This book is dedicated to my beautiful and wonderful wife, Debby.
Without her love and support, I would never be able to write these books.

Acknowledgments

I want to thank my team at CleverMedia: William Follett, Brian Robbins, and Jay Shaffer.

I couldn't have written this book without the help of Jeremy Clark, Francis Cheng, and the rest of the Macromedia Flash team.

Thanks to my family, Jacqueline, Jerry, and Larry Rosenzweig, and Anne, Tage, and Andrea Thomsen.

Thanks to all the people at Sams who worked on this book: Betsy Brown, Damon Jordan, George Nedeff, and Jeff Schultz.

Tell Us What You Think!

As the reader of this book, *you* are our most important critic and commentator. We value your opinion and want to know what we're doing right, what we could do better, what areas you'd like to see us publish in, and any other words of wisdom you're willing to pass our way.

You can email or write me directly to let me know what you did or didn't like about this book—as well as what we can do to make our books stronger.

Please note that I cannot help you with technical problems related to the topic of this book, and that due to the high volume of mail I receive, I might not be able to reply to every message.

When you write, please be sure to include this book's title and author as well as your name and phone or fax number. I will carefully review your comments and share them with the author and editors who worked on the book.

Fax: 317-581-4770

Email: `graphics@samspublishing.com`

Mail: Mark Taber
Associate Publisher
Sams Publishing
201 West 103rd Street
Indianapolis, IN 46290 USA

Introduction

ActionScript is the powerful programming language inside Macromedia Flash. Learning ActionScript is your key to taking your Flash movies to the next level. Fortunately, learning ActionScript is easy.

This book teaches you how to write programs in ActionScript. It is divided into 24 short lessons. Each lesson builds on the previous ones. By the time you are finished with this book, you will be able to use ActionScript to make your movies completely interactive.

The *Sams Teach Yourself in 24 Hours* books are designed to teach the fundamentals of a topic from the ground up even if you have little or no experience in the topic. The books are for readers who want to learn the subject quickly. They use the tutorial method with plenty of examples and step-by-step instructions.

Sams Teach Yourself Flash MX ActionScript in 24 Hours quickly introduces you to the fundamentals of ActionScript. You don't need to know anything about ActionScript beforehand, but you should already know the basics of Flash drawing and animation. Most lessons include tasks that take you through building a small Flash movie that demonstrates a concept. By reading the material, you will learn ActionScript, and doing the tasks will reinforce what you have learned.

Who Should Read This Book

This book is for ActionScript beginners. Many people fit into this category. For instance, you could be an animator who has worked with Flash for a while but has not yet used ActionScript to add interactivity. Or, you could be someone who has not yet used Flash, but you know that you will want to add interactivity to your movies right away.

What You Should Already Know

This book teaches ActionScript. It does not teach Flash. ActionScript is the programming language inside Flash. This means that you should already be familiar with the Flash drawing tools, timeline, movie publishing, and symbols. This describes many Flash illustrators and animators.

If you are totally new to Flash, you should first take the time to learn Flash basics. Flash MX comes with a walk-through tutorial that explains everything you need to know. Run through that tutorial before starting to read this book. You may also want to glance through the user manuals, or try *Sams Teach Yourself Flash in 24 Hours* for greater detail.

What You Will Learn

This book assumes that you have never used a programming language before. Hour 3, "Learning to Program," explains the basic concepts that you need to know. The other lessons will add more concepts as they are introduced.

If you already know a programming language, this book will help you translate what you already know into ActionScript.

Although this book contains many examples of real Flash movies, it is not a complete book of examples of everything possible with ActionScript. If you have an idea of what you want to do with Flash, chances are you will not find that exact movie here. Instead, you will find examples that teach the fundamentals, which will later help you create your specific idea.

This book is about Flash MX, also known as Flash 6. You will need to have Flash MX to use the examples. Earlier versions of Flash will not be able to open any of the example movies. In addition, some of the commands I will teach did not exist in Flash 5 and earlier. Please do not try to use this book with any version of Flash previous to Flash MX.

Is This Book Right for You?

So you are trying to decide whether this book is the one you are looking for. Take a look through the table of contents. It gives you a good idea of what the book covers.

This is not a reference book. It does not go into every command and function of ActionScript. Instead, it teaches you the concepts and commands that will take you from beginner to intermediate skill. From there, you can begin to investigate on your own and learn new commands and techniques.

Here is a list of reasons why this book might fit your needs:

- You want to learn ActionScript quickly.
- You have tried to learn ActionScript before, but couldn't grasp some concepts.
- You have learned some ActionScript on your own, but feel that there is much more to learn.
- You don't care so much about programming, but need to add interactivity to your movies.
- You have used ActionScript tutorials online, but need a complete set of tutorials to round out your ActionScript knowledge.

How This Book Is Organized

This book is arranged in a linear fashion, with concepts and tasks getting more complex as you move along. If you are already familiar with programming, for instance, you could skip Hour 3. If you have already dabbled in ActionScript for a while, you might want to skip Hour 1, "Your First Look at ActionScript;" Hour 2, "Using the Script Editing Window;" and Hour 4, "Writing Code In Flash."

Each lesson in this book builds on the concepts learned in earlier lessons. As you advance, your knowledge will get both deeper and broader.

Although you can skip directly to a task in a lesson that fits your immediate need, you may find that you won't understand what you are reading because you missed something covered earlier. Some readers are able to use books in this way, whereas others need to take it step-by-step.

Conventions

The lessons all include a summary at the end. If you already know a bit of ActionScript, you can use these summaries to determine whether the lesson is critical for you. Otherwise, the summary is a great way to review what you have learned.

After the summary comes a set of questions and answers. These cover some questions that you may have after reading the lesson. Usually, the questions and answers take what you have learned to the next level by giving you ideas about how to expand on what you have learned.

Each lesson also includes a workshop. This is a set of four questions that test your knowledge of what you just read. I usually take this opportunity to make sure that you understand key points. Missing one of the quiz questions means that you should probably go back and review that part of the lesson. Otherwise, you may find that you don't know all you need to know to use that concept in that lesson.

Inside each lesson are tips, notes, cautions, and coffee breaks. A tip is a suggestion that will save you time and effort, or give you an idea about how to use what you have learned. A note is a piece of information that gives you a little more insight into a concept. A caution explains a typical pitfall that people fall into when first using the technique. A coffee break is an aside that gives you an interesting, but unimportant, piece of information about the topic.

Almost all the lessons in this book provide one or more tasks. You can follow along with the step-by-step instructions to use what you have learned to build a Flash movie. If you feel you understand the concept completely, you can simply follow along with the tasks. If you want to really reinforce what you have learned, you should do each step of the task.

Each task results in a Flash movie. You can find these movies on the book's CD-ROM. Each lesson has its own folder. The names of all example movies are mentioned in the book, but you can also usually find them by matching the concept with the file name.

Additional Information

After you complete this book, you may want to continue your ActionScript education. There are plenty of commands to learn, and programmers are always developing new and interesting techniques. Many times, programmers take Flash beyond what Macromedia even thought possible. It is a good idea to keep up with current ActionScript tricks and techniques.

The best way to do this is online. There are dozens of active Flash Web sites and mailing lists. Every Flash programmer should belong to at least one list and check out at least one site on a regular basis.

I have set up a site called Developer Dispatch at `http://www.developerdispatch.com`. On this site, you will find a long list of other Flash sites and mailing lists. Developer Dispatch also has a Flash message board that you can use to talk with other developers.

I have also written another book called *Flash ActionScript for Fun and Games*. That book goes further than this one with many complex game examples and will be especially useful to you if you are learning ActionScript to build games.

If you want to check for updated CD-ROM files or read about my games book, go to my Web site: `http://www.garyrosenzweig.com`. You can also find out how to contact me and receive information about future books.

PART I

Getting Started with ActionScript

Hour

HOUR 1

Your First Look at ActionScript

ActionScript is the programming language built into Macromedia Flash. It is like other programming languages, such as JavaScript, Java, and C++. However, you don't need to know any other programming languages to learn ActionScript.

To start learning ActionScript, let's first begin by looking at exactly what ActionScript is, what it can do, and how it relates to the rest of Flash MX.

In this hour, you will:

- Find out where ActionScript came from
- Get a glimpse of what an ActionScript program looks like
- Learn what sort of things ActionScript can do
- See where to put ActionScript programs

What Scripts Are

ActionScript is a *programming language*. A programming language is a list of instructions that tell a computer what to do. A computer will obey these instructions exactly as they are stated.

Little Programs Inside Flash

NEW TERM A list of instructions for the computer is called a *program*. Another name for a program is a *script*. From now on, I'll refer to these lists of instructions as *scripts*.

A program or script exists inside an environment. In the case of ActionScript, that environment is the Flash movie. A script can tell the Flash movie what to do. In some cases, a script can tell other things, such as the user's Web browser or computer's operating system, what to do. But for the most part, scripts can control only what's inside the Flash movie.

Scripts can be as small as one line, or as long as thousands of lines. They can be placed in one central part of the Flash movie or sprinkled throughout the Flash movie. Some people will refer to an entire Flash movie that uses scripts as a program, whereas other people will refer to each individual script in the movie as a program. Both definitions are technically true because a single program can be defined as many smaller programs. It is just a matter of semantics.

For the most part, scripts are little programs placed on various frames and elements inside Flash movies. Later in this hour, we'll examine exactly where in the Flash movie these programs can be placed.

You may already be familiar with some programming languages. JavaScript is the language understood by most Web browsers and is commonly used to make Web pages interactive. Internet Explorer understands JavaScript and a similar language called VBScript. HTML (Hypertext Markup Language) is an unusual programming language that you might be familiar with. It issues a series of instructions to the Web browser about how to display text and images.

If you have used Macromedia Director before, you may have written some programs with Lingo, its programming language. Even though Director and Flash have many similarities, Lingo and ActionScript are very different languages.

In high school or college, you may have taken a course in programming. Many people are taught BASIC (Beginners All-Purpose Instruction Code), Pascal, or even COBOL.

With the exception of HTML, all the languages mentioned use similar constructs: loops, conditions, variables, and so on. You'll be able to apply these skills to ActionScript as soon as you know the specific syntax that ActionScript uses. However, if you have never learned a programming language before, don't worry. I'll show you everything you need to know in the upcoming hours.

Origins of ActionScript

So where does ActionScript come from? It actually has its roots in many different places. Let's take a moment to learn about where computer languages came from.

When digital computers were first created, the only way to program them was in their native language: binary code. This is simply a list of 1's and 0's. When different groups of 1's and 0's are combined and fed into a computer, it can trigger the computer to behave in different ways. A long program written this way might perform a simple task such as adding two numbers together.

Instead of rewriting binary code every time someone wanted to add two numbers together, this code was written in such a way that it could add together *any* two numbers. Instead of writing the code over again, you could simply reuse the code, but feed it different numbers each time. Little functions like this were soon created to handle all sorts of tasks such as addition, subtraction, multiplication, comparisons, looping, and so on. Pretty soon, instead of writing in binary code, you could use these prewritten functions to perform almost any task.

Today's modern computer languages are much easier to understand and use than binary code and its immediate successors. For one thing, modern computer languages look like English. Words such as "go," "for," "begin," and "if" are used, as well as operators such as +, -, and =.

Some computer languages, such as BASIC, Pascal, and Macromedia Director's Lingo, can almost be read like English sentences. They are easy to learn and understand. Other languages, such as C and Fortran, look very technical. They are more powerful in the hands of experienced programmers. More recent languages form a balance between these two sides. Languages such as C++, Java, and JavaScript are readable, yet powerful. ActionScript is similar to these recent languages.

Flash follows the standard created by the ECMA (European Computer Manufacturers Association). ActionScript is actually similar to ECMAScript, a language developed by that organization. JavaScript also attempts to follow this standard. So rather than ActionScript being based on JavaScript, as many people think, both ActionScript and JavaScript are based on a common ancestor.

Flash always had some capability for interactivity. The earliest versions could use navigation controls and buttons with some simple scripted instructions. But basically, Flash was a vector-based animation tool. It caught on like wildfire because of the needs of Web site designers. They needed a tool to be able to create graphically intense, but low bandwidth sites. Because vector shapes are defined by lines, curves, and fills rather than pixels, they make much smaller files than do bitmap images. Thus, Flash allowed designers to create nice Web pages without leaving out the people using slow modems.

Even though Flash was meant primarily for illustration and animation, there was a need for some scripting. For instance, designers wanted buttons that allow the user to navigate to another Web page.

When Flash first appeared, it was actually called FutureSplash. Later on, it was bought by Macromedia, renamed, and added to Macromedia's product line.

Scripting in early versions of Flash was simple. It wasn't until Flash 4 that standard programming structures, such as conditional statements and loops, were added. But Flash scripting was still done with pull-down menus and fill-in-the-blank forms. It could barely be considered a programming language.

Real ActionScript was born with Flash 5. Programmers could type their programs directly and attach them to the elements of the Flash movie. Flash MX expands ActionScript even further. ActionScript now provides more than 300 commands, functions, operators, and constructs. It is truly a full-featured programming language.

What Scripts Look Like

Scripts are basically English words with mathematical symbols and punctuation. Here is an example:

```
on (press) {
    gotoAndPlay ("my frame");
}
```

You can decipher what this code does by examining the key words in it. The word "press" suggests that the user is clicking on something, in this case a button. The long word on the next line can be read "go to and play" and suggests that the script is commanding Flash to go to a specific point in the movie and play the movie from that point on.

This script demonstrates that ActionScript can control the flow of a Flash movie. We'll look at the script shown previously in more detail later on. Before we go further, let's examine what other powers ActionScript can have over the Flash movie.

What Scripts Can Do

A Flash movie consists of scenes. Each scene has a timeline. Each timeline starts with frame 1 and continues from there. The natural state of a Flash movie is to move forward at a constant rate from scene 1, frame 1, to the end of scene 1 and then on to scene 2 and so on. You can set a movie to play through all the frames of all the scenes and stop. Or, you can set the movie to loop.

The primary purpose of ActionScript is to change this linear behavior. A script can stop a movie on a certain frame, loop back to a previous frame, or even give the user control of what frame is shown next. ActionScript can be used to make a movie completely break away from the passive linear mode of standard Flash movies.

But that's not all that ActionScript can do. It can also turn a Flash movie from an animation into an interactive computer program. Let's look at some of the basic functions that ActionScript can perform.

- **Animation** You don't need ActionScript to create animation in Flash. But scripting can help to create some complex animation. For instance, a ball can bounce around the screen in a seemingly endless path with ActionScript. It can even obey the laws of physics, being pulled down by gravity. If you were to animate such a thing without ActionScript, you might need thousands of frames. But a script can do it in one frame.
- **Navigation** Instead of the movie moving forward at a constant pace, you can pause it at a menu of choice and let the user decide where to go next.
- **User Input** You can ask the user questions and use that information in the movie or send it to a server. A Flash movie with some ActionScript can be a better way to do a Web form. Or, the movie itself can use the information to customize the user's experience.
- **Get Data** A script can interact with the server in the opposite direction, too. You can get up-to-date information and present it to the user.

- **Calculations** ActionScript can take numbers and perform calculations with them. It can predict a mortgage payment or add up the cost of items in a shopping cart.
- **Graphic Alterations** Scripts can be written to alter the size, angle of rotation, or even the color of movie clips in your movie. You can even duplicate or remove items from the screen.
- **Examine the Environment** You can use ActionScript to examine the playback environment of a Flash movie. You can find out what time and date it is and what location the movie is being played from.
- **Play Sounds** ActionScript is a good alternative to the Flash timeline for playing sounds. You can even control the balance and volume of a sound.

Expanding the Possibilities of Flash

The most important thing that ActionScript can do for you is something I can't list here—because it hasn't been thought of yet. A powerful programming language such as ActionScript, combined with a strong imagination, can bring new and innovative results.

The purpose of this book is to teach you the basics of ActionScript so that you can use these building blocks to create your own masterpieces.

Next, we'll get a little more technical and look at exactly where ActionScript code fits into a Flash movie.

Where Scripts Go

The first question many developers have when learning ActionScript is "Where do the scripts go?"

Flash is a complex multimedia authoring environment. If you have used Flash for a while, or have just run through the tutorials that come with Flash MX, you know the basic elements that make up this environment. There are three places where scripts can be placed among these elements.

Scripts in the Timeline

Each scene in a Flash movie has a timeline. Each key frame in this timeline can hold a script. In addition, you can have multiple scripts on the same frame by placing them in different layers in the timeline.

To place a script in the main timeline, first select any key frame. If you are starting a new movie, there should be one empty key frame in the timeline. Figure 1.1 shows an empty timeline, with the default key frame selected.

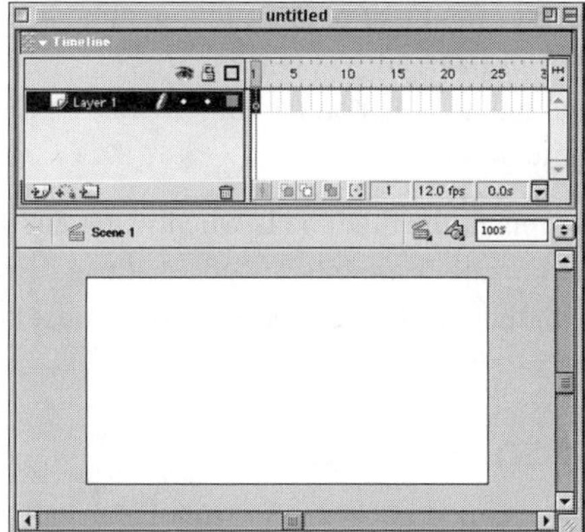

FIGURE 1.1
This is how the timeline looks when you create a new Flash movie. A script can be placed on the one key frame that is automatically inserted for you.

With a key frame selected, you just need to bring up the Action panel to see what script is there, or to start writing a new script.

There are several ways to bring up the Actions panel. You can choose Window, Actions from the menu, or use the keyboard shortcut F2.

> If you are familiar with Flash's complex Movie Explorer, you can also find and view scripts using the series of expandable lists in the window.

Figure 1.2 shows the Actions panel. The Actions panel is actually titled Actions—Frame because the script will be applied to this frame. If this is a new movie, the Actions panel will be blank. We'll soon fill it with all sorts of scripts. In Hour 2, "Using the Script Editing Window," we'll look at how to use the Actions panel.

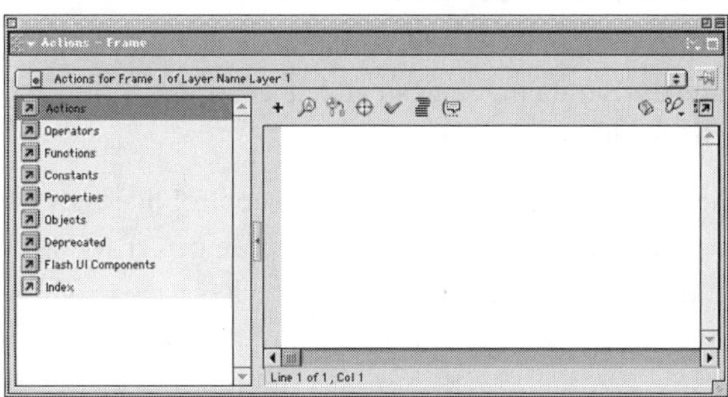

FIGURE 1.2
The Actions panel is where you view scripts placed in a frame.

Scripts in the timeline execute when that point in the timeline is encountered as Flash is playing back the movie. For instance, if you place a `stop()` command in the script attached to a key frame, the movie will stop moving forward at that point. It will continue only if another script tells it to.

Another reason to place scripts in the timeline is when you want to use functions as part of your ActionScript code. Functions are bits of code that can be reused. For scripts throughout the movie to call these reusable functions, they must be placed in the main timeline.

Scripts Attached to Buttons

NEW TERM Elements in Flash are called *symbols*. A symbol is usually a graphic element. There are three types formally called *graphics*, *movie clips*, and *buttons*. Graphics cannot have scripts attached to them; they are simply static or animated images. Movie clips are like graphics, except that they can have scripts attached to them.

The third type of symbol, buttons, can also have scripts attached. As a matter of fact, buttons are useless without scripts—they can't do anything without scripts.

To attach a script to a button, first select the button on the stage. Then choose Window, Actions from the menu. Or use the keyboard shortcut F2.

Notice that the Actions panel has a different title. It looks just like the window in Figure 1.2, but this time, it is titled Actions—Button.

As you might guess, scripts attached to buttons usually contain instructions for Flash to perform if the user clicks the button. Scripts can also react to when the mouse enters or leaves the button's space. Buttons can also react to key presses. This makes it easy to script a button that has a keyboard shortcut.

Scripts Attached to Movie Clips

Movie clips differ from plain graphic symbols in that they can be named, and they can have scripts attached to them. You can attach a script to a movie clip in the same way that you attach a script to a button.

Scripts attached to movie clips can be used to control that movie clip or to control other movie clips on the same timeline. Your scripts can detect when a movie clip first appears on the screen, and when a frame in the timeline has passed. This allows you to write scripts that execute repeatedly, once each frame. You can use such scripts to control animation.

In addition to attaching a script to a movie clip, you can also place scripts inside movie clips. After all, a movie clip is just another Flash movie. Inside a movie clip, there is another timeline. You can place timeline scripts on this timeline just like you can with the movie's main timeline. You can even place buttons inside a movie clip and attach scripts to it. A complex example would be a button with a script inside a movie clip, which is inside another movie clip, which is on the main timeline.

Task: Your First Script

1. Create a new movie.
2. Place three key frames in the movie by pressing F7 twotimes with the timeline selected.
3. Use your Flash drawing skills to create different graphics on each frame. For example, you could place a 1 on the first frame, a 2 on the second frame, and a 3 on the third frame.
4. Now if you run the movie by choosing Control, Test Movie, you will see the movie loop through the three frames.
5. Return to the main timeline and select the second key frame. Press F2 to bring up the Actions panel.
6. The left side of the Actions panel shows an expandable list of keywords. Find the `stop` keyword and double-click it. You will find it under Actions, Movie Control. Now the script window should contain one line that looks like this:

   ```
   stop ();
   ```

7. Close the Actions window and choose Control, Test Movie to run the movie again. You can also press Command+Return on the Mac or Control_Enter in Windows. It should show you frame 1, frame 2, and then stop. You'll never see frame 3.

   ActionScript has taken control. You've created your first script and thwarted Flash's intentions of looping through all three frames.

Summary

ActionScript is a relatively new programming language that borrows from other modern languages such as Java, C++, and JavaScript. ActionScript uses English words and symbols to provide a set of instructions for the Flash movie to follow. It exists so Flash movies can be more interactive than just plain linear animations.

ActionScript can control the flow of a Flash movie, alter movie clips in the movie, allow for user input, communicate with an Internet server, perform calculations, and even play sounds.

You can place ActionScript scripts in the timeline, on buttons, or on movie clips. You can see what scripts are in these locations by selecting the key frame, movie clip, or button and opening the Actions panel.

Q&A

Q What elements of a Flash movie can a script control?

A Scripts can control the flow of a movie, making it stop on a frame or jump to any frame in the movie. In addition, scripts can control movie clips. Although buttons can contain scripts, they cannot be controlled by scripts.

Q How do I know whether a script is attached to a key frame, movie clip, or button?

A In the case of key frames, you will see a little "A" in the timeline if the key frame contains a script. However, there is no way to determine whether movie clips or buttons contain scripts. You just have to select them and open up the Actions window to see. Alternatively, you can use the Movie Explorer panel to seek out scripts.

Q If I learned how to program in ActionScript with Flash 4 or earlier, will that help me to learn ActionScript for Flash MX?

A Real ActionScript was only introduced with Flash 5. If you've scripted Flash in versions 4 or earlier, some of the concepts may be familiar to you. Unfortunately, the leap between Flash 4 and 5 was so great that you pretty much have to start learning Flash scripting all over again. However, if you learned Flash 5 ActionScript, then Flash MX ActionScript is only a little more advanced.

Workshop

The quiz questions are designed to test your knowledge of the material covered in this hour. The answers to the questions follow.

Quiz

1. Which version of Flash first contained modern ActionScript?
2. What elements of Flash can have scripts placed on them?
3. Do you have to know ActionScript to be able to tell what a script does?
4. How do you bring up the Actions window?

1

Quiz Answers

1. Flash 5 was the first version to contain what we now know as ActionScript. However, Flash 4 did contain the basic programming constructs, such as conditional statements, loops, and variables.
2. The main timeline, movie clips, and buttons can have scripts placed on them.
3. No. Because ActionScript uses English words, you can usually decipher what a script does just by picking out keywords in the script. Writing your own script, however, takes more skill.
4. There are two ways. Both require that you first select a key frame in the timeline, a movie clip, or a button. Then you can choose Window, Actions, or use the keyboard shortcut F2 for that menu item.

HOUR 2

Using the Script Editing Window

The ActionScript programmer's home is the Actions panel. This is where you write, view, and edit scripts. Getting to know this panel is important if you want to learn ActionScript.

In this hour, you will:

- Learn how to bring up the Actions panel
- Learn how to use the Normal mode of the Actions panel
- Find out how to access Flash's online help system to look up ActionScript topics
- Discover the Actions panel Expert mode

Accessing the Actions Panel

Flash MX uses a panel system to help you access information and properties of various Flash elements. When you run Flash MX for the first time, you will be asked about how you plan to use Flash, and then your default panel layout will be decided. You can switch between defaults in the Window, Panel Sets menu. This will also determine the size of the ActionScript window, but you can always stretch that window to any size you want.

You can always bring up or close the Actions panel with the F2 key. You can click and drag its title bar to undock the panel from the right side of the screen. You can click and drag the bottom right corner of the screen to enlarge the size of the window, something that you will need to do if you want to write large programs.

Using panels in Flash is simple in some ways and complex in others. It seems complex mostly because so many options are available. It is worth the time to get to know the panels and how they work.

Normal Mode

The Actions panel has two different modes. The default mode is Normal mode. In this mode, you cannot directly type scripts character for character. Instead, you must choose from the menu of keywords on the left side of the screen.

This is similar to how scripting in Flash 4 worked. It also makes it nearly impossible to make simple mistakes.

Tour of the Actions Panel in Normal Mode

Figure 2.1 shows the Actions panel in Normal mode. It is a complex window with many items to review.

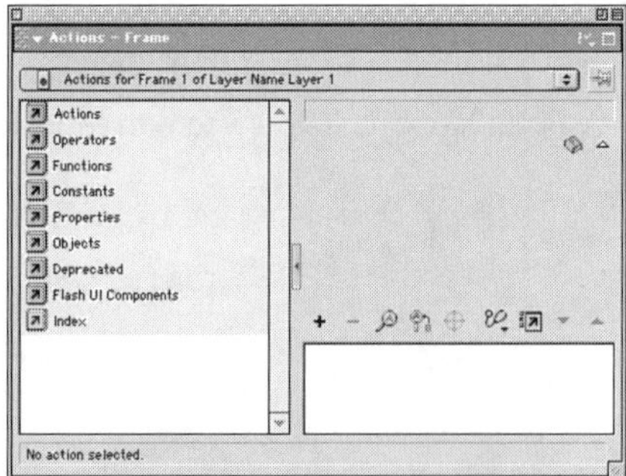

FIGURE 2.1
The Actions panel can be used in Normal mode (shown here) or Expert mode.

The top of the panel shows a pop-up menu that shows exactly which script you are currently editing. In Figure 2.1, it reads Actions for Frame 1 of Layer Name Layer 1. This is just a fancy way of saying that it is the script on frame 1, layer 1.

On the left side of the panel is a list of ActionScript commands, sorted into categories. Click a category to expand it and see the subcategories or commands inside.

On the right side of the panel is a large blank space where options appear as you enter various commands and functions. Figure 2.2 shows the Actions panel after you choose to insert the command `goto`. Notice the Movie Control category has been expanded on the left. The `goto` command was double-clicked to insert it into the script.

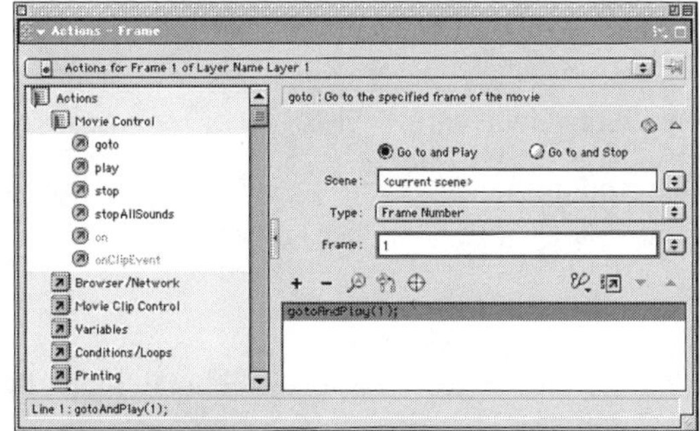

FIGURE 2.2
The Actions panel in Normal mode as it looks after a `goto` *command has been inserted.*

At the top-right side of the panel is a short definition of the command `goto`. Below that is a custom set of options that apply directly to the `goto` command.

It looks like a small form with fields for Scene, Type, and Frame. This is the parameters area for the selected command. It changes depending on what type of ActionScript command is selected.

The first option for the `goto` command is whether it is a Go to and Play or a Go to and Stop command. In this case, a Go to and Play command is selected. Both commands are similar, except that the first stops the movie at the destination frame, and the second takes it to the destination frame and continues moving forward to the next frame. We'll look at these two commands in depth in Hour 5, "Controlling the Flow of the Movie."

This command needs some additional information to make it work. Namely, it needs to know what frame you want to jump to. The Scene field indicates which scene the destination frame is in. In this case, it is the current scene. The next field is a pop-up menu that lets you determine how you want to define the destination frame. You could define it by Frame Number, Frame Label, or Expression. We'll look at the other two options later, but for now Frame Number simply means that you will indicate the exact number of the frame, in this case 1.

Under all this are two buttons that have a plus (+) symbol and minus (–) symbol in them. These allow you to quickly insert and delete commands in your script. However, they are rarely used alternate methods for doing this. You can delete commands by just using the Delete or Backspace key. You can insert commands by using the category list on the right side of the panel.

Next to the + and – buttons are other buttons used for various things. You can search or find and replace text in the script. You can add debugging breakpoints. You can switch between Normal and Expert modes. You can also choose to see line numbers listed next to each line of the script. The little up and down arrows to the far right allow you to select the next or previous lines of code.

At the bottom-right side of the Actions panel is your script. In Figure 2.2, you can see the one-line script `gotoAndPlay(1);`. I placed this script there before taking the screenshot. That line is also highlighted by a dark shade of blue. This means that this line is selected.

At the bottom of the Actions window, you can see `Line 1: gotoAndPlay(1);`. This information area tells you what line number you are at and repeats the line for you.

Categories

The categories on the left side of the Actions panel break up all the ActionScript keywords into organized groups to make them easier for you to find. You are probably curious about what each category contains. We'll go into detail about specific keywords and symbols in later hours. For now, here is a summary:

- Actions In this category, you'll see the simplest ActionScript commands and more. This category provides commands to test conditions, loop, create reusable functions, duplicate and create movie clips, and load data from a server. The keywords here form the meat of ActionScript. They are divided into the subcategories of Movie Control, Browser/Network, Movie Clip Control, Variables, Conditions/Loops, Printing, User-Defined Functions, and Miscellaneous Actions.
- Operators These are keywords and symbols used in mathematical and comparative operations—for instance, the + symbol, which performs addition, or the == symbol, which compares two items. They are divided into the subcategories of Arithmetic Operators, Comparison Operators, Logical Operators, Bitwise Operators, Assignment Operators, and Miscellaneous Operators.
- Functions ActionScript functions allow you to change data in some way or return some information, such as the version of Flash. For instance, you can convert the characters "123" into the number 123 with a function. The term *functions* can also be used to describe reusable bits of code that you create. In addition to some basic functions, there are two subcategories of Mathematical Functions and Conversion Functions.

- Constants Constants refer to special keywords that represent specific values such as `true`, `false`, `null`, and the `newline` character.
- Properties Properties are keywords that give you access to information about elements in Flash, such as movie clips. For instance, the `_x` property returns the horizontal position of a movie clip on the screen.
- Objects This category is the most diverse and most difficult to explain at this stage of the game. This is a catch-all for different concepts in ActionScript. All object keywords are divided into four subcategories: Core, Movie, Client/Server, and Authoring. One subcategory in Movie is Movie Clips. The keywords here relate to the manipulation of movie clips. Another subcategory is Math, which contains functions such as square root and cosine. You'll learn how to use the diverse set of commands and functions in the Objects category throughout the day.
- Depreciated This category contains keywords that are obsolete but still work in Flash MX. Avoid these keywords at all costs because they may not be supported in future versions of Flash.
- Flash UI Components This category contains keywords that specifically apply to special components, such as radio buttons and scrollbars.
- Index The Index category is an alphabetical list of all keywords in ActionScript. Every keyword is listed both under its category and in this index.

Sometimes the categorizations in the Actions panel help you find keywords. At other times, they make it harder. For instance, you might think that `_x`, the horizontal position of a movie clip, might be found under Objects, Movie, MovieClip, Properties. But it is just under the Properties category at the main level. You might think that `sqrt` would be under Functions, but it is under Objects, Core, Math, Methods.

Task: Writing Code in Normal Mode

To write scripts in Normal mode, you don't have to type much. Instead, you just point the mouse and click a lot. Let's try to create a short script from scratch.

1. Create a new movie.
2. Select the default key frame that is in frame 1, layer 1.
3. Choose Window, Actions to open the Actions panel. Close all the other panels to make it easier to use the Actions panel.
4. Click the Actions category to expand it.
5. Click the Movie Control subcategory to expand it.

6. Double-click the `goto` command. This places `gotoAndPlay(1);` in the script area. At the bottom of the screen, you will see Scene, Type, and Frame fields.
7. Change the **1** in the Frame field to a **5**.

The Normal mode of the Actions panel makes it easy to write script. Before we go any further, it will be useful to take a look at Flash's online help system.

Using Flash's Help System

So far, you have seen a lot of ActionScript syntax, but little explanation of what these keywords do. We'll be getting to most of these in the next 22 hours.

However, even when you are finished with this book, it is impossible to keep it all in your head. The best programmers rely on documentation to remind them of how commands and functions work.

Flash uses ToolTips throughout the program and an extensive HTML-based help system. You will need to know how to use these to become proficient in ActionScript.

Short Definitions

If you played with the keyword category listings in the Actions window, you might notice that small definitions appear near the top on the right when you select a keyword in the category list. Usually you see "To add item, double-click or drag item to the script window below it."

In the case of the Go To command, you will see a ToolTip that reads "Go to the specified frame of the movie." That's a short summary of what the command will do.

Click on some other commands and see what the short definitions for those commands say. Spend some time investigating before you move on.

Reference Panel

Flash also has a special panel specifically for helping you remember how to use ActionScript syntax. The Reference panel can be brought up by choosing Window, Reference or by using the keyboard shortcut Shift+F1. Figure 2.3 shows this panel.

Notice that the left side of the panel looks the same as the category list on the left side of the Actions panel. As a matter of fact, you can access the Reference panel from the Actions panel: Click a little booklike button in the Actions panel to bring up the Reference panel. It automatically goes to the keyword that you have selected in your script.

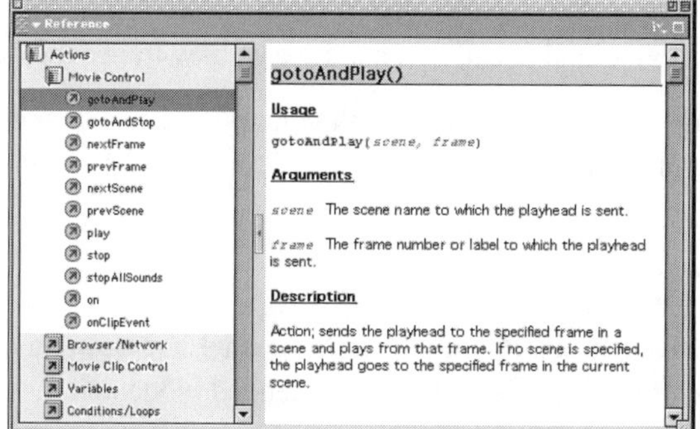

FIGURE 2.3
The Reference panel contains a complete ActionScript dictionary.

Online HTML Help

To get more detailed information about an ActionScript command, choose Help, ActionScript Dictionary. Your browser launches and displays a page that looks like Figure 2.4.

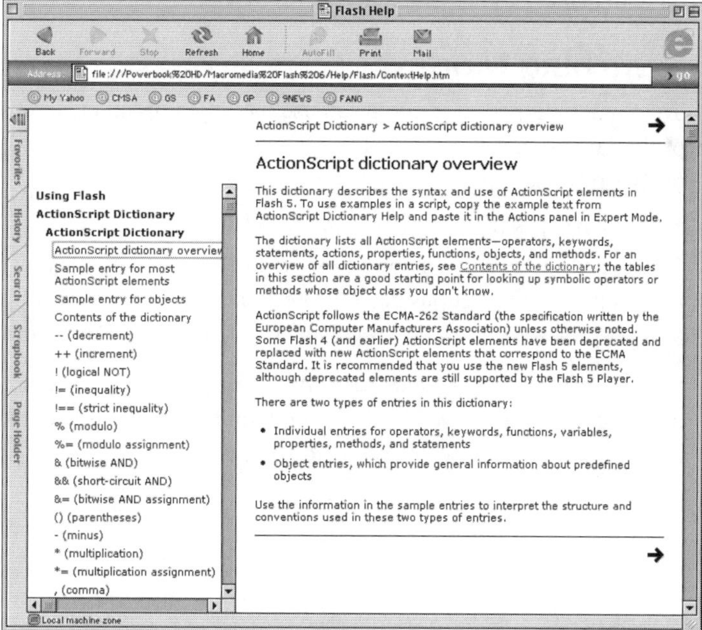

FIGURE 2.4
The ActionScript dictionary appears inside your Web browser.

On the left side of the browser window is a list of contents that includes all the ActionScript commands and functions. If you select one of these, it either expands to a list or brings up information on the right.

2

The main entry for each keyword appears on the right side of the browser window. It includes a description and usually an example of how to use the keyword in a script.

Spend some time getting to know the online help system. You will need to refer to it often while learning Flash and will still need it occasionally even after you are an expert.

Expert Mode

Now that you have learned to use the Actions panel in Normal mode, it is already time to advance to Expert mode. This is the recommended mode and the one that most ActionScript programmers use.

In Expert mode, you don't need to use the category list to the left. Instead, you can just type the keywords that you want to use. Because the Actions panel allows you to type almost anything, it is easy to make mistakes.

However, you can still use the category and keyword list to the left to insert standard ActionScript commands, functions, and operators. It also comes in handy when you can't quite remember a command, or how to spell it.

Switching Modes

To switch to Expert mode, you can use the little pop-up menu in the upper-right corner of the Actions panel. The first two choices are Normal Mode and Expert Mode. Switch it to Expert Mode.

You can also use the keyboard shortcuts Command+E and Command+N on the Mac and Ctrl+E and Ctrl+N in Windows to switch between Normal and Expert modes. However, make sure that the Actions panel is the frontmost window, with full focus. Otherwise, these keys will map to File, New Document, and Edit, Edit Symbols in the menu.

Figure 2.5 shows the Actions panel in Expert mode. The area of custom command parameters disappears, as well as the short definition area. Instead, the main code typing area takes over almost the whole right side of the screen.

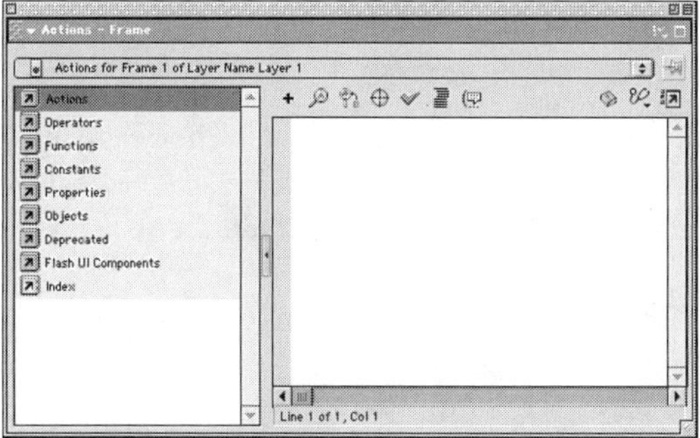

FIGURE 2.5
The Actions panel in Expert mode includes a larger area for typing in code.

Switching from Normal to Expert mode is easy and always works. However, switching from Expert to Normal mode works only if there are no syntax errors in your code. This is a shame because I find that I often want to switch to Normal mode to have access to the helper forms at the bottom of the window. However, unless I have already correctly formatted the command or function I am working on, Flash won't let me switch. Then, after I have found the correct format, I no longer need to switch.

The Actions Panel Pop-Up Menu

The Actions window pop-up menu has several other commands that will be useful while you use the Actions panel, especially in Expert mode.

You can use the standard find and replace functions to search through your code. The keyboard shortcut Command+F on the Mac and Ctrl+F in Windows quickly brings up the Find dialog. The keyboard shortcut Command+H on the Mac and Ctrl+H in Windows brings up the Replace dialog. You can also find something once and then press F3 to find its next occurrence.

Another function in this menu is the `Goto Line` function, which quickly takes you to a specific line number.

The `Check Syntax` function looks at the script in the window and determines whether there are any obvious errors. If it doesn't find any, you get a message that says `This script contains no errors.`

> Often, this message lies to you. The `Check Syntax` function determines only whether there are any obvious errors with your code. It does not try to run your code to see whether it is viable. Therefore, it is easy to write code that results in an error that will not be caught by the `Check Syntax` function. Each line of the code is correct, but taken as a whole, there is a problem.

Still, the `Check Syntax` function can come in handy, especially for beginners. It catches things such as the misuse of operators or a missing bracket.

The Auto Format and Auto Format Options menu choices relate to the fact that Flash is always cleaning up your code as you type it. It indents the code and colors it in. You can change how this works with the Auto Format Options dialog, shown in Figure 2.6.

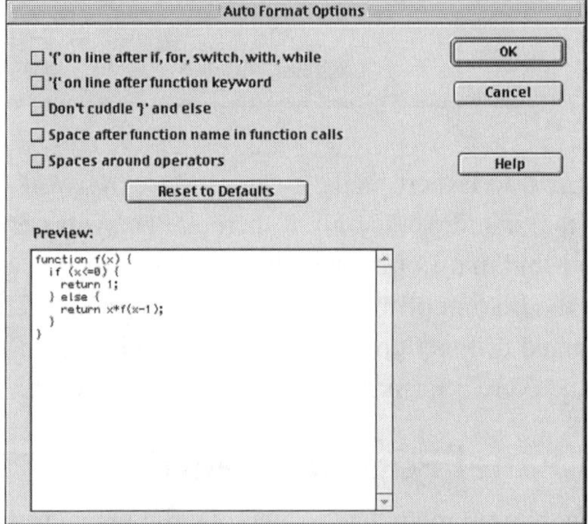

FIGURE 2.6
The Auto Format Options dialog allows you to customize how Flash formats your code.

In addition, selecting the Preference menu option lets you select the colors that Flash uses in your code, the indentation width, and even the font used in the Actions panel. You can also get to this dialog by choosing Edit, Preferences and then selecting the ActionScript Editor tab. Figure 2.7 shows this dialog.

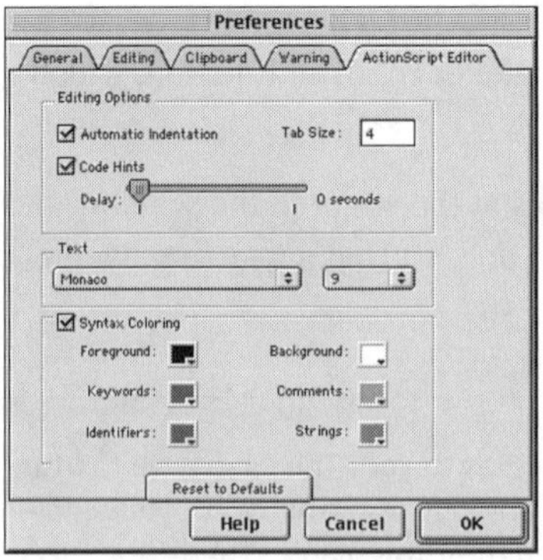

FIGURE 2.7
The Preferences dialog allows you to customize how the ActionScript Editor displays your code.

Script colorization is a great help when programming. When this is on, you'll see official ActionScript keywords in one color, with constructs that you create, such as variable names and values, in another color. This can be a great help for beginners, as a correctly typed keyword such as `gotoAndPlay` should turn blue as soon as you type it. If it does not, then you may have mistyped the command.

The remaining options in the Actions panel pop-up menu allow you to export or import text files. This means that you can write your scripts in a text editor of your own choice and then import them into Flash. You can also print your script using this menu.

I don't recommend writing your code in another program. The Actions panel is not the fastest text editor in the world, but you can only write code so fast anyway. It is much better to write scripts inside the Flash environment where you can quickly refer to the keyword category list, the names of your movie clips, and the names and locations of frames. Plus, you can quickly switch between different scripts stored in different locations inside the Flash movie.

Typing Code in Expert Mode

Ironically, the Actions window is simpler to use in Expert mode than in Normal mode. This is because all you need to do is type; there are no forms to fill out at the bottom of the window. It is just a simple text editor.

The downside is that it is also much easier to make mistakes. In Normal mode, Flash keeps you in line. But in Expert mode, you are free to mistype command names or put the wrong parameters in the wrong place.

In Expert mode, you simply place the cursor in the typing area and type away. Flash doesn't leave you completely on your own, however. Your text will automatically be formatted with indentations. The different keywords will also follow the color scheme specified in the preferences.

You can also use the button that looks like a check mark to check your script for obvious syntax errors. The formatting button next to it will format all your script, although each line will automatically format after you press Return on the Macintosh or Enter in Windows.

The Actions panel also contains a great help function called Code Hints. These are little pop-up menus that appear as you are typing. You can ignore them and keep on typing, or you can use them to select from a list of options. You will notice these Code Hints as you use the Actions panel more and more.

Task: Writing Code in Expert Mode

Now let's create the same script that we used in the first task, but in Expert mode.

1. Create a new movie.
2. Select the default key frame that is in frame 1, layer 1.
3. Choose Window, Actions to open the Actions panel. Close all the other panels to make it easier to use the Actions panel.
4. Use the pop-up menu to switch to Expert mode.
5. Click in the typing area.
6. Type the following line there:

```
gotoAndPlay(5);
```

Your Actions panel should now look like Figure 2.8.

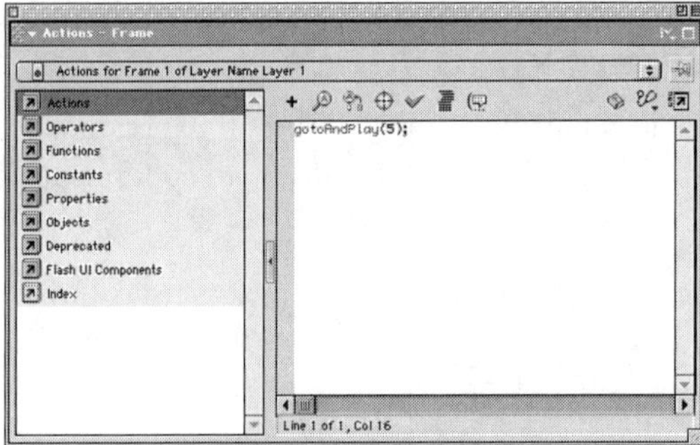

FIGURE 2.8
The Actions panel in Expert mode, with a short script that was manually typed in.

Summary

The Flash Actions panel is part of a system of panels in Flash MX that allow you to modify almost any element. The programmer spends most of his time working with the Actions panel, so it is worthwhile to undock this panel from the right side of the screen and customize its size and options.

The Normal mode of the Actions panel allows you to select from a list of keywords and prompts you to fill in all the options that apply. On the other hand, the Expert mode allows the programmer the freedom of typing in the code directly.

To become a proficient programmer, you should be familiar with the Actions window and Flash's online ActionScript help system.

Q&A

Q Can I write complex programs in Normal mode?

A Certainly. However, the better you become at ActionScript, the more the Normal mode will slow you down. Think of the Normal mode as training wheels for novice programmers.

Q If I write a program in Normal mode, can I go back and edit it under Expert mode?

A Yes. You can always switch from Normal mode to Expert mode and continue to modify the same code. However, you can only switch from Expert mode back to Normal mode if there are absolutely no syntax errors or incomplete commands in the code.

Q How do I know whether the online help file I am using is up-to-date?

A Check the Macromedia Web site occasionally for updates to the online help system. If they update it, they will include an installer or instructions on how to update your help.

Q Typing in the Actions panel seems slow. Is there any way to speed it up?

A If you have a slower machine, the Actions panel can seem slow. You can speed it up by closing all other panels and turning off some of the formatting and colorization options.

Workshop

The quiz questions are designed to test your knowledge of the material covered in this hour. The answers to the questions follow.

Quiz

1. How do you switch between Normal and Expert mode?
2. Can you use the category lists of keywords in Expert mode?
3. What is a quick way to check for syntax errors in Expert mode?
4. Why shouldn't you use commands in the Depreciated category?

Quiz Answers

1. You can use the pop-up menu at the upper-right corner of the Actions panel. You can use the View Options button inside the panel. You can also use the keyboard shortcuts, Command+N and Command+E on the Mac or Ctrl+N and Ctrl+E in Windows.

2. Yes. You can insert keywords into the script with the category list of keywords even in Expert mode.
3. You can use the Check Syntax button in the Actions panel in Expert mode to make sure that you don't have any syntax errors.
4. These commands are all obsolete. They may not be supported in future versions of Flash. In addition, there are more modern alternatives for each of them.

HOUR 3

Learning to Program

Programming is both a science and an art. You will need both knowledge of the programming language's syntax and a lot of creativity because there is rarely only one way to write a program. Ten different programmers will write 10 different programs to accomplish the same task.

As you learn ActionScript, you will develop your own style. At first, you will probably pick up the style that I use in this book. But later this will slowly develop as you adapt techniques you invent yourself.

Some basic programming concepts hold true for just about every programming language. Let's review those concepts in this hour before learning the specifics of how they are implemented in Flash.

In this hour, you will:

- Understand how computers think
- Find out what elements make up a program
- Learn about variables
- See how conditions and loops make programs flow
- Learn how to break a large problem into smaller parts
- Find out how to write bug-free code

How Computers Think

Actually, computers don't think at all. They mindlessly follow instructions. They take these instructions very literally.

A Flash script is a list of instructions. However, it is best not to think of them as a list of instructions addressed to the computer but to the Flash runtime environment. Scripts tell Flash what to do.

When you look at a code listing, you can "play computer" by reading the code and predicting what the computer will do each step of the way.

To play computer, you pretend that you are the computer, or more specifically, that you are Flash. You read each line of the program and pretend that it is an instruction that you must carry out.

For instance, if you are supposed to jump from one frame in the Flash movie to another, you imagine that the Flash movie is now on the destination frame and waiting for the next instruction. You then read the next line and follow that instruction.

By playing computer, you can predict what your scripts will do. You can troubleshoot your scripts this way and fix problems in them before you even run the program once. Soon, playing computer will be something that you do naturally as you program. When you write a line of code, you will imagine what Flash will do with that instruction. As you write a whole script, you will constantly be checking your code by doing this.

Computer programs are like onions. Take a Flash movie, for example. It is a .swf file that runs inside the Flash plug-in. The Flash plug-in, in turn, is running inside your Web browser. The Web browser is running as an application inside your computer's operating system. The operating system uses a complex toolbox of programs to do things such as display pixels on the screen; this toolbox is running on the microprocessor inside your computer.

All these levels depend on the ones below; each level must support everything that runs on top of it. This makes for a complex and delicate system.

Fortunately, as an ActionScript programmer, you are shielded from everything but the top layer. You don't have to know how the microprocessor, operating system, or Web browser works. You don't even have to know how Flash works—just what it is capable of doing and how you go about doing it.

Commands, Functions and Operations

So far, I have used the term *keywords* to describe elements of ActionScript. For instance, `gotoAndPlay` is a keyword. It is also a command.

New Term A *command* is an element of ActionScript that tells Flash to do something specific. Commands are obeyed as long as they make sense. For instance, if you use `gotoAndPlay` with a frame label that doesn't exist, the command cannot be executed.

Commands are the most basic element of programming. In Flash, little can be done without using at least one command. We'll be learning many commands throughout the rest of the book.

New Term *Functions* are terms in ActionScript that perform a calculation and return a result. For instance, a function might take a single number and return the square root of that number.

New Term Both commands and functions can take one or more *parameters*. A parameter is a value passed to the command or function. The `gotoAndPlay` command needs at least one parameter to work: the name or number of the frame to go to. A square root function would need a single number value as a parameter.

New Term Different than commands and functions are *operators*. These are usually symbols, not words. For instance, the + operator performs addition between two values.

You'll be using commands, functions, and operators throughout your ActionScript programming.

Variables

All sophisticated programming languages use variables to store information. You may store information for a number of reasons. A variable has two parts: its name and a value.

Storing Information

You will need to store information to write complex computer programs. Sometimes you will only store the information for a short period of time. For instance, you may want your program to repeat a set of commands 10 times. In that case, you will need to count the number of times the commands have been repeated and continue on after this counter reaches 10.

In other cases, you will want to store information for longer periods of time. For instance, you can ask the user to enter her name and then you can store this information in a variable. Later in the Flash movie, you can display this name.

Variable Names

The name of a variable is usually a word or group of words. Sometimes it is a single letter. In general, you should make the name of the variable as descriptive as possible.

For instance, if you want to store the name of the user in a variable, `userName` is a good choice for the variable name. A bad choice would be *n*, which is too short, or *name*, which could be confused with the name of something else in the Flash movie.

In ActionScript, a convention has arisen that many programmers follow when inventing variable names. The variables usually start with a lowercase letter but then use an uppercase letter when a new word begins in the name. The variable name `userName` is a good example. A longer example would be `currentUserFirstName`.

Spaces cannot be used in variable names, and neither can special characters. But numbers can be used. So a variable name may be `player2`.

Variable Types

You can store many different types of information in variables. Numbers are the simplest. You can store the number 7 in a variable, for instance.

NEW TERM You can store two different types of numbers in variables. An *integer* is a number that has no decimal component. The numbers 7, 335, -5, and 0 are all good examples of integers.

NEW TERM The other type of number is called a *floating point number*, or *float*. This is a number that has a decimal component. Good examples of floats include 0.1, 532.23, and -3.7.

NEW TERM You can store characters and words in variables too. These are called *strings*. A string is a sequence of characters. It can be one or more characters, or even a string without characters, which is called an empty string. "Hello", "This and that", "a", and "" are examples of strings.

When writing about strings, quotes are used to define that the value is a string and not another type of variable. For instance, 7 is the number 7, whereas "7" is a string with a single character, the digit 7.

In other programming languages, you would normally have to decide in advance what type of information each variable would hold and write that at the beginning of your program. For instance, you would declare that there is a variable named `userName` and that it holds a string. However, in ActionScript, you don't have to declare variables in advance. You just use them, and Flash creates the variables on-the-fly the first time they are used.

In addition, the variables are not restricted to holding only one type of information. The variable `userName` could hold a string at one point and a number at another point.

This flexibility is rarely needed, but it is one less thing for ActionScript programmers to worry about.

> Another thing that ActionScript programmers don't have to worry about is garbage collection. This is when you reclaim the memory used by a variable after the variable has ceased to be useful. Most modern computer languages such as ActionScript automatically perform garbage collection, so you don't have to worry about it.

There are other types of variables besides numbers and strings. For instance, arrays can hold lists of information instead of a single piece of information. We'll look at arrays and other data types later in the book as they are needed.

Conditions

Your programs can make decisions. No, they can't tell you which laundry detergent to buy. But they can take pieces of information, compare them, and then perform different tasks depending on the outcome.

For instance, suppose that you want to check the name a user provides and make sure that the user gives a name at least three characters long.

The decision that the program needs to make is based on this one fact. If the user's name is three characters long or longer, the program does one thing; if the user's name is less than three characters long, the program does something else.

There are actually two parts to this decision. The first part is to test to see whether the condition is met. If the name is three characters long, the condition is met, or we say that it is *true*. Otherwise, the condition is not met, or it is *false*. All conditions are either true or false.

NEW TERM A value that is either true or false is called a *boolean* value.

The second part of the decision-making process is to choose which piece of code to execute based on the true/false condition. Sometimes, there is only one option: Some code is executed if the condition is true. If the condition is false, no code is executed at all. Sometimes, there is an alternate set of code to execute if the condition is false.

Get used to phrasing questions and comparisons as conditions. Computers always think in terms of true and false, not in abstract terms such as "what does this mean?"

For instance, if you want the computer to perform three different tasks based on whether a variable is 1, 2, or 3, you might phrase it like this:

- Is the variable's contents equal to 1? If so, then do this…
- Is the variable's contents equal to 2? If so, then do this…
- Is the variable's contents equal to 3? If so, then do this…

So instead of asking the computer something complex such as "do one of these things based on the value of the variable," you ask it three separate questions that have true or false results.

Conditions are almost always based on a comparison. You can compare the values of two variables to see whether they are equal. You can also compare them to see whether one is less than the other or greater than the other. If the variables are strings, you can compare them to see whether one appears alphabetically before or after the other.

Loops

Computers are great for doing repetitive tasks. Whereas a human gets bored doing the same thing a few times in a row, a computer is happy to repeat the same task hundreds or even millions of times. In fact, repetitive tasks are where computers really excel.

Looping is an important part of every programming language. ActionScript is no exception. You can repeat a set of instructions a certain number of times, or until a certain condition is met.

In fact, conditions are an important part of looping. All a loop needs is a starting and ending point, plus a condition that signifies the end of the loop.

For instance, if you want to loop 10 times, a variable will be used to start counting at 0. Each time the loop loops, the counter is incremented by 1. When it reaches 9, the loop ends and the program continues past the end of the loop. The following is an illustration of a typical program loop:

1. Some command before loop.
2. Start of loop, counter set to 0.
3. Some command in loop.
4. Some other command in loop.
5. Counter incremented by 1.
6. If counter is less than 9, go back to step 3.
7. Some command after loop.

In the preceding seven steps, step 1 only happens once. Then step 2 signifies the beginning of the loop. Steps 3, 4, 5, and 6 are executed 10 times. After the 10th time, step 7 is executed, and the program continues from there.

So if the loop is to occur 10 times, why does it check to see whether the counter reaches 9? This is because the counter starts at 0. This is typical of most computer programming languages. The counter counts from 0 to 9 instead of from 1 to 10.

Another important part of loops is when, exactly, the condition is examined. In some cases, it is examined before the commands in the loop are executed, and in other cases it is examined in the end.

There are also ways to break out of loops prematurely, and ways to skip the rest of the commands in a loop and start back at the beginning. We'll look at the ways to do this in ActionScript in Hour 4, "Writing Code in Flash."

Achieving the Impossible

Commands, functions, operations, variables, conditions, and loops are the fundamentals of computer programming. The tough part is putting the program together.

Programming is problem solving. Your programs are just sets of instructions to solve a big problem. So the first step in programming is to define what problem you want to solve.

A good example in the real world is going to the market to get milk. The problem would be "I need to get milk." But is that a clear enough definition to allow you to solve the problem?

What sort of milk do you want? whole? two percent? skim? How much do you want? a gallon? a pint? a liter? Where do you want to go to get the milk? the nearby supermarket? the convenience store? the local organic food store?

A better defined problem might be "I need to go to the nearby supermarket to get a gallon of skim milk."

Now that you have defined the problem, you need to determine what you want to do to solve it. You probably want to get in the car, drive to the store, find the milk, take it to the check-out line, pay for it, take it back to the car, drive home, and get out of the car. Breaking it down to these steps makes it easier to see exactly what is needed.

Each of these steps, however, can be broken down even further. Getting in the car involves opening the door, climbing in, placing the key into the ignition, turning it, and so on.

You can go even further. Opening the car door involves reaching for the handle, pulling gently on the handle, and then pulling on the door to open it. If the car was locked, you may also have had to take out your key, place it in the lock, turn the key, and so on.

Did you realize that so much was involved with going to get some milk? These steps seem so minor and detailed that you just don't think about them normally, but you have to do them.

As a computer programmer, you need to include every minor step in your program so that the computer knows how to perform the entire task.

If it helps, think of Flash as an alien from another planet or a prehistoric man thawed from ice. You have to explain every step of everything you want him to do, and you can't assume that he knows anything.

For instance, suppose that you want to make a space invaders game, just like the classic arcade game. It seems like a pretty big order at first, so you break it into steps. You've got the invaders, the shields, and the player.

Focus on the player's ship first. It should be able to move left and right, and fire bullets.

Focus on the movement first. The left and right arrow keys make it move from side to side. The program also needs to check to make sure that the ship doesn't move past the edge of the screen.

Focus on the movement to the left first. You've got to detect when the user presses the left arrow key and then reposition the ship slightly to the left when he does.

This last focus doesn't seem nearly as big a problem as the original one—building a space invaders game. You can achieve this step easily if you just know a few basic keywords.

This is the secret to computer programming. You need to break the problem down into smaller and smaller problems until you can handle each one.

If you are ever having difficulty figuring out how to solve a problem, it is probably because you have not broken it down into small enough pieces. Programming is partly knowing how to break down a big problem into smaller ones, and partly having the patience to implement each and every small step.

I can't stress this point enough. It is the single most important piece of information in this book. You must break down programming problems into smaller and smaller steps until you can solve each problem. About 90 percent of the time that people ask me for advice on how to do something on the computer, their problem turns out to be that they aren't breaking down the problem into small enough pieces.

Writing Bug-Free Code

A *bug* is an error or other problem with the program that you have written. Sometimes, bugs are obvious things that you are warned about while writing the program. Flash warns you about syntax errors and things that it doesn't understand.

The term *bug* came about because the first computer bug was actually a real bug. A moth got caught in an early computer, attracted by the light of the vacuum tubes inside. The term bug has been used to describe computer problems ever since.

Other bugs don't show up until you run the program. These are problems that look okay to Flash but make the program perform in a way other than what you wanted.

Simple Solution

The easiest way to write a bug-free program is not to put the bugs in there in the first place. This sounds a little ridiculous, but it makes sense.

Take time planning and writing your code. Check and double-check variable and function names. Think about how each line of the program will work as you write it.

One way to make it easier to do this is to write your program one piece at a time. After you have completed each piece, test it out before going any further.

For instance, if you are making a space invaders game, try just making the player's ship react to the left arrow key first. Set up everything you need in your movie to make this one thing happen. Then, test it. If you keep working with just small steps like this, you'll avoid having to make a lot of bug fixes when you are finished.

The Hard Truth About Bugs

The hard truth is that it is nearly impossible to write a program that doesn't have any bugs at first. Even the best programmers who have been writing programs all their lives can't do it.

So don't try to be a perfectionist as you write your code. You will have to spend some time testing and fixing bugs anyway at the end.

This is a tough point for some people who are first learning to program. It seems that programming is something that has a certain amount of precision and should be easy to get right the first time. But it is more like an art, you work at a program, making adjustments and changes, until it runs the way you want it to.

> Dealing with bugs this way seems contradictory. On the one hand, take the time to write bug-free code, but, on the other hand, don't waste time trying to be a perfectionist. Find a balance between these that will optimize your time and effort.

Preparing for Bugs

You can do many things to prepare for fixing bugs later. The primary one is to comment your code. Most programming languages allow you to add comments to your code, and ActionScript is no exception. You can designate one or more lines, or even part of a line, to a comment. A comment can be anything you want; it is ignored by Flash.

The idea behind commenting your code is to leave hints for yourself so that you can return to the code later and remember what it does. It also helps if someone else will be using your code later.

At times, it may seem like overkill to comment code. After all, when you write a section of code it is obvious to you what the code is doing. But consider that some bugs may not pop up for weeks or months. You may be several projects down the road when you find that you need to open up an old Flash file and make changes. Comments will be a huge help at that point.

In addition to comments, you can also make your code easier to read by using descriptive variable names and function names. Three months after writing the program, you may not remember what s was supposed to stand for, but `gameScore` will still make sense.

Debugging

So, how do you get rid of bugs? This is a process called *debugging*.

Sometimes debugging is straightforward. You simply see what the program did wrong, think about what could have caused it, go into the program, and make a change.

However, it is more often the case that you will need to investigate a little to determine what is wrong. Sometimes you need to make a change, test the program, and make some more changes. A single bug can sometimes take hours to track down.

Flash includes some debugging tools that will help you fix your programs. You can track variable values and even set breakpoints in your code. We'll look at some of these tools in Hour 4.

Summary

Computers follow your program as a set of instructions, taking each command literally. You must spell out every step to the computer so that it understands what you want it to do.

Computer programs are made up of commands, functions, operations, conditional tests, and loops. Commands give the computer a specific instruction. Functions perform calculations and return a value. Operations take several values and combine them in some way. Conditions test one or more values to get a true or false result. Loops allow the program to repeat a set of instructions many times.

Variables are containers for storing numbers or strings of characters. Variables have names and contents.

Writing a program takes patience. You must first define the problem that the program is meant to solve. Then you must break down the program into smaller and smaller steps until you have steps so small that they are easy for you to handle.

After a program is finished, it may still contain problems called bugs. You have to allow some time for debugging so that your program runs correctly when you are finished.

Q&A

Q Do functions always need some sort of data going into them?

A No. It is common to have functions that don't need any parameters. For instance, a function could return the current date, or the position of a movie clip on the screen.

Q Can I perform an operation between two numbers, if one is an integer and the other a float?

A Yes. Flash allows you to mix integers and floats in calculations. The result will be a float.

Q If I compare two strings, will upper- and lowercase make a difference?

A Yes. Flash considers uppercase letters to come before lowercase letters. This is not true in some other programming languages.

Q What if I create a loop that never ends? What happens?

A This is called an *infinite loop*. It is a bug of the worst kind. Flash will detect that the program is taking an abnormally long time to run and ask whether you want to stop the program. It is then up to you to fix the problem with the loop.

Workshop

The quiz questions are designed to test your knowledge of the material covered in this hour. The answers to the questions follow.

Quiz

1. What is the difference between a command and a function?
2. If you created a variable and placed "7" inside it, what type of variable would it be?
3. Name four important parts of a loop.
4. Should good programmers be able to write bug-free code?

Quiz Answers

1. Both commands and functions can perform various actions, but a function always returns some sort of value.
2. It could be either a string with one character, the digit 7, or it could be an integer with the number 7. Because the question placed quotes around the "7", it is more likely that it is referring to a string.
3. A loop has a start point, an end point, a condition test, and some contents.
4. Even a good programmer will have some bugs in her program when it is first complete. However, a good programmer will also test the code and use debugging techniques to eliminate these bugs before finishing.

HOUR 4

Writing Code in Flash

Some basic structures can be found in almost every programming language. ActionScript is no exception. You can store information in variables, repeat code, perform tests, and break up code into subroutines.

In this hour, you will:

- Learn about the basic parts of a script
- Find out how to use the Output window
- Use variables to store information
- See how to perform tests
- Use operations to change values
- Learn about loops
- See how to place code into functions
- Understand how dot syntax works
- Find out why you should comment your code
- Learn how to debug your code

Parts of a Script

When you write your own scripts, you will use all sorts of different keywords and characters. To learn these, it will be useful to look at a real script and examine its parts.

We'll use the following script as an example. It is a button script that runs when the user clicks the button that the script is attached to. It doesn't perform any particular function, but rather demonstrates several major ActionScript constructs.

```
on (press) {
    var myVariable = 7;
    var myOtherVariable = "Macromedia";
    for (var i=0; i<10; i++) {
        trace(i);
        if (myVariable + 3 == 5) {
            trace(myOtherVariable);
        }
    }
}
```

The first line of the script identifies the rest as something that executes when the user first presses the button. The `on (press)` construct can be used only in button scripts. You can also use `on (release)` if you want the code to execute when the user completes the button press.

The curly bracket, {, at the end of the first line signifies that this is the beginning of a code segment. From the open bracket, {, to its corresponding closing bracket, }, all the code inside the brackets is part of a set of code that belongs together. In this case, the code segment represents all the code that is executed when the button is pressed.

Notice that the indentations of the code example follow the brackets. The line after an open bracket is indented one tab stop farther, and every line that follows it is at the same level until the corresponding close bracket, or another open bracket takes the code one tab stop farther. This type of indentation makes it much easier to read the code and is common among computer languages. In fact, Flash will indent your code for you by default.

The first line of this code segment creates a new local variable called *`myVariable`*. It assigns the value of 7 to it. The new line assigns the string `"Macromedia"` to the variable *`myOtherVariable`*. We'll look more at Flash variables in the section "Local and Global Variables" later this hour.

The semicolon at this end of this line, and many other lines, signifies the end of the instruction. Put a semicolon after every line that is a complete instruction.

The `for` structure starts a loop. In this case, it loops 10 times, with the variable `i` starting at 0 and increasing to 9. We'll look at loops in the section "Loops," later this hour. The bracket at the end of the `for` line signifies the start of the code segment that will be the body of the loop.

The `trace` command sends its contents to the Output window. We'll see more of that command in the upcoming section "The Output Window."

The `if` command is called a conditional statement. It tests the statement that follows it, `myVariable + 3 == 5`, to see whether it is true. If so, the code segment in the brackets is executed. If not, this whole code segment is skipped.

The code segment in question is a single `trace` command that sends the variable *`myOtherVariable`* to the Output window.

The rest of the example consists of three close brackets. The first closes the `if` statement. The second closes the `for` loop, and the third bracket closes the `on (press)` segment.

Now that you have seen a complete, though small, ActionScript program, let's take a closer look at some specific parts of ActionScript.

Output Window

The Output window is a special programming tool that only appears if you are testing a movie while running Flash. Error messages and some other information appear in the Output window. In addition, the ActionScript command `trace` writes out information that you specify to the Output window.

The Output window is useful when you are debugging a program. You can use the Output window to track the values of variables and tell you what part of an ActionScript program is currently running.

The Output window can also be used to help you learn ActionScript. We can write short little programs that do nothing but send information to the Output window. This will help you see the results of your first simple program.

Task: Send a Message to the Output Window

The best way to become familiar with the Output window is to use it. Let's write a simple program that sends a message to the window.

1. Start Flash MX and create a new movie.
2. Select the default first frame of the movie and then open the Actions panel, if it is not already open. Expand the Actions panel so that it is much bigger than the default size.

3. Use the pop-up menu in the upper-right corner of the Actions panel to set the Actions panel mode to Expert.
4. Click in the script area of the Actions window so that you see an insertion cursor there.
5. Type the following script in the Actions panel:

   ```
   trace("Hello World");
   ```

   The result should be an Actions panel that looks like Figure 4.1.

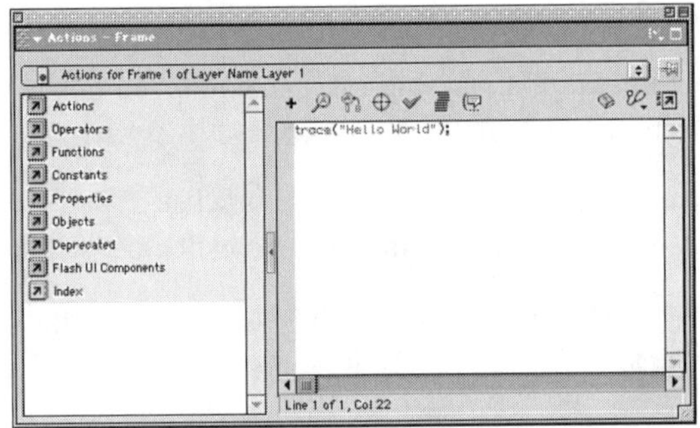

FIGURE 4.1
The Actions panel contains a simple one-line script that sends a message to the Output window.

6. Choose Control, Test Movie to run the movie.

The movie takes a second to run. You end up with a blank window that represents your running movie. Because no graphics are in your movie, there is nothing to show.

The Output window also appears with the words "Hello World," as you might expect. Figure 4.2 shows this simple window.

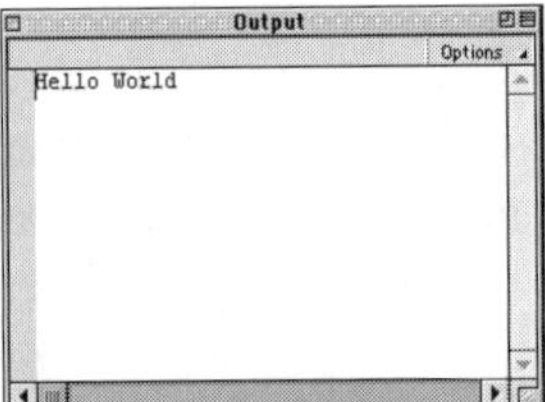

FIGURE 4.2
The Output window contains the message that the `trace` *command specified.*

Like the Actions panel, the Output window has a small pop-up menu in the upper-right corner. You can use it to copy the text in the Output window or clear all the text. You can also search the text in the window, save it to a file, or print it.

One last option in the pop-up menu lets you set the current debug level. You can choose only to have error messages displayed, have minor warnings displayed as well, or have no error messages displayed at all.

We'll use the Output window throughout the rest of this hour and in many other times throughout the book.

Local and Global Variables

In Hour 3, "Learning to Program," I mentioned variables. They are little containers for storing information.

Setting Variables

Using variables in ActionScript is easy. All you need to do is assign a value to a variable name. Here is an example:

```
myVariable = 7;
```

The preceding line creates the variable named *myVariable* and places the number 7 inside it. Note that the name *myVariable* was chosen arbitrarily by me. You could name the variable anything. For instance, *numberContainer*, *a*, or *fred* would all work.

To see variables in action, you can test them with the Output window. Here is a short program that you can place in the first frame of a blank movie:

```
myVariable = 7;
trace(myVariable);
```

When you run this movie, the Output window appears with the number 7 in it. The number 7 was stored in *myVariable* and then the `trace` command was used to place the contents of *myVariable* in the Output window.

Global Variables

A *global* variable is one that is accessible throughout the entire level of the Flash movie. You can set it in one frame, and it will still contain its contents in another frame.

You don't need to do anything special to create a global variable. Just using it, like in the previous example, automatically makes the variable a global one.

In most programming languages, global variables are available everywhere. However, Flash movies use a system of levels. The main movie timeline is the *root* level. Any movie clips are actually small Flash movies inside the main one. The graphics and scripts inside a movie clip are one level down from the root level. Global variables at the root level aren't accessible inside a movie clip—at least not directly.

Local Variables

NEW TERM *Local* variables, unlike globals, are only available in the current script. In the next frame, the variable won't exist. You can certainly create a new variable with the same name, but the previous contents from the last frame will not be in it.

The point of local variables is to create modular code. If a variable is local, it is removed from memory when the script is finished. Otherwise, if it is a global variable, the variable and its value will hang around until the movie ends.

To create a local variable, you need to use the `var` keyword. For instance, you could create a local variable named *`myLocal`* and place the number 9 in it like this:

```
var myLocal = 9;
```

After you set the variable with the `var` keyword, you don't have to use `var` again in that local piece of code. For instance, the following code creates the local variable, sets it to 9, changes its value to 11, and then sends it to the Output window:

```
var myLocal = 9;
myLocal = 11;
trace(myLocal);
```

When deciding when to use local variables and when to use global variables, the rule of thumb is to always use local variables unless there is a good reason to use a global. We'll mostly use local variables.

Comparisons and Operations

Comparing two things in ActionScript is simple. You use standard mathematical symbols, such as =, <, and >.

Are the Values the Same?

You have already seen how the = symbol is used to assign a value to a variable. To differentiate between times when you want to assign a value and times when you want to compare two values, the double equals symbol, ==, is used when you want to compare two things. The single equals operator is used to assign values to variables.

So, if you want to see whether variable *a* is the number 7, use ==. Here is an example that places the results in the Output window:

```
var a = 7;
trace(a == 7);
```

This code assigns the value 7 to the variable `a` by using the single equals symbols. It then compares `a` with 7 by using the double equals symbol.

When you test this code, the Output window will show "true." If you set *a* to 8 instead, the Output window will show "false" because 7 is not equal to 8.

> It is a common mistake, even for experts, to accidentally use a `=` in the place of a `==`. This can lead to a bug that is difficult to find because the difference can easily be missed by the eye. Watch out for this.

You can also use the == comparison to compare two strings. The following code compares a variable that contains a string with another string:

```
var myString = "Hello World.";
trace(myString == "Hello World.");
trace(myString == "hello world.");
```

When you run this program, you get both a "true" and a "false." This is because the first comparison matches the variable to exactly the same string, whereas the second comparison demonstrates that comparisons of strings take case into account.

Suppose that you want to test to see whether two values are not equal to each other. In this case, you use the special operator `!=`, which just means "not equals":

```
var a = 7;
trace(a != 9);
trace(a != 7);
```

The first `trace` statement produces a "true" because a is not equal to 9. The second `trace` statement produces a false because a is indeed equal to 7, but we are trying to test for it not to be 7.

Less Than or Greater Than

You can also compare two things to see whether they are less than or greater than each other. To do this, use the standard mathematical symbols < and >. Here is an example:

```
var a = 7;
trace(a < 8);
trace(a > 6);
trace(a < 1);
```

You should get a "true," "true," and "false" from this program. The variable a contains 7, which is less than 8, greater than 6, but is certainly not less than 1.

You can also use the <= or >= comparisons = (greater than or equal to) operator>=) operator>to find out whether a number is less than or equal to, or greater than or equal to, another number. Here is an example:

```
var a = 7;
trace(a <= 9);
trace(a >= 5);
trace(a >= 7);
```

All three of the preceding statements are "true."

Operators

You can also modify the values of variables with operations. They are also standard mathematical symbols such as + and - for addition and subtraction. For multiplication, we use the * symbol. For division, we use the / symbol.

For instance, to add 4 to a variable that contains the number 7, we just use a second assignment statement that sets the value of the variable to its current value, plus 4:

```
var a = 7;
a = a + 4;
trace(a);
```

The result is 11, of course. ActionScript actually has some shorthand for performing the same addition. The += operation takes the current variable and adds the next number to it. Here is some code that does exactly the same thing as the previous code:

```
var a = 7;
a += 4;
trace(a);
```

There is another piece of shorthand that you should be familiar with. The ++ operator is like the += operator, but it adds exactly 1 to the number. Here is an example:

```
var a = 7;
a++;
trace(a);
```

The result is 8. Now try this:

```
var a = 7;
trace(a++);
trace(a);
```

The result is first a 7 and then an 8. What happened here? Well, the first `trace` command placed the current value of a in the Output window. Then the ++ operator added one to a. The second `trace` statement placed the new value in the Output window.

Now try this:

```
var a = 7;
trace(++a);
trace(a);
```

You will get two 8s this time. This is because when you place the ++ operator before the variable, the addition is performed before the command.

You can use -- as well as ++ to subtract rather than add. You can also use -= to subtract a number and *= and /= to multiply or divide a variable by a number.

Task: Operations Quiz

Look at the following bits of code and see whether you can determine the value of a before you read the solution:

```
var a = 7;
a++;
a--;
trace("a");
```

The result is 7. 1 is added to a and then 1 is taken away.

```
var a = 7;
a += 6
a *= 2;
trace(a);
```

The result is 26. a starts at 7, changes to 13 when 6 is added to it, and then is multiplied by 2 to get 26.

```
var a = 7;
var b = 3;
a -= b;
a++;
trace(a);
```

The result is 5. b is subtracted from a leaving 4. Then 1 is added to a.

```
var a = 22;
var b = 6;
var c = 13;
a = b + c;
a -= 2;
b++;
trace(a);
```

The result is 17. a starts off as 22, but the value is completely replaced by b + c, which is 19. Then 2 is subtracted from a, leaving 17. The b++ changes b to 5, but does not affect a at all.

Conditions

Now that you know how to compare variables, you can use this information for something besides sending "true" and "false" to the Output window.

The `if` Statement

The `if` statement allows you to use the results of a comparison to change the way the Flash movie works. Here is a simple `if` statement that compares a to see whether it is 7 and jumps to another frame if it is.

```
if (a == 7) {
    gotoAndPlay(10);
}
```

The `if` statement starts with the word "if," followed by a comparison. Always place parentheses around the comparison. Then there is the open bracket.

The next lines, until the close bracket, contain the code to be executed if the comparison is true.

`else`

You can also include an optional extension to the `if` statement that executes some code if the condition is not met. Here is an example:

```
if (a == 7) {
    gotoAndPlay(10);
} else {
    gotoAndPlay(15);
}
```

You can also extend an `if` statement even further with `else if` clauses:

```
if (a == 7) {
    gotoAndPlay(10);
} else if (a == 8) {
    gotoAndPlay(15) {
} else if (a == 13) {
    gotoAndPlay(20);
} else {
    gotoAndPlay(25);
}
```

You can make an `if` statement as long as you want. You can even compare different variables in the `else if` clauses; there is no restriction to keeping it to a similar comparison.

Compound Comparisons

You can also compare more than one thing in an `if` statement. Suppose that you wanted to go to a frame only if `a` was 7 and `b` was 15. You could do that this way:

```
if ((a == 7) and (b == 15)) {
    gotoAndPlay(20);
}
```

The `and` operator takes two comparisons and combines them, returning true only if they are both true. Place parentheses around both comparisons individually to make it clear how Flash should interpret them.

You can also use `or` to combine two comparisons, but return true if either one or the other is true.

```
if ((a == 7) or (b == 15)) {
    gotoAndPlay(20);
}
```

In this code, the movie jumps to frame 20 if `a` is 7, or if `b` is 15. If both are true, it also jumps to frame 20. However, if `a` is not 7 and `b` is not 15, the `gotoAndPlay` command is not executed.

Loops

The syntax for creating loops in ActionScript is a little more complex than the simple `if` statement. Fortunately, it is almost identical to how loops are created in languages such as C, C++, and Java.

The `for` Loop

The primary type of loop is the `for` loop. It looks like this:

```
for(var i=0;i<10;i++) {
    trace(i);
}
```

If you run this code in a frame script, you get the numbers 0 through 9 placed in the Output window. The loop counts from 0 to 9, changing the local variable `i` along the way.

As you can see, a `for` statement has three parts. Each part is separated by a semicolon.

The first part is a variable declaration. In this case, the local variable `i` is created and set to 0. This first part of the `for` statement is executed once, before the loop starts.

The second part of the `for` statement is a condition. In this case, it tests to see whether `i` is less than 10. The `for` loop continues to run as long as this condition is true. When the loop starts, `i` is equal to 0, which is certainly less than 10, so the loop begins.

The third part of the `for` statement is an operation to be performed every time the loop loops. In this case, `i` is incremented by 1. This operation is performed after each iteration of the loop because the `++` operator is placed after the `i`. If it were placed before the `i`, such as `++i`, the operation would take place before the commands inside the loop are executed.

Inside the brackets are the commands to be executed each time through the loop. Let's play computer and see how the example works:

1. The local variable `i` is created and set to 0.
2. A check is made to make sure that `i` is less than 10. Because it is, the loop is allowed to continue.
3. A note is made that the variable `i` should be incremented by 1 when each iteration of the loop is complete. For now, `i` remains at 0.
4. The `trace` command then sends the contents of `i` to the Output window, in this case 0.
5. The iteration of the loop ends, and `i` is increased by 1.
6. The loop starts again, and the check is made to see whether `i` is less than 10. It is, because `i` is now 1, and the loop is allowed to continue.
7. The `trace` command sends the contents of `i` to the Output window, in this case 1.

This continues, with `i` increasing by 1 each time, until the 10th time through the loop. Then the following happens:

8. The iteration of the loop ends, and `i` is increased by 1. Its value is now 10.
9. The loop starts again, and the check is made to see whether `i` is less than 10. It is not because `i` is equal to 10. The loop ends.
10. The next line after the closing bracket at the end of the loop executes, and the loop is over.

Other Kinds of Loops

The `for` loop is the most common kind of loop. However, two other kinds of loops are the `while` loop and the `do` loop.

The `while` loop looks like this:

```
while (a != 7) {
    // more code here
}
```

As you can see, this is a much simpler loop than a `for` loop. It actually looks just like an `if` statement, except that the code in the brackets will continue to run over and over again until the condition is met. This being the case, it is easy to create undesirable infinite loops. You would have to make sure that the code inside the loop alters `a` in some way so that it eventually achieves the value of 7 and the loop ends.

The sibling to the `while` loop is the `do` loop. Here is what it looks like:

```
do {
    // more code here
} while (a != 7);
```

The `while` and `do` loops are actually the same thing, except that the condition is checked in different places. In the `while` loop, the condition is checked before each iteration of the loop, whereas in the `do` loop, it is checked after each iteration of the loop. The difference is that the `do` loop always runs at least once.

Breaking Out of Loops

All three kinds of loops can use two optional commands to change the flow of the loop. The first command, `break`, stops the loop and jumps right to the instruction following the loop.

The other command, `continue`, terminates the current pass through the loop but starts the next pass through the loop right away.

For instance, if instructions A, B, and C are inside the loop, and instruction B performs a `continue` command if a certain condition is met, instruction C will be skipped, and the loop will start again at A. If it was a `break` command instead, C would be skipped and the loop would end.

It is difficult to show valid examples of `break` and `continue` without a complex example, so we will save that for later in the book when we need it.

Functions

Until now, we've placed all our code in short scripts attached to the first frame of the movie. This works well for short, simple programs, but these scripts can get very long if you try to make the program complex.

Functions allow you to organize and reuse your code. You place functions in the timeline just as we have been doing. Here is a simple function:

```
function myFunction(num) {
    var newNum = num + 3;
    return newNum;
}
```

A function starts with the keyword `function` followed by the function name. Function names can be anything you want, just like variable names. But they should usually be something that relates to what the function does.

After the function name comes a left parenthesis. Then follows a list of parameters. A *parameter* is a variable that is defined when the function is called. Think of it as the input to a function. In this case, you are going to give the function a number to do something with.

You can have one, many, or no parameters. Either way, you close off the parameters section with a right parenthesis and then use an open bracket to start the function.

All the lines between the open and close brackets are the instructions inside the function. In this case, a new local variable is created, called *newNum*. The value of *newNum* is set to whatever *num* is, plus 3. So if you pass a 7 in to the function as *num*, *newNum* is now 10.

The `return` command is a special command used only inside functions. It completes the function and sets a value as the result of the function. In this case, *newNum* is the result of the function.

To use this function, call it like it was a standard ActionScript function or command, such as `trace`. Here is an example:

```
var a = myFunction(7);
```

This line of code creates a new local variable called `a`. It places in it the results of `myFunction(7)`. To determine this value, *myFunction* is called with the number 7 as its only parameter.

When the function starts, it creates a local variable called *num* and places 7 inside it. It then runs the code inside, which ends with the `return` command sending the value 10 back to the thing that originally called the function. In this case, `a` gets set to 10.

A great thing about functions is that you can reuse them. Here are three lines of code that reuse the function to produce three different results:

```
trace(myFunction(7));
trace(myFunction(13));
trace(myFunction(2));
```

When you run this code, along with the function included before it, you will get the results 10, 16, and 5. Another advantage to using functions is that you can make one change in the function, and it will affect all the commands that use that function. For instance, if you change the `+ 3` in the function to `+ 4`, the results of the preceding three lines become 11, 17, and 6.

Dot Syntax

Something else that you will be seeing a lot of as you learn ActionScript is dot syntax. Dot syntax is a way of grouping objects and functions that is used in many object-oriented programming languages.

Here is an example of dot syntax. Suppose that you want to take the square root of a number. Flash has a built-in square root function. It is a part of a group of math functions called the math object. To use the square root function, you first have to use the name of the math object, which is simply `Math`. The name of the function is `sqrt`. So this is how you would use the math object's square root function:

```
var a = Math.sqrt(4);
```

We'll look at the math object and its functions, as well as other objects like it, throughout the book.

Another common way to use dot syntax is to address a property of a movie clip. Suppose that you have a move clip named myClip and you wanted to determine its horizontal position on the screen. That would be the _x property of the movie clip. So the code would look like this:

```
var a = myClip._x;
```

We'll look at all the different movie clip properties as we need to use them in future hours, particularly in Hour 7, "Moving and Changing Movie Clips."

You can also use dot syntax to reference global variables inside other movie clips. So if you have code in a movie clip and are using a global variable inside that movie clip, you can access it from the root level like this:

```
var a = myClip.myVariable
```

Don't worry if you aren't sure about objects, movie clip properties, or movie clip levels. We'll examine each of these more throughout the book as we use them, particularly in Hour 6, "Controlling Movie Clips," and Hour 7. Right now, it is just important that you understand what dot syntax looks like.

Comments

Some of the most important lines of code in your programs don't do anything at all. They are comments, which Flash just ignores.

Comments, however, help you organize your code and remind you what a particular piece of code does. Here is a simple example:

```
// add 2 to the number
num += 2;
```

The previous example shows a line that is completely a comment. It begins with two forward slashes. The rest of the line is whatever you want it to be.

You can also place a comment at the end of a line. Here is an example:

```
num += 2; // add 2 to the number
```

Whenever you use the double slashes, the rest of the line is ignored by Flash.

If you have ever studied computer programming in college, you probably already know how important comments are. Most teachers will severely penalize a programming assignment if it is turned it with inadequate comments.

There are many different ways to use comments in your code. Programmers usually place one or more lines of comments before each function that explain what the function does. You can also place comments before individual lines if you feel they need more explanation.

Debugging

No matter how careful you are writing your program, every programmer has to eventually deal with bugs. To stamp out these pesky things, you should be as skilled in debugging techniques as you are in programming. Three methods are useful for debugging: logical deduction, sending messages to the Output window, and the ActionScript debugger.

Logical Deduction

Most bugs that occur are simple and easy to track down and fix. You won't need any special tools. When the bug occurs, you will have a pretty good idea of what it is and where it is.

Even if you don't know where the problem is at first, if you act like a detective and look through your code, you can usually find it. Think of all the information that you have as clues: When did the problem happen? What happened? What should have happened instead? What else unusual went on that might be another symptom of the bug?

No one knows your program better than you do. If you use logical deduction, you should be able to find your bug and fix it. However, some bugs are a little trickier, so you will need to use some helpful tools.

Output Window

A simple but effective tool in debugging is the Output window. You can place `trace` commands in your program that send information to the Output window. This information can tell you what your code is doing.

For instance, suppose that you have a simple loop that doesn't seem to work right. By adding a few `trace` commands, you can get a list of actions in the Output window that should point you in the right direction.

```
for(var i=0;i<9;i++) {
    trace("starting loop");
    trace(i);
    a += i;
    trace(a);
    trace("ending loop");
}
```

In this example, you will get a series of `"starting loop"` and `"ending loop"` messages, with two numbers representing the variables *i* and *a* between them. You can then watch the progression as these two variables change.

4

Debugger

A more heavy-duty tool is the debugger. This is a Flash window that shows you all sorts of data about your Flash movie and ActionScript code as your movie plays.

To use the Debugger window, choose Control, Debug Movie rather than Control, Test Movie. Your movie will compile and launch, but this time with the Debugger window shown.

Figure 4.3 shows the Debugger window. It contains several panes. The pane on the left has several tabs that allow you to examine different types of things in the Flash movie. The pane on the right shows you your ActionScript code.

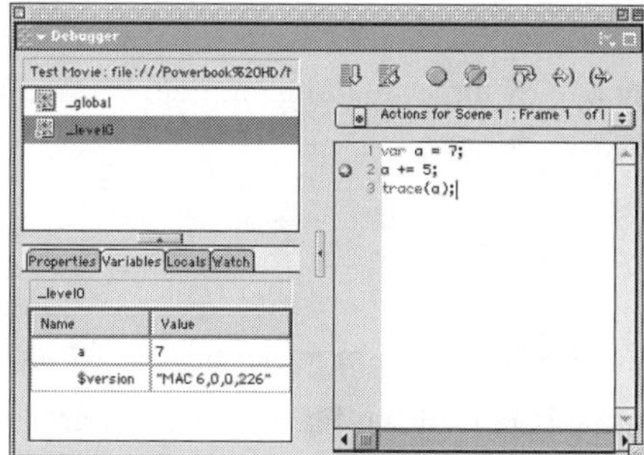

FIGURE 4.3
The Debugger window is a complex tool that will help you track down bugs.

One way to use the Debugger window is to set *breakpoints*. A breakpoint is an indicator placed next to a line of code in your scripts. When you test the movie in debug mode, the movie automatically stops at a breakpoint and allows you to examine the current state of the movie, including variable values. You can then proceed to step, line-by-line, through the code.

Because you are just getting started with ActionScript, the Debugger window is a needlessly complex tool. However, as you advanced from novice to expert, you will find yourself needing it more.

Summary

A script uses a set of symbols that you need to become familiar with to read and write ActionScript. Curly brackets surround segments of code that belong together. Dots, or periods, tie together objects and their properties.

There are two types of variables. Global variables are available to the entire movie level, whereas local variables are available only to the current function or script. You can set variable contents with `=`, and use `+`, `-`, `/`, and `*` to perform operations on variables and numbers. The shorthand `++` and `--` will add and subtract 1 from a variable, whereas `+=` and `-=` will add or subtract a specific number from the variable.

You can compare two values to see whether they are equal by using the `==` symbol. You can also use <, >, <=, and >= to test values. A test always results in a true or false value that can be used by an `if` statement to run code only if the test is true.

There are several kinds of loops, but the main one is the `for` loop that counts with a variable from one value to another. The `for` statement has specific syntax that you should get to know well.

Functions can be used to group bits of code together so that they can be used by many different parts of your program. They can accept values, known as parameters, and return a value as well.

Debugging can be done by one of three methods: logical deduction, use of the `trace` command, or Flash's built-in debugger.

Q&A

Q Will the Output window show up in my final movie if I use a `trace` command?

A No. The output window is part of the Flash authoring application and will not show up when your Flash movie is on a Web site.

Q What happens when I divide a number by 0 in ActionScript?

A You get a special ActionScript value indicated by "Infinity". However, you should consider any division by 0 as a bug and avoid it.

Q Is there any limit to how many `else if` statements I can use?

A No, but there is a better way to implement a long list of conditions. The `case` statement allows you to test one variable against a list of possible values.

Q If I place a function in one frame's script, is it available to scripts in other frames?

A Yes, as long as it is on the same timeline. Functions inside movie clips, however, can be directly accessed inside that movie clip only.

Workshop

The quiz questions are designed to test your knowledge of the material covered in this hour. The answers to the questions follow.

Quiz

1. What is the difference between = and ==?
2. Can you access global variables inside a function?
3. When you make a comparison, how many possible outcomes are there?
4. How many different types of loops are there in ActionScript?

Quiz Answers:

1. A single equals symbol is an assignment. It is how you set a variable to a value. A double equals symbol is a test. It compares the values on either side.
2. Yes. You can access global variables anywhere in that timeline. However, you can access local variables only in the code segment, such as a function, in which they appear.
3. Only two: true or false. Either the comparison works out, or it doesn't.
4. Three: the `for` loop, the `do` loop, and the `while` loop.

PART II

Navigation and Animation with ActionScript

Hour

HOUR 5

Controlling the Flow of the Movie

The simplest, but in some ways the most powerful, thing that ActionScript can do is control the flow of the Flash movie. You can stop a movie on a certain frame, or jump around from frame to frame. This frees the Flash movie from its even-paced linear movement that it has by default.

In this hour, you will:

- Learn how to stop the movie on a frame
- Find out how to jump from one frame to another
- Create buttons to allow the user to control the Flash movie
- Make a simple slideshow
- Create a full presentation with Flash

Stopping the Movie

Perhaps the simplest command in ActionScript is the `stop` command. When issued, it simply stops the movie in its tracks on the current frame.

Most of the time, you will want to place the `stop` command in a frame on the timeline. Although only `stop` is necessary, the Flash reference material shows the command with the optional parentheses, so we will use them here as well:

```
stop ();
```

When you use the `stop` command, the movie is really just paused on the current frame. Any animation inside movie clips or graphic symbols on the frame continues to animate. However, animation on the main timeline stops.

For the movie to continue, you need to issue another ActionScript command. The simplest one is the `play` command. This pushes the movie forward to the next frame, and it continues playing.

We'll look at the `play` command in the section, "Creating Buttons," later in this hour. For now, let's just look at an example of the `stop` command.

The movie stop.fla on the CD-ROM is a simple example. The first frame contains a large graphic of the letter "A" on it. The second and third frames contain the letters "B" and "C," respectively.

The second frame of the movie also contains a script. It is a simple script with just the `stop` command. Figure 5.1 shows the work area and timeline for this movie. Notice that there is an "a" in the second frame, signifying a script there. The Actions panel is also shown in Figure 5.1. In it, you can see the script.

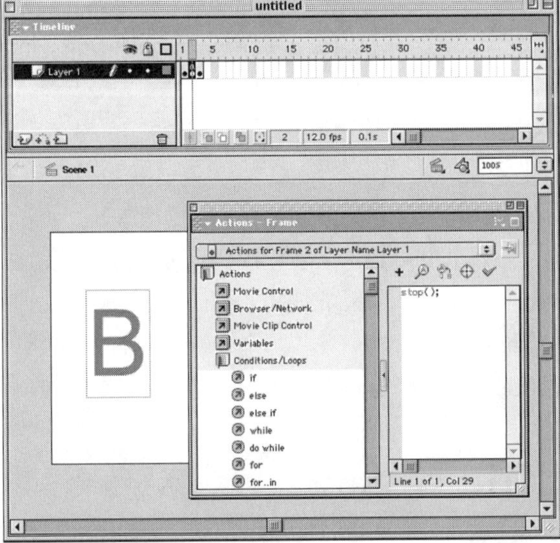

FIGURE 5.1
The "a" indicates a script in frame 2 of the timeline.

When you test the movie, the first frame with the "A" quickly appears. Then the movie moves on to the second frame with the "B." At this point, the `stop` command executes, and the movie stops on frame 2. Frame 3, with the "C" on it, never appears.

Jumping from Frame to Frame

Another basic ActionScript command is the `gotoAndPlay` command that we have already seen many times in examples. This command jumps from the current frame to any frame you specify. You can use a number or a frame marker name. Here are some examples:

```
gotoAndPlay(7);
gotoAndPlay(20);
gotoAndPlay("my frame label")
```

You can also specify a scene if your movie uses more than one. If you use `gotoAndPlay` with just one parameter, that parameter is the frame. But if you use it with two parameters, the first is the scene name and the second is the frame number or name.

```
gotoAndPlay("My Scene","My Frame");
```

When you use the `gotoAndPlay` command, the movie jumps to the frame specified and immediately continues playing. However, if you want the movie to jump to another frame and stop on that frame, you should use the `gotoAndStop` command. It works the same way as `gotoAndPlay`, with the same option of using one or two parameters.

There are also two simple commands that work just like `gotoAndStop` but take the movie to the next frame or the previous frame. You can use `nextFrame` or `prevFrame` in cases where you just want to advance or go back one frame.

To see all these commands in action, it is useful to have a movie with buttons. So let's take a look at how to create buttons before going any further.

Creating Buttons

Buttons are one of the three main types of symbols that you use in Flash. The others are movie clips and graphics.

Making a New Button

There are many ways to create a button. One method is to choose Insert, New Symbol from the menu. You are presented with a dialog asking you to name the symbol and to choose whether it is a movie clip, button, or graphic. Choose Button.

The main Flash window now changes to show the button's timeline instead of the movie's main timeline. There are four frames in a button timeline. They are labeled Up, Over, Down, and Hit. They represent the three button states, and the active area of the button.

If you place a graphic, such as a circle, in the first frame and nothing in the other three frames, the Over and Down states of the button will be the same as the Up state. The active area of the button will be the same as well.

On the other hand, you can create a different graphic for each key frame. Figure 5.2 shows four different views of the main Flash window, each with a different key frame selected. In this example, I used a simple circular button with a slight variation for each state. The Hit frame represents the entire area of the button so that it is easy for the user to click it.

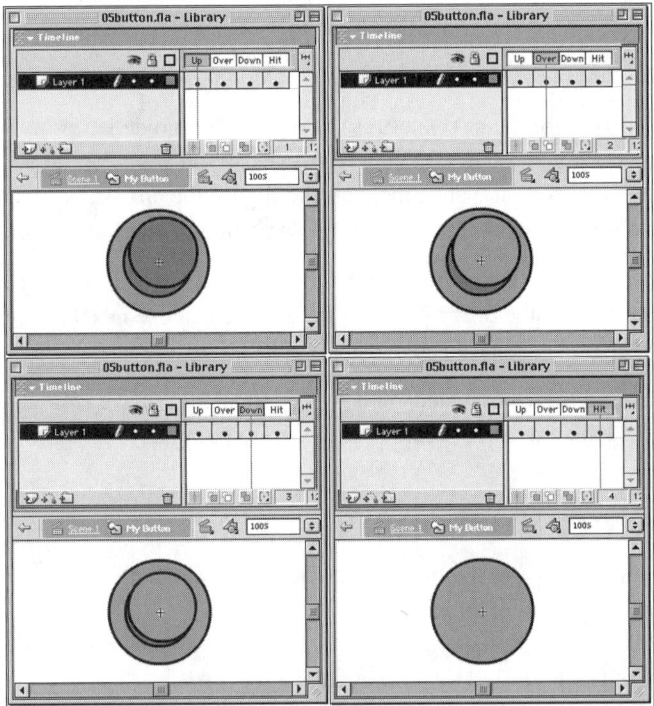

FIGURE 5.2
The four different key frames of a button.

When you are finished creating your button, return to the main timeline by clicking the name of the scene, usually Scene 1, where it appears just under the timeline.

Now, open up the library by choosing Window, Library. You should see the button in the library. Drag it to the work area in the main window.

Adding a Script to a Button

To add a script to a button, first select the button. Then bring up the Actions panel. Alternatively, you can right-click the button in Windows, or Control+click the button on the Mac. Select Actions from the menu that appears.

Make sure that the Actions panel is set to Expert mode. You can check this in the pop-up menu that is activated at the upper-right corner of the window.

Here is a typical button script. You can place this in the script window and then test the movie to see whether it works. Figure 5.3 shows the Actions panel with the script in it.

```
on (release) {
    trace("You clicked the button!")
}
```

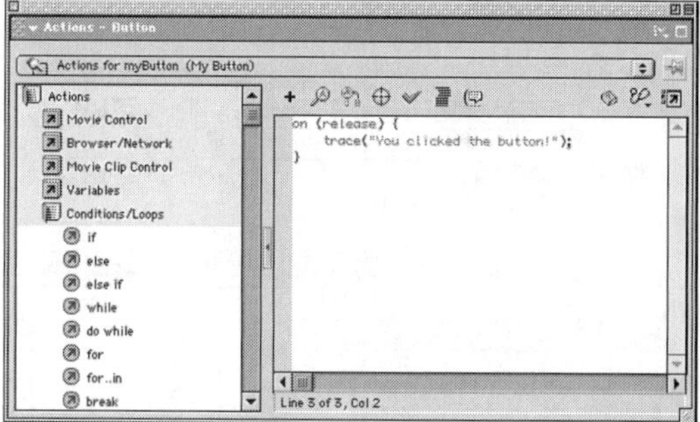

FIGURE 5.3
The Actions panel with a simple button script.

NEW TERM Button scripts use a special syntax that starts with the `on` keyword. This creates a *handler*. It is called that simply because it "handles" an event. In this case, the event is `release`, which is what happens when the user clicks the button and then releases. That is the most common type of button event.

You could also use the alternative event `press` in place of `release`. The difference is that the handler will run when the user first clicks the button and will not wait for the user to release the mouse button.

When a handler is activated, the code inside the brackets is executed. In this case, just a `trace` command is there. It sends a message to the Output window to let you know that the script worked.

Now let's put our knowledge of ActionScript navigation commands and button scripts to work.

Task: Slideshow

A slideshow is a simple presentation where you have various screens, or slides, presented one after the other. This is similar to how a plain Flash movie would work, except that without scripts, the movie would continue rather quickly through these frames.

Instead, we'll use scripts to pause the movie on each frame. To continue it, we will use buttons that allow the user to advance to the next frame whenever she wants.

1. Create a new Flash movie. Place four different pieces of text or graphic on the first four frames. The example movie 05slideshow.fla contains the words "Frame 1" through "Frame 4" and a different shape on each frame.

   I've also placed the text "Slideshow Example" above everything else, stretched across all frames on its own layer. The result is partially shown in Figure 5.4. You can see the contents of Frame 1, plus the way the timeline is set up.

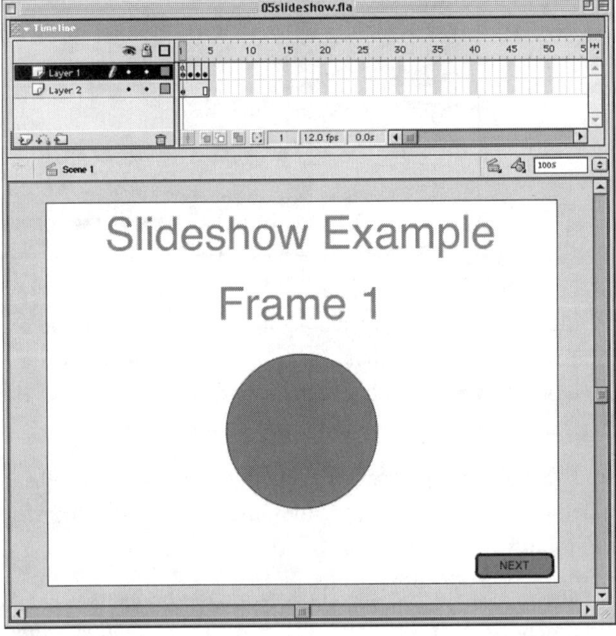

FIGURE 5.4
The slideshow movie is set up with individual elements on each of the four frames plus some elements across all the frames.

2. Create a button. It can be as simple or as complex a button as you want. In Figure 5.4, you can see my Next button at the bottom right.
3. Make sure that the button is placed on a layer so that it stretches across all four frames of the movie. Check the example movie if you are not sure how this should look.

4. Attach a script to the button. Make sure that you have the button and not the frame selected. The Actions panel should have the title Actions - Button at the top. Here is the script:

```
on (release) {
    nextFrame();
}
```

5. Now, select the first frame of the movie. In Figure 5.4, you can see that one of the layers, Layer 1, has four separate key frames, and the other layer, Layer 2, has one key frame that stretches across all four frames. Select the first key frame in Layer 1 and open the Actions panel. Its title should now be Actions - Frame. Looking at the title of the script panel is a good way to confirm that you are writing a frame script, not attaching one to a movie clip. Place this simple script in the script panel:

```
stop();
```

   This stops the movie from rapidly advancing from Frame 1 through Frame 4. We want it to stop at Frame 1 and await the user.

6. Choose Control, Test Movie to see it in action. The movie starts at Frame 1 and then pauses. You can then click the Next button to advance to Frame 2. You can keep advancing until you get to Frame 4.

   The movie will not advance past Frame 4 because the `nextFrame` command will simply do nothing if there are no more frames. You could have placed the Next button in every frame except the last one so that the button will not even appear there.

Next, we'll build a much more complex presentation movie.

Task: Simple Presentation

Now let's build a more complex presentation. We'll start with the basic functionality of the slideshow example and build from there.

The first thing we will add is a Back button to match the Next button. We'll also place these buttons only on frames where they apply. So there will be no Next button on the last slide and no Back button on the first slide.

The major advancement for this movie will be the addition of a main menu screen. This will be the new first frame of the movie, and it will have buttons that link to every other frame of the movie. This means that the user can start anywhere in the movie that he wants. If he wants to jump right to the third slide, then he can.

Figure 5.5 shows the main menu screen. There is a movie title and a screen title. Under that are four simple buttons with the names of the frames that they link to on the right of each button.

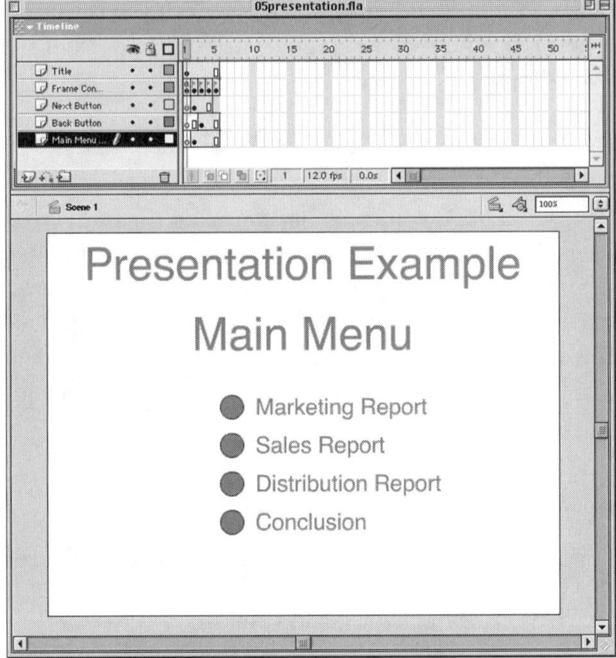

FIGURE 5.5
The main menu screen has links to all the slides in the presentation.

In Figure 5.5, you can also see the main timeline. I have done a lot more to separate out the elements onto layers and to label the layers.

You can see that the Next button is present on only the first three out of four slides, and the Back button is present only on the last three out of four slides. You can also see that the main menu screen precedes these slides.

The little flags in the Frame Contents layer of the timeline show that I have labeled the four slide frames. This means that we can refer to each slide by a name rather than a frame number.

Now, let's build this movie. You can refer to the example movie on the CD-ROM named 05presentation.fla if you want.

1. Create a new movie, or start with the movie from the slideshow in the previous task.
2. The title of the movie is on a layer by itself. It is just a piece of text at the top, in this case "Presentation Example."

3. The elements of the main menu are all in the Frame Contents layer, in a key frame that stretches across only the first frame of the movie. It includes a piece of text reading "Main Menu" and four buttons. The four buttons are actually one button in the library. I just dragged the button onto the work area four times. The buttons are just simple circles. Next to each button is a piece of text with the name of the slide that the button links to.
4. The script on each button uses the `gotoAndStop` command. Here is the script in the first button:

   ```
   on (release) {
       gotoAndPlay("marketing");
   }
   ```

   As you might guess, the first slide, which will be in the second frame of the movie, is labeled Marketing. I could have used `gotoAndPlay(2);` and avoided using labels at all, but labels make the code much easier to work with. For instance, suppose that we wanted to add more frames at the start of the movie. Then slide 1, the marketing slide, would no longer be located in Frame 2 of the movie. This means that you would have to go back and change this script. However, by using a name rather than a number, you can shift things around in your movie without having to update your scripts.

   The other three buttons use the same script but with different markers. They are Sales, Distribution, and Conclusion to match the names of the rest of the frames.
5. Create the other four key frames in the Frame Contents layer. Instead of using the simple "Frame X" titles as in the slideshow example, I used real-world titles: Marketing, Sales, Distribution, and Conclusion. This makes the example seem a little like a corporate presentation or Web site.

   Figure 5.6 shows the second slide, which is the Sales slide. You can see the name of the slide, a shape to give the slide some content, and some buttons at the bottom. Pretend that the shape is actually some complex and boring graphic showing the rise in sales of a fantastically successful Internet company.
6. The buttons at the bottom of the slide in Figure 5.6 are actually placed on several frames. Each button has its own layer in the timeline. The Next button stretches across all but the last slide. The Back button stretches across all but the first slide. The Main Menu button stretches across all the slides. None of these buttons stretches back to the first frame of the movie, which is the main menu.

   Create these three buttons and place them in their own layers stretched across the appropriate frames.

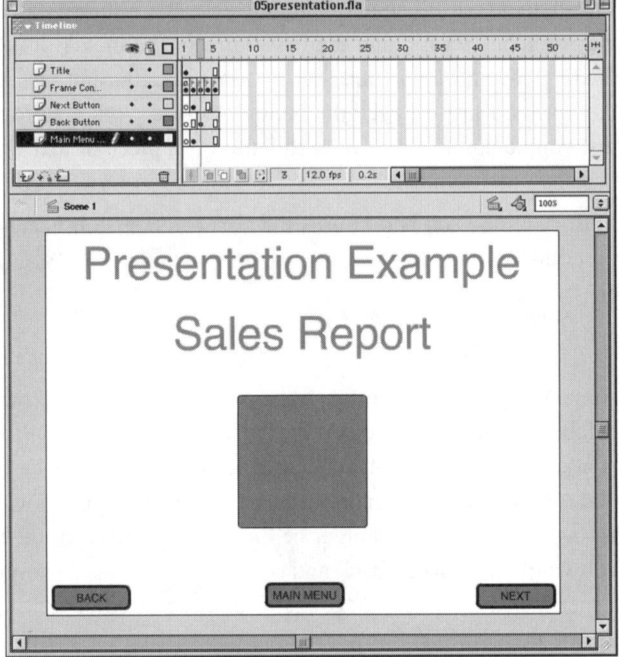

FIGURE 5.6
The Sales slide includes a title, some content, and a row of buttons at the bottom.

7. The script for the Next button is identical to the script used in the previous example:

```
on (release) {
    nextFrame();
}
```

8. The script for the Back button is similar. It just uses the `prevFrame` command instead:

```
on (release) {
    prevFrame();
}
```

9. The script for the Main Menu button is a simple one as well. It uses `gotoAndStop` to take the user back to the first frame:

```
on (release) {
    gotoAndStop("main menu");
}
```

   Make sure that you also label the first frame as `"main menu"`.

10. The only script remaining is the one that needs to be placed on the first frame to prevent the movie from animating through all five frames when it starts:

```
stop();
```

This completes the presentation movie. Test the movie to make sure that it works. Look over all the scripts again to make sure that you understand what each one is doing.

A movie like this can be used for many things. For one, it can be the entire contents of a Web site. The main menu can link to frames that explain a company's mission, services, and contacts. Or, it could be a personal home page with frames about the owner's history, interests, and other bits of information.

The important thing to realize is that Flash is no longer just an animation tool to you. You now control the movement of the Flash movie and can make it do other things besides a plain linear animation.

Summary

You can use many commands to control the flow of a Flash movie. Here is a list:

- `stop` Pauses the current timeline on the current frame.
- `play` Continues the flow of a movie after a `stop` command.
- `gotoAndStop` Jumps to a frame name or number and pauses the movie there.
- `gotoAndPlay` Jumps to a frame name or number and lets the movie continue animating from there.
- `nextFrame` Moves the movie to the next frame and stops it there.
- `prevFrame` Takes the movie back one frame and stops it there.

The `stop` command is usually placed in a frame script to pause the movie and let the user take control of what happens next. The other movie control commands are usually placed in `on (release)` button handlers.

Q&A

Q If you use the `stop` command and the movie stops, why do movie clips still animate and buttons still work?

A The `stop` command affects only the flow of the main timeline. Symbols on the screen, such as movie clips and buttons, still move and respond at a normal rate.

Q The `nextFrame` command goes to the next frame and then stops there. What if I want to go to the next frame and then have the movie continue at its normal animation pace?

A You can use the `nextFrame` command to go to the next frame and then immediately follow it with a `play` command.

Q Can I place functions inside button scripts?

A No. Functions can be placed only in the main timeline. You can only put `on` handlers in button scripts.

Q Can I place buttons on a frame but make them inactive?

A Not as easily as you think. You can place a button on a separate key frame and then just not attach a script to it. The button won't do anything, but it will still look active. A better method would be to create a graphic symbol that looks like an inactive version of the button and place it in the same spot where the button would normally appear.

Workshop

The quiz questions are designed to test your knowledge of the material covered in this hour. The answers to the questions follow.

Quiz Questions

1. If you have a movie with several frames, how do you prevent the movie from automatically animating through all the frames?
2. What is the difference between `gotoAndPlay` and `gotoAndStop`?
3. What are the two `on` handlers that will respond to a button click?
4. Why should you avoid using frame numbers in `gotoAndStop` and `gotoAndPlay` commands?

Quiz Answers

1. Place a `stop` command on the first frame.
2. The `gotoAndPlay` command jumps to a frame, and the movie continues to flow forward. The `gotoAndStop` command stops the movie on the destination frame.
3. You can use `on (press)` to trigger code when the user clicks the button and `on (release)` to trigger code when the user releases the button.
4. If you use frame numbers, and later insert or remove frames from your timeline, you will have to go back and adjust the frame numbers in your code. On the other hand, if you use frame names, your code will always go to the right frame.

Hour 6

Controlling Movie Clips

The primary element used by Flash animators and programmers alike is the movie clip. These little Flash movies inside your main Flash movie allow you to modularize your program, grouping elements and establishing levels of interactivity. Much of ActionScript is concerned with controlling movie clips.

In this hour, you will:

- Learn how to tell movie clips what to do
- Create an animation playback controller
- Find out what it means to target a movie clip
- See how to make a movie clip script
- Make a movie clip that plays backwards

Telling Movie Clips What to Do

Suppose that you have a movie that contains a simple animated movie clip. The main movie is simple: just one frame with a movie clip on it. The movie clip itself is a long animation of some sort, but it is all self-contained inside the movie clip. It contains no ActionScript code at all.

The first thing that you need to do to control a movie clip is to name it. Naming movie clips in Flash is confusing because all movie clips have two names: the name of the original movie clip in the Library, and the name of the movie clip instance in the work area. The reason for the two names is that you can have more than one instance of the same movie clip on the screen at the same time.

So, for instance, you could have a movie clip called "gear animation" in the Library, and a "gear1" movie clip instance on the screen. You could also have a "gear2" movie clip instance. They are both taken from the original "gear animation" movie clip in the Library.

Figure 6.1 shows the property panel when a movie clip is selected. To bring up the property panel, select the movie clip in the work area and choose Window, Properties.

FIGURE 6.1
The properties panel shows the name of the movie clip instance and allows you to change that name if you want.

In Figure 6.1, you can see that I have named the movie clip instance "gears". It also shows the name of the original Library element as "gear animation".

The name of the movie clip instance on the screen is the critical one to an ActionScript programmer. This name is what you will need to refer to the movie clip in your programs.

For example, if you have a movie clip instance named "gears", you would refer to it with that name. Then, using dot syntax, you could give it a command, such as `stop`. Here is an example:

```
gears.stop();
```

You can also send other commands to a movie clip. For instance, if you want to tell a movie clip to go to a certain frame, you can use `gotoAndStop`.

```
gears.gotoAndStop(5);
```

Note that this is how you send commands to a movie clip that is at the current level. If you want to place a command on a frame inside this movie clip, you shouldn't use the name of the clip, just `gotoAndStop`. If you were to use the name of the movie clip, Flash would look for a movie clip instance named "gears" inside the current movie clip instance "gears" inside the main timeline—two levels down rather than one.

Task: Animation Playback Controller

Now let's put this knowledge to work. In the example movie 06animationplayback.fla there is a movie clip named "gears". Other elements on the main timeline are buttons that will control this movie clip.

The "gears" movie clip is nothing special. It contains 60 frames of animation. No scripts or markers are in it at all.

The goal here is to build a movie that controls the movie clip completely. It allows the user to click buttons to advance the movie clip frame-by-frame, play the movie clip at its normal rate, stop the movie clip, and send the movie clip back to the first frame.

1. Create a new Flash movie. Create movie clip animation in it, or simply steal the "gear animation" movie clip from the sample movie.
2. Drag the movie clip from the Library to the work area. Choose Windows, Properties so that you can change the name of the movie clip to "gears".
3. Place a script in the first and only frame of the main timeline. This script prevents the movie clip from animating when you first run the movie:

```
gears.stop();
```

4. Create a set of buttons. You will need a button for the following actions: Advance, Previous, Play, Stop, and Rewind. Place them all in the work area under the movie clip. Figure 6.2 shows how this looks in the sample movie.

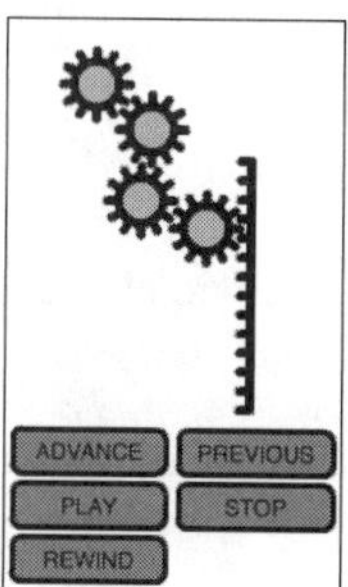

FIGURE 6.2
The sample movie features a movie clip animation and five buttons.

6

5. The Advance button uses the `nextFrame` command, addressed to the movie clip, to advance the clip one frame at a time.

```
on (release) {
    gears.nextFrame();
}
```

6. The Previous button uses the prevFrame command, in the same manner, to move the movie clip back one frame.

```
on (release) {
    gears.prevFrame();
}
```

7. The Play button uses the play command to let the movie clip advance and loop as it would normally.

```
on (release) {
    gears.play();
}
```

8. Likewise, the Stop button issues a stop command to the movie clip.

```
on (release) {
    gears.stop();
}
```

9. The Rewind button does something a little different. It uses the gotoAndStop command to send the movie clip back to Frame 1 and have it wait there.

```
on (release) {
    gears.gotoAndStop (1);
}
```

   Test this movie. If none of the buttons seem to work, the most likely reason is that the movie clip is not named properly.

Imagine this same example movie, but with a cartoon or other animation instead of the simple one here. The Flash movie then acts like a viewer for the animation.

Targeting Movie Clips

We have already seen the simplest way to target a movie clip. Just use its name, followed by a dot, followed by the command you want to send.

However, there are plenty of other ways to target a movie clip as well. First, let's learn how to target different levels of the Flash movie.

The most basic target level in a Flash movie is the main timeline. You can target it with the _root keyword. That is an underscore followed by the word "root."

For instance, if you want to send a gotoAndStop command to the main timeline, you can do this:

```
_root.gotoAndStop(7);
```

If you issue this command from the main timeline, there is no need for the _root target; however, it will work either way. But if you are writing code that is inside a movie clip, and you want that movie clip to tell the main timeline one level above it to do something, _root is one way of doing it.

You can also use _parent to target the level exactly one above the current level. So, if you are one movie clip down from the root level, and you use _parent, it is the same as using _root. However, if you are two levels down, _parent means the level above, whereas _root means two levels above.

It can help to number the levels. The root level, which is the main timeline, is level 0. A movie clip on the root level is at level 1. If there is a movie clip inside that movie clip, it is at level 2. From level 2, _parent refers to level 1, and _root refers to level 0.

So what about the other way? If you are at level 0, and you want to refer to a movie clip named "gears", you have already seen that you can refer to it by name. You can also use the term _root followed by square brackets, with the name of the movie clip inside it. Here are two lines of code that mean exactly the same thing, provided they are at the root level:

```
gears.gotoAndStop(7);
_root["gears"].gotoAndStop(7);
```

Another way to do this would be to use the keyword this. When you use this, you are referring to the current level. So this at the root level is the same thing as _root. However, this inside the movie clip "gears" will be the same as gears. the following three lines mean the same thing at the root level:

```
gears.gotoAndStop(7);
_root["gears"].gotoAndStop(7);
this["gears"].gotoAndStop(7);
```

So which one should you use? The advantage of using _root and this is that you can refer to movie clips by variables. For instance, you could do this:

```
var whichClipToUse = "gears";
this[whichClipToUse].stop();
```

The advantage of using this over _root is that you will not always have everything happening at the root level. Sometimes movie clips will issue commands to other movie clips at lower levels, and you will need to use this to make it work. Therefore, this wins out as the best way to refer to movie clips. However, in simple cases, it will be better to just refer to movie clips by name like we did in the last example.

Movie Clip Scripts

You have already seen how to attach movie clips to frames and buttons. Now it is time to attach them to movie clips.

Movie clip scripts, like button scripts, use handlers. Instead of using the `on` keyword that button scripts use, we will use the `onClipEvent` keyword. Here is an example of a movie clip script:

```
onClipEvent (load) {
    trace("This clip has been loaded.");
}
```

The `load` event happens when a movie clip first appears on the screen. It happens one time only.

Remember that when you stop the main timeline, the movie clips on the main timeline continue to animate. That fact is important to movie clip scripts because the next event, `enterFrame`, occurs every time a new frame is reached in the movie clip. Even when the main timeline is stopped, the movie clip continues to move along its own timeline, looping back to the beginning when it reaches its end. This means that `enterFrame` events happen at a continuous rate. Whenever an `enterFrame` event occurs, our `onClipEvent (enterFrame)` handler will be called. Here is a sample:

```
onClipEvent (enterFrame) {
    trace("This clip has entered a new frame.");
}
```

The sample movie 06enterframe.fla contains a simple movie clip with this script attached to it. Run it, and your Output window will look like this:

```
This clip has been loaded.
This clip has entered a new frame.
This clip has entered a new frame.
This clip has entered a new frame.
This clip has entered a new frame.
```

This last line will repeat as long as you let the movie run. This timed repetition will allow us to do all sorts of things in the hours to come. It will be the bedrock of our scripts.

Task: Backward Movie Clip

For now, let's write a simple movie clip script that demonstrates how it works. We'll make a movie clip run backward.

We will start the movie clip at the last frame and then use a `prevFrame` command to send the clip back one frame at a time.

1. Start a new movie. Place a simple, animated movie clip on the screen. You can use the "gear animation" from the previous example.

   In this case, it doesn't matter what you name the movie clip. We will never need to refer to it by name because the script will be attached directly to the movie clip.

2. Select the movie clip and bring up the Actions panel. The title of the Actions panel should be Actions—Movie Clip.

3. Two handlers are in this script. The first one is an `onClipEvent (load)` handler that sends the movie clip to the last frame, in this case frame 60:

   ```
   onClipEvent (load) {
       gotoAndStop(60);
   }
   ```

   This handler is called only once, when the movie clip first appears.

4. The second handler is an `onClipEvent (enterFrame)` handler that executes once per frame. It pushes the movie clip to the previous frame:

   ```
   onClipEvent (enterFrame) {
       prevFrame();
   }
   ```

Test the movie to see it in action. In the example movie, 06reverse.fla, you can see the same "gear animation" animation play backward.

Task: Clips Controlling Other Clips

Movie clips can also control other movie clips. By using the `_root` or `_parent` keyword, you can send your commands up one level. Then, by using the name of the movie clip you want to address, you can send the commands back down to another clip. Here is an example. Suppose that you want the movie clip "gears1" to send a command to its sibling, "gears2":

```
_parent.gears2.gotoAndStop(7);
```

If "gears1" and "gears2" are at level 1, `_parent` addresses level 0. Adding "gears2" addresses the command back down to level 1, but to another movie clip entirely. Another way to do this would be with square brackets:

```
_parent["gears2"].gotoAndStop(7);
```

Now let's use that technique to create a movie with three movie clips. The first one has a movie clip script that advances it one frame at a time. Inside this movie clip is a script triggered on the 15th frame. It tells the next movie clip to move forward one frame. This second movie clip does the same thing to a third movie clip. The result is that the first movie clip animates quickly, one frame per normal movie frame. The second movie clip animates one frame for every 15 frames that the first clip animates. The third movie clip animates one frame for every 15 frames the second clip animates.

Take a look at the example movie 06clipcommunication.fla to see what this looks like before trying to build it yourself.

1. Create a new Flash movie. Make a movie clip that has 15 frames of animation. Name it “cog”.
2. Inside the movie clip, place a `stop()` script on the first frame. This prevents it from animating all by itself. Instead, we will control its animation through ActionScript.
3. On the 15th frame of the movie clip, place the following script:

```
_parent[clipToTell].nextFrame();
gotoAndStop(1);
```

   This code does two things. First, it tells a sibling movie clip with the name stored in the variable *`clipToTell`* that it should advance to the next frame. Second, it sends itself back to the first frame to start again.

4. Now we just have to define the variable *`clipToTell`*. We’ll do this in the movie clip script, so exit the editing of the “cog” movie clip and return to the main timeline. Place an instance of the “cog” movie clip in the work area and name it “cog1”.

   Now attach a movie clip script to it. Here is the script:

```
onClipEvent (load) {
    clipToTell = "cog2";
}

onClipEvent (enterFrame) {
    nextFrame();
}
```

   The first thing that happens when the movie clip starts is that the variable *`clipToTell`* is set to “cog2”. This means that when the movie clip gets to frame 15, it uses the previous script in step 3 to tell “cog2” to advance one frame.

   The `onClipEvent (enterFrame)` handler is used to advance this movie clip by one frame for each main movie frame.

> It can be confusing to see that the movie clip script and the frame scripts inside the movie clip are at the same level. After all, you can only get at and edit the movie clip script while viewing the main timeline, and you can only get at and edit the movie clip’s frame scripts by viewing the movie clip’s timeline. Despite this, these scripts are all at the movie clip level. This is why the global variable *`clipToTell`* is available to both.

5. Now drag the "cog" movie clip to the work area a second time. Name this instance "cog2". Place the following script on it:

```
onClipEvent (load) {
    clipToTell = "cog3";
}
```

   This is all the second movie clip needs. It does not need a `onClipEvent (enterFrame)` handler because it does not advance one frame for every frame the main movie does. Instead, it gets its instruction to advance from "cog1".

   The second clip, however, has a value of "cog3" for the *`clipToTell`* variable. That means that when it gets to frame 15, it tells "cog3" to advance by one frame.

6. Create a third instance of the "cog" movie clip. Name this one "cog3". No script is needed on this movie clip at all. There will be no "cog4" in this example, so "cog3" does not need to worry about telling another movie clip that it is time to advance.

This movie demonstrates more than just clip-to-clip communication. It also demonstrates how movie clip scripts and a movie clip's frame scripts can share a global variable. This global is available only inside the movie clip and not to other sibling movie clips or the main timeline.

Summary

You can target movie clips by using dot syntax or bracket notation. Using square brackets lets you target movie clips by name with the name contained in a variable.

You can target the top level of a Flash movie with `_root` and the level above the current level with `_parent`.

Movie clips can have scripts attached to them that control what they do. Movie clip events include `load` and `enterFrame`. These events can trigger `onClipEvent` handlers.

Q&A

Q A lot of things in ActionScript use the underscore, _, as the first character. What does that mean?

A The underscore is a standard way in some modern programming languages of identifying a predefined reserved property. You'll see many more properties like it in Hour 7, "Moving and Changing Movie Clips."

Q How do I address a movie clip that is two levels down?

A Using dot syntax, you can address the movie clip "innerClip" inside "outerClip" like this: `innerClip.outerClip.stop();`. Similarly, you can use brackets to do it like this: `this["innerClip"]["outerClip"].stop();`.

Q In the last task, the global variable *`clipToTell`* is available only inside the movie clips. What if I wanted to get that value from the root level?

A You could use dot syntax or brackets to address the variable the same way that you send commands to that movie clip—for instance, `cog1.clipToTell`.

Q In the last task, if the first movie clip assigns one value to *`clipToTell`* and the second movie clip assigns another value to *`clipToTell`*, doesn't the second assignment replace the first?

A No. The global *`clipToTell`* exists as separate variables inside each movie clip. Think of the first one as `cog1.clipToTell` and the second one as `cog2.clipToTell`.

Workshop

The quiz questions are designed to test your knowledge of the material covered in this hour. The answers to the questions follow.

Quiz

1. If you have a movie clip at level 1, what is the difference between using `_root` and `_parent` in scripts inside this movie clip?
2. How many names does a movie clip have?
3. What is the advantage of using brackets rather than dot syntax in referring to a movie clip?
4. If scripts in the main timeline are at level 0, and frame scripts inside a movie clip are at level 1, at what level is the script attached to the movie clip?

Quiz Answers

1. Basically, none. Both refer to the main timeline at level 0. However, if you move this clip around and place it inside another movie clip so that it is at level 2, `_root` will refer to level 0 and `_parent` will refer to level 1. So you will want to be careful which one you use anyway.

2. Two. It has a name in the Library. It also has a name for the specific instance of the movie clip. There is only one Library name for the clip, but you will need as many instance names as there are instances.
3. Brackets allow you to use the contents of a variable as the name of a movie clip. With dot syntax, the name is hard-coded as part of the script.
4. Level 1. Movie clip scripts are at the same level as the frame scripts inside the movie clip.

HOUR 7

Moving and Changing Movie Clips

Movie clip instances have properties that you can examine and change. By using these properties, you can change the screen location of a clip, rotate it, scale it, and even hide it.

In this hour, you will:

- Learn how to change the position of a movie clip
- Find out how to determine the cursor location
- Learn how to rotate a movie clip
- Learn how to scale a movie clip
- See how a movie clip can be made invisible

Position

New Term Every element in the Flash work area has a position. This position is measured in *pixels*. The upper-left corner of the screen is at 0, 0. That is, it is horizontal position 0 and vertical position 0.

If you use Flash's default movie dimensions, the bottom-right corner will be at 550, 400. That is, horizontally 550 pixels from the left side and 400 pixels down from the top.

Every spot in the work area can be identified as a position. For instance, the exact center of the area is 225, 200. Figure 7.1 shows the work area with several spots labeled.

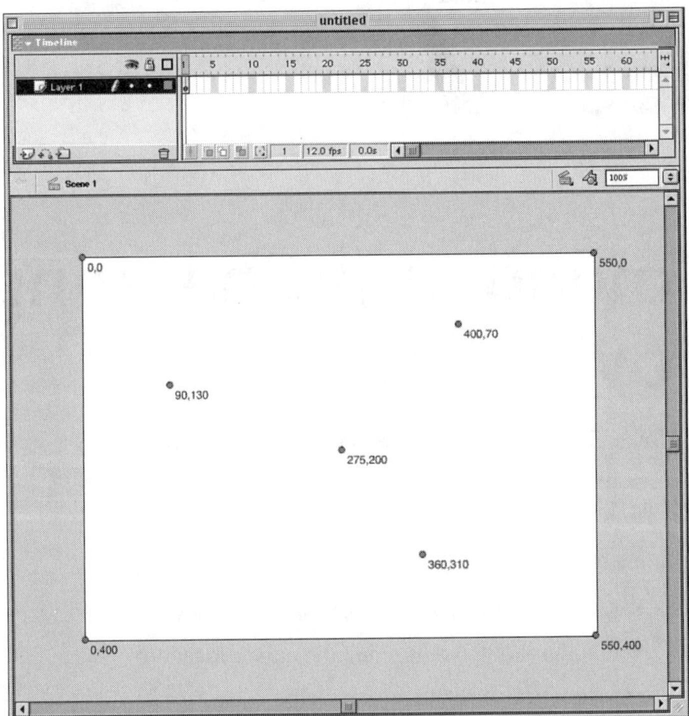

Figure 7.1 *The work area with several positions.*

Another name for the horizontal coordinate of a position is *x*. The vertical coordinate of a position is *y*. A position is then expressed in *x*, *y* coordinates.

In many programming languages, you need to use integers to express x and y coordinates; not in Flash. You can use floating point numbers to precisely position movie clips. For instance, a movie clip might lie at 218.45, 143.9.

To examine the position of a movie clip, you need to use the _x and _y properties. For instance, if you have a movie clip named myClip, you could use the following lines to send the x and y coordinates of that clip to the Output window:

```
trace(myClip._x);
trace(myClip._y);
```

You can also see the location of a movie clip by selecting it in the work area and bringing up the Info panel. You can do this by choosing Window, Info or by using the keyboard shortcut Command+I on the Mac or Ctrl+I in Windows. Figure 7.2 shows this panel.

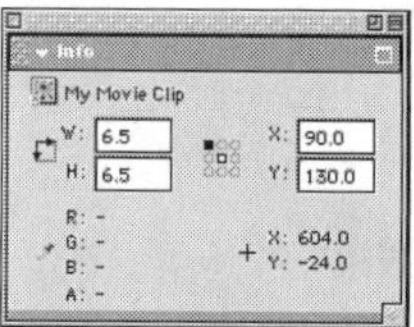

FIGURE 7.2
The Info panel shows the position of the movie clip selected. The second X and Y readings at the bottom show the mouse location.

To change the position of a movie clip when the movie is running, all you need to do is set the _x and _y properties of the movie clip. Here is an example:

```
myClip._x = 200;
myClip._y = 250;
```

You can alter the _x and _y properties in the same way that you alter variables. You can use +=, -=, ++, and -- to make changes based on the original value of the property. For instance, to move a movie clip five pixels to the right, you could do this:

```
myClip._x += 5;
```

If you want to move a movie clip one pixel down, you could do this:

```
myClip._y++;
```

If you want to refer to the _x or _y property of the current movie clip, the one that contains your code, you can refer to _x or _y without a prefix, or you can use `this` as the object reference. So either of these will work to increase the horizontal position of a movie clip, if the code is attached to that clip:

```
_x++;
this._x.++;
```

Because using _x and _y by themselves affects the current movie clip, what do they affect if you use them in the main timeline? As you might be able to predict, they change the position of the entire movie, shifting it so that all the elements are offset by _x and _y. There's not much use for this functionality, however.

Task: Bouncing Ball

1. Start a new Flash movie. Create a movie clip that has a ball graphic inside it. See the movie 07bouncingball.fla for an example.
2. You can name the instance of the movie clip, myClip, but our code will not depend on the name of the clip.
3. Attach the following code to the movie clip:

   ```
   onClipEvent(enterFrame) {
       this._x += 5;
   }
   ```

   This code acts once per frame. It pushes the movie clip over by one pixel each frame. The result is a clip that moves slowly across the screen until it reaches the other side. It actually continues even past there.
4. To alter the code so that it bounces off the right wall, we'll need to make a few changes. The horizontal speed of the movie clip will be stored in a variable named `speedX`. Change the movie clip script to this:

   ```
   onClipEvent(load) {
       speedX = 5;
   }

   onClipEvent(enterFrame) {
       this._x += speedX;
   }
   ```

   If you run the movie now, it behaves exactly as it did before. The variable `speedX` is set to 5, and that value is used to increment the horizontal position of the movie clip.
5. Now it is time to make the clip bounce off the right wall. To do this, we will test to see whether the clip's horizontal position is at, or past, the right wall. If so, `speedX` is reversed so that the ball moves back the way it came.

   ```
   onClipEvent(load) {
       speedX = 5;
   }
   ```

```
onClipEvent(enterFrame) {
    this._x += speedX;
    if (this._x >= 550) {
        speedX = -speedX;
    }
}
```

Now the ball bounces off the right side of the screen and comes back toward the left wall.

6. To make sure that it bounces off the left wall, we'll want to test for the horizontal location of the ball being less than 0 and reverse its direction in that case too.

```
onClipEvent(load) {
    speedX = 5;
}

onClipEvent(enterFrame) {
    this._x += speedX;
    if (this._x >= 550) {
        speedX = -speedX;
    } else if (this._x <= 0) {
        speedX = -speedX;
    }
}
```

7. Now let's make the ball move in a vertical direction as well. There is nothing new in this next alteration of code. It is just the same things we have been doing, but applied to both the horizontal and vertical directions.

```
onClipEvent(load) {
    speedX = 5;
    speedY = 5;
}

onClipEvent(enterFrame) {
    this._x += speedX;
    this._y += speedY;

    if (this._x >= 550) {
        speedX = -speedX;
    } else if (this._x <= 0) {
        speedX = -speedX;
    }

    if (this._y >= 400) {
        speedY = -speedY;
    } else if (this._y <= 0) {
        speedY = -speedY;
    }
}
```

When you run the movie now, the ball bounces off all four walls. It keeps going and going. It is a good example of an animation easily done with ActionScript but next to impossible with frame-by-frame manually created animation.

Figure 7.3 illustrates this example.

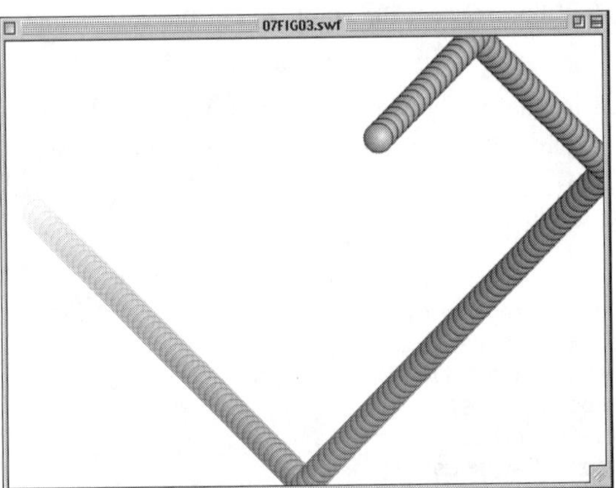

FIGURE 7.3
In the 07bounce.fla example movie, the ball ricochets off all four walls. This figure uses shading to show the ball over many frames. The example movie shows only the current ball location.

You may notice that the ball seems to go slightly beyond the edges of the screen. That is because the horizontal and vertical location of the movie clip refers to the middle of the ball. If the ball is 20 pixels in diameter, the ball might appear to go about 10 pixels past the edge. You can adjust for this in your calculations in many ways. The simplest would be to use 10, 10, 540, and 390 as your screen edges, not 0, 0, 550, and 400.

Mouse Location

Not only can you get the location of a movie clip on the screen, you can even get the location of the mouse, also known as the cursor.

What is the difference between the *mouse* and the *cursor*? The mouse is the physical device attached to your computer. You may even have a track pad or tablet instead. The cursor is the graphic that moves around the screen as you move your mouse. So, technically, *cursor* is the term I should be using here. However, ActionScript uses the term *mouse* in its keywords. I will therefore use *mouse* and *cursor* interchangeably.

Two special properties of the Flash player tell you the horizontal and vertical positions of the cursor on the screen. These are the `_xmouse` and `_ymouse` properties.

But what are they properties of? If used by themselves, `_xmouse` and `_ymouse` are properties of the object they are contained in. So if you use them in the main timeline, they are root properties. If you use them in a movie clip, they are movie clip properties.

What's the difference? Well, `_xmouse` and `_ymouse` measure the mouse location from registration point of the object. So if you are using the root properties, you get the location of the mouse from the upper-left corner of the movie. If you use them inside a movie clip, you get the mouse location from the center of the movie clip.

In most cases, you will want these properties as they relate to the main movie. To ensure this, you can use `_root._xmouse` and `_root._ymouse`.

Here is the code inside the example movie 07mouse.fla. It contains a movie clip with this script on it. In every frame that passes, the script will write the x and y location of the mouse to the Output window, followed by a blank line to separate the pairs of numbers.

```
onClipEvent (enterFrame) {
    trace(_root._xmouse);
    trace(_root._ymouse);
    trace("");
}
```

When you run this movie, you will see the pairs of numbers stream through the Output window. Move the mouse around and watch the numbers change. Bring the cursor up near the upper-left corner of the screen to see them get close to 0, 0 and then to the lower-right to see them get close to 550, 400.

Notice that if you move the cursor outside the Flash test window, the values of `_xmouse` and `_ymouse` don't change. If you move the cursor from the center of the movie to a point outside the movie fast enough, the old value stays until the cursor re-enters the active area. This is an unfortunate fact of life with Flash and something that you will have to plan for when using `_xmouse` and `_ymouse`.

Task: Follow the Mouse

7

Now that you know how to get the mouse location, and you know how to set the location of a movie clip, you can combine these two pieces to make a movie where a movie clip follows the cursor around the screen.

1. Create a new Flash movie.
2. Make a simple movie clip. Something like a small circle will do.
3. Attach the following script the to movie clip:

```
onClipEvent (enterFrame) {
    this._x = _root._xmouse;
    this._y = _root._ymouse;
}
```

That's all there is to it. Check out the sample movie 07followthemouse.fla. When you test the movie, the movie clip immediately snaps to the location of the mouse, provided that the mouse is over the test window.

In Hour 13, "Rollovers," we'll look at how to use a similar technique to create custom cursors.

Move Clip Rotation

Another property like `_x` and `_y` is the movie clip property `_rotation`.

The `_rotation` property accepts a value in degrees. A circle is divided into 360 degrees. The values used by `_rotation` range from -180 to 180. You can use integers or floating point values.

The value of `_rotation` always stays between -180 and 180, no matter what you set it to. For instance, if you set it to 179, it stays 179. However, if you set it to 181, it wraps around to -179.

To change this property, simply set it to a value. You can also use operators such as ++ and += to change the value. Here are some examples:

```
myClip._rotation = 90;
myClip._rotation++;
_root["myClip"]._rotation = 45;
this._rotation += 0.5;
```

Task: A Rotating Movie Clip

You can easily write a movie clip handler that rotates the movie clip at a constant rate. All you need to do is increase the `_rotation` property.

1. Start with an empty Flash movie.
2. Place a simple movie clip in the middle of the screen. Don't use a simple circle, though, because it will not appear to change while it rotates.

3. Attach the following script to the movie clip:

```
onClipEvent(enterFrame) {
    this._rotation += 1;
}
```

When you run the movie, the movie clip rotates 1 degree per frame. This means that it will take 360 frames to rotate completely around. At 15 frames per second, that's 24 seconds for a complete turn. That is, of course, if your computer can handle the full rate of animation. If you keep the movie clip and any other elements in the movie simple, this should not be a problem.

4. To make the movie clip spin twice as fast, change the 1 to a 2. Try other values as well.

5. To make the movie clip rotate in the opposite direction, change the number to a negative value, such as -1. Alternatively, use `-=` instead of `+=`. Check out the example movie 07rotation.fla to see an example.

Stretching and Shrinking Movie Clips

You can also change the horizontal and vertical scaling of a movie clip. This means that you can stretch it and shrink it, changing its width, height, or both.

Scale Properties

The properties for doing this are `_xscale` for the horizontal scale of the movie clip and `_yscale` for the vertical scale of the movie clip.

The values you need to set these two properties to is a percentage. That means that 100.0 is 100 percent of the original scale of the movie clip. You can use smaller values, such as 50, to shrink the movie clip. Or, you can use larger values, such as 200 to stretch the movie clip. You can even use negative values to flip the movie clip.

The example movie 07mousescale.fla contains the most complex script that we have seen so far. It checks the `_xmouse` and `_ymouse` properties to get the location of the mouse. Then it determines how far away the mouse is from the center of the movie clip. It uses this distance, both the horizontal and vertical components, to calculate a percentage of scale to apply to the movie clip. The result is that the movie clip stretches and shrinks so that the bottom-right corner matches the location of the mouse. Here is the code:

```
onClipEvent (load) {
    // get the original width and height of the mc
    origWidth = this._width;
    origHeight = this._height;
}
```

```
onClipEvent (enterFrame) {
    // get the distance from the center of the mc to the mouse
    dx = _root._xmouse-this._x;
    dy = _root._ymouse-this._y;

    // calculate the percentage of scale
    sx = 100*dx/(origWidth/2);
    sy = 100*dy/(origHeight/2);

    // set the scale of the mc
    this._xscale = sx;
    this._yscale = sy;
}
```

Figure 7.4 shows this example movie in action. The bottom-right corner is locked to the mouse location, and the whole movie clip scales so that this remains true.

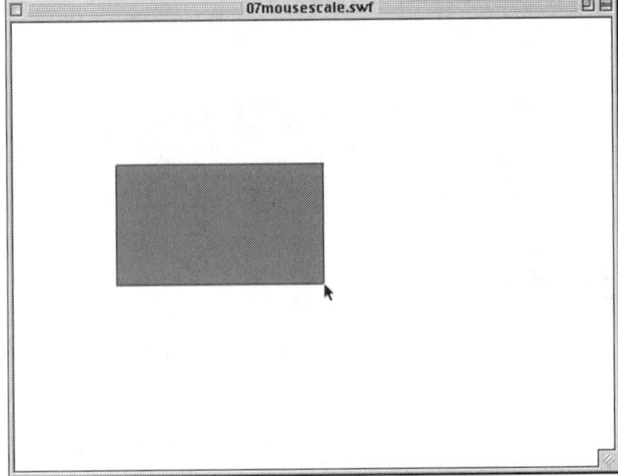

FIGURE 7.4
In the 07mousescale.fla example movie, the movie clip scales according to the mouse location.

Notice that this code includes two new properties of a movie clip that we have not yet seen. `_width` and `_height` are values that return the current width and height, in pixels, of the movie clip. We need to grab and store these values in the `onClipEvent(load)` handler because this is the only point where we can get the original values for this movie clip. If we were to get the `_width` and `_height` later, they would reflect the changed values as the user moves the cursor around.

Width and Height Properties

You can also set the `_width` and `_height` properties of a movie clip. This gives you two ways to stretch or shrink a movie clip.

The difference between using _xscale and _yscale versus _width and _height is simple. The scale properties have a normal value of 100, representing 100 percent of the width or height of the movie clip. The _width and _height properties have pixel values instead of a percentage.

So if a movie clip is 75 pixels wide and 40 pixels high, its _width and _height properties will be 75 and 40, but its _xscale and _yscale properties will both be at 100.

In most cases, you can actually accomplish the same task with either pair of properties. Here is some code that accomplishes the same thing that the previous example did, but by setting _width and _height instead of _xscale and _yscale. You can see it on the CD-ROM as 07mousescale2.fla.

```
onClipEvent (enterFrame) {
    // get the distance from the center of the mc to the mouse
    dx = _root._xmouse-this._x;
    dy = _root._ymouse-this._y;

    // set the scale of the mc
    this._width = dx*2;
    this._height = dy*2;
}
```

As you can see, this code is much simpler than the previous example. It doesn't even use the onClipEvent(load) handler because the original width and height don't need to be stored. This is clearly a case where using _width and _height has an advantage over using _xscale and yscale.

Task: Simulated 3D Scaling

Although Flash is not capable of real 3D graphics, the kind seen in popular computer games, you can create the illusion of 3D by using scaling.

Scaling an object is a great way to give your movie depth. After all, when an object is far away, it should look smaller. When it is closer, it should look bigger.

Figure 7.5 shows the same movie clip in two different locations on the screen. This is the same movie clip, except that the one in the lower-left corner is scaled higher than the one in the upper-right. This makes the first one appear closer.

FIGURE 7.5
One airplane appears closer simply because it is larger.

You can further strengthen this illusion with movement. Let's create a movie that makes the airplane travel from one corner of the screen to another, growing in scale at the same time:

1. Start with a new Flash movie.
2. Make a movie clip out of a drawing of an airplane or other object. You can use the airplane in the 07airplane.fla example movie if you want. You can place the movie clip anywhere on the screen.
3. Attach this code to the movie clip:

```
onClipEvent(load) {
    scaleAmt = 10;
    x = 525;
    y = 25;
}

onClipEvent(enterFrame) {
    scaleAmt++;
    x -= 5;
    y += 5;

    this._xscale = scaleAmt;
    this._yscale = scaleAmt;
    this._x = x;
    this._y = y;
}
```

The code starts by setting three variables to their initial values. The variable `scaleAmt` holds the scale value for the movie clip. The variables `x` and `y` are the location of the movie clip.

For each frame that passes, all these values will change. The *scaleAmt* variable increases by 1. The *x* variable decreases by 5, sending the movie clip to the left. The *y* variable increases by 5, sending the movie clip down.

How did I get the values 1, 5, and 5 for the variable changes? Simple: trial and error. I could have tried to calculate the best values to use, but it was easier to just try different values until I found ones that worked. This technique is usually the best way to create simple effects like this one.

Both the `_xscale` and `_yscale` properties of the movie clip are set to *scaleAmt*. The `_x` and `_y` are set appropriately.

The result of this movie is that the airplane appears to fly from the upper-right corner to the lower-left corner, getting closer to the user in the meantime. The illusion created makes it appear as if you are viewing the plane from above. If you draw the airplane in the right perspective, you can make it approach or move away in any direction you want.

To give you an example of how programming styles can differ, here is the same program condensed into fewer lines. It is useful to see variations like this because it gives you an idea of the artistic freedom that programmers have when writing their scripts.

```
onClipEvent(load) {
    this._x = 525;
    this._y = 25;
}

onClipEvent(enterFrame) {
    this._xscale++;
    this._yscale++;
    this._x -= 5;
    this._y += 5;
}
```

Visibility

Another property that you should know about is the `_visible` property. This property takes a simple Boolean value, true or false, and shows or hides the movie clip accordingly. Here is an example:

```
myClip._visible = false;
```

If you want to see this property in action, look at the example movie 07visible.fla. There are two buttons: one to set the `_visible` property to true, and the other to set it to false.

7

But suppose that you don't want the movie clip to completely disappear. You can set the transparency amount with the _alpha property. You can set this to any value from 0 to 100. Here is an example:

```
myClip._alpha = 50;
```

> The _alpha property of a movie clip refers to the fourth color channel, also called the *alpha channel*. The first three color channels are red, green, and blue, which are the three colors needed to create the full rainbow of color. The fourth channel is the amount of transparency for that particular pixel.
>
> You'll see reference to the alpha channel in software such as PhotoShop, Illustrator, and Fireworks.
>
> When you hear that a graphic is 32-bit, this refers to the fact that there are four color channels, each taking up 8 bits of data. A 24-bit image means that there are only red, green, and blue channels.

When you set an _alpha to 0, the movie clip is completely transparent. When you set it to 100, the movie is completely visible and opaque. When it is transparent or semitransparent, anything behind it partially shows through.

Figure 7.6 shows the same movie clip three times. The first one on the left is with an _alpha setting of 100. The last one on the right has an _alpha setting of 10, which makes it barely visible. The middle one is at 50.

FIGURE 7.6
The same movie clips, but each at a different _alpha *setting.*

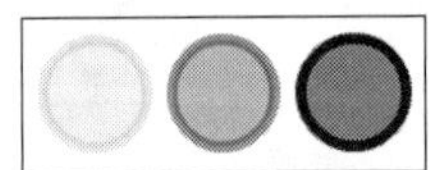

Task: Fading Movie Clip

If you can set a movie clip's transparency value, it follows that you can gradually change that value to make it appear as if the movie clip is fading away. Here's how to do it:

1. Start with a new Flash movie.
2. Create a simple movie clip. Any simple shape will do.
3. Attach the following movie clip script:

```
onClipEvent(enterFrame) {
    if (this._alpha > 0) {
        this._alpha -= 5;
    }
}
```

This script uses an `if` statement to determine whether the `_alpha` value is not yet at 0. It starts at 100 and then decreases by 5 area frames. If it is 0, it fails the `if` statement, and the `_alpha` property no longer decreases.

The example movie 07fadeaway.fla contains this script. Give it a try.

Summary

You can use a variety of movie clip properties to alter the location and appearance of a movie clip. The `_x` and `_y` properties allow you to set the horizontal and vertical location of a movie clip. You can use `_xscale` and `_width` to change the horizontal scale of a movie clip, and `_yscale` and `_height` to change the vertical scale of a movie clip.

You can rotate a movie clip with the `_rotation` property. You can also make a movie clip semitransparent or completely invisible with the `_alpha` and `_visible` properties.

You can get the horizontal and vertical position of the cursor with the `_xmouse` and `_ymouse` properties.

Q&A

Q Can I use `_x` and `_y` values that are less than 0 or greater than the width or height of the work area?

A Yes. You can use almost any reasonable value for `_x` and `_y`. You can position movie clips off the edge of the work area. You can still see them if you adjust the test window properly, but they will be partially or completely hidden when played back in the browser.

Q Is there any way to detect the mouse location when it is outside the work area?

A No. But you can use the technique of making the work area much bigger than what you need so that there is some extra space around the edge of your graphics where the mouse location can be detected.

Q When you rotate a movie clip, what determines the point at which it rotates around?

A When you edit a movie clip in the work area, you will notice a small cross at the center of the screen. This is the movie clip's registration point. This point corresponds to the location of the `_x` and `_y` properties of the movie clip and the point of rotation.

Q If a movie clip already contains a semitransparent graphic, does the `_alpha` property override it?

A No. The semitransparency of the graphics and the `_alpha` property are combined to determine the final transparency of the movie clip parts.

Workshop

The quiz questions are designed to test your knowledge of the material covered in this hour. The answers to the questions follow.

Quiz

1. What is the difference between the `_width` property and the `_xscale` property?
2. If you set the `_rotation` property of a movie clip to 185, what will the value of the `_rotation` property be?
3. What is the difference between setting the `_alpha` property of a movie clip to 0 and setting the `_visible` property of a movie clip to false?
4. If you set the `_x` and `_y` position of a movie clip to 0 and 0, will the movie clip be completely visible?

Quiz Answers

1. The `_width` property is measured in pixels and starts as the exact number of pixels that the movie clip is wide. The `_xscale` property is a percentage and starts at 100 percent.
2. The `_rotation` property can be a value from -180 to 180. If you set it to 185, it will resolve itself around to -175.
3. Nothing. They will both make the movie clip completely invisible.
4. No. This will place the movie clip's registration point at 0,0, which means that only the bottom-right quarter of the movie clip will be in the work area and visible in the player.

HOUR 8

Selecting and Dragging Movie Clips

The most basic actions in most modern computer programs use object selection and dragging to help the user express what he wants to do. If all you do is move files around on your desktop, you are doing a lot of selecting and dragging.

It makes sense, then, to learn how to re-create this functionality in your Flash movies.

In this hour, you will:

- Learn how to create selectable movie clips
- See how to allow the user to drag movie clips around the screen
- Use draggable movie clips to allow the user to make choices
- Create a simple matching game

Selection

You have already learned how to make buttons that allow the user to click and make an action occur. A different type of user interface element, however, allows the user to select an item on the screen.

The difference is that a user clicks to make a selection, and that movie clip changes its appearance. But nothing else happens. This way, the user can make or change her selections. After that, the user can click another button or perform another action.

We'll use selections as the first step toward learning how to drag and drop movie clips, the goal of this hour.

Button Inside the Movie Clip Method

A movie clip cannot simply react to a mouse click. Unlike a button, it cannot use an `on (release)` or `on (press)` handler.

So you have to be tricky. You put a button inside a movie clip. The button can handle the mouse clicks as long as it is big enough to cover the entire movie clip.

The example 08buttoninmc.fla illustrates this. When you look at the movie, you will see that it has a single movie clip on the screen. Inside that movie clip is a single button.

To turn this into a selectable movie clip, we'll have to make this into a multiframe movie clip. The first frame contains the button named Off Button. This button has the following script:

```
on (release) {
    this.gotoAndStop(2);
}
```

By referring to `this`, the button is referencing the movie clip that it is in. Frame 2 of the movie clip contains a similar button named On Button. The difference is that the On Button is a little brighter, indicating that the movie clip has been selected. The script on this movie clip is similar:

```
on (release) {
    this.gotoAndStop(1);
}
```

As you might guess, by clicking the button on frame 2, the movie clip goes to frame 1, where the original Off Button is located. By clicking the buttons in the movie clip over and over again, the movie clip goes back and forth between frames 1 and 2.

The only thing left is to place a `stop();` command on the first frame of the movie clip. You can go to the example movie 07buttoninmc.fla to try this out.

`hitTest` Method

You can detect a mouse click in a movie clip without a button. However, this method is a little trickier. After you learn it, though, it is a much cleaner solution.

To detect a mouse click on a movie clip without a button, use the `onClipEvent(mouseDown)` or `onClipEvent(mouseUp)` movie clip handlers. For instance, you can place the following script on a movie clip:

```
onClipEvent (mouseUp) {
    this.gotoAndStop(2);
}
```

The example movie 08twomcs1.fla contains two instances of the same movie clip with this same script applied to both. Two frames are in the movie clip, each with a different colored circle. A `stop();` command is on the first frame of the movie clip.

When you try this movie, you will see right away why the `onClipEvent(mouseUp)` handler is different from the `on(release)` handler used on buttons. If you click on one movie clip, they both react.

This is because all movie clips get the `mouseUp` event sent to them. It is not exclusive to just the movie clip under the cursor.

Determining Which Movie Clip Was Clicked

There is a way to determine which movie clip has been clicked. The `hitTest` function tests a mouse location with a movie clip to see whether the location is inside the movie clip. So, by modifying the script, we can only send the correct movie clip to its second frame. You can see this one in example 08twomcs2.fla.

```
onClipEvent (mouseUp) {
    if (this.hitTest(_root._xmouse, _root._ymouse)) {
        this.gotoAndStop(2);
    }
}
```

The `hitTest` function can work a variety of different ways. In this case, it is fed the x and y values of the mouse location. It is prefaced with `this` so that it refers to the current movie clip. When the user clicks anywhere, the `onClipEvent (mouseUp)` handlers in all the movie clips get triggered. Then, both of the movie clips perform the `hitTest` test; only one that is under the mouse will test positive and jump to frame 2.

A Selection Script

To change this into a selection script, we have to allow the user to click the movie clip multiple times and change the state of the movie clip from off to on and back to off again.

The script has to determine which state the movie clip is currently in and then send the clip to the other frame. The script can determine the current state by looking at the current frame of the movie clip. This can be done with the aptly named `_currentFrame` property. This property reads 1 when the movie clip is on the first frame and 2 when it is on the second.

Here is the new script. You can see it in 08twomcs3.fla. This is a complex script because it first tests the location of the mouse and then tests the current frame of the movie clip.

```
onClipEvent (mouseUp) {
    if (this.hitTest(_root._xmouse, _root._ymouse)) {
        if (this._currentFrame == 1) {
            this.gotoAndStop(2);
        } else {
            this.gotoAndStop(1);
        }
    }
}
```

Now you have seen two completely different ways of making selectable movie clips. I like the second way better because you don't end up with the extra library symbols of the buttons. The advantage of using buttons, however, is that they can easily contain up, down, and over states, which are sometimes nice for user feedback as users make their choices.

Task: Keypad Lock

Now let's put your knowledge of selectable movie clips to use. In this example, we'll create a movie that acts like a keypad lock. The screen looks like Figure 8.1, a simple numeric keypad. Each one of these keys, 12 in all, is a movie clip instance.

FIGURE 8.1
This keypad is made up of 12 instances of the same movie clip, plus a layer of numbers on top.

In the example movie 08keypad-noscripts.fla, you'll find all the movie clip instances in place but no scripts there yet. You will also see a layer that contains the 10 digits and the * and # characters. I placed these on top of the movie clips so that I didn't have to build 12 different but similar movie clips. Instead, I could reuse the same movie clip and make it appear different by placing a different number on top of it.

1. Start with the movie 08keypad-noscripts.fla. Or, you can create your own movie with 12 instances of the same movie clip.
2. These movie clips should all have two frames. The first frame is the off state of the key. It looks like all the keys in Figure 8.1. The second frame is similar, but you can tell that the key is lit up, or somehow highlighted.
3. Place a `stop();` command on frame 1 of the movie clip. This prevents it from animating when the movie starts. We want it to stay at frame 1 and wait.
4. Each movie clip instance must have a name. Name the 10 numbers one, two, three, and so on. Name the other two movie clips asterisk and pound.
5. Start with the movie clip at the upper-left corner. In Figure 8.1. It has the number 7 on top of it. It should be named seven. Place the following script on it:

   ```
   onClipEvent (mouseUp) {
       if (this.hitTest(_root._xmouse, _root._ymouse)) {
           if (this._currentFrame == 1) {
               this.gotoAndStop(2);
           } else {
               this.gotoAndStop(1);
           }
       }
   }
   ```

   This is exactly the same script that we used in the previous example. It determines whether a mouse click took place with the mouse over this movie clip and sends it either to frame 2 or frame 1, depending on where it is now.
6. Place the exact same movie clip script on all 10 number keys. Do not place it on the asterisk or pound keys.
7. Test the movie. You should be able to click on any number key and see it light up. Click on it again and see it turn off. Test all 10 number keys. If it does not work, go back and double-check your work. Make sure that the right scripts are in the right places. You can use the example movie 08keypad.fla to see how this should work.
8. Place this script on the asterisk key:

   ```
   onClipEvent (mouseUp) {
       if (this.hitTest(_root._xmouse, _root._ymouse)) {
           _parent.clearAll();
       }
   }
   ```

   Instead of sending the movie clip to frame 1 or 2, this script calls a function named `clearAll` that is one level up from this movie clip. One level up is the root level; we will have to make a function at the root level named `clearAll`. We'll get to that in a minute.

9. Place this script on the pound key:

```
onClipEvent (mouseUp) {
    if (this.hitTest(_root._xmouse, _root._ymouse)) {
        _parent.checkCode();
        }
    }
}
```

This is a similar script except that it calls `checkCode` instead. Next, let's create these two functions.

10. In the main timeline, on the first and only key frame, add this script:

```
function clearAll() {
    one.gotoAndStop(1);
    two.gotoAndStop(1);
    three.gotoAndStop(1);
    four.gotoAndStop(1);
    five.gotoAndStop(1);
    six.gotoAndStop(1);
    seven.gotoAndStop(1);
    eight.gotoAndStop(1);
    nine.gotoAndStop(1);
    zero.gotoAndStop(1);
}
```

The `clearAll` function tells each numbered movie clip to go to its off frame. This essentially resets the keypad. You can test the movie again at this point if you want. Try clicking a few keys, and then click the asterisk key to clear them all. Check the 08keypad.fla movie if you are unsure about where this script goes.

11. Add this function to the same key frame script as the previous function. They should come one after the other in the same script.

```
function checkCode() {
    var correct = true;
    if (zero._currentFrame == 2) correct = false;
    if (one._currentFrame == 1) correct = false;
    if (two._currentFrame == 1) correct = false;
    if (three._currentFrame == 2) correct = false;
    if (four._currentFrame == 2) correct = false;
    if (five._currentFrame == 2) correct = false;
    if (six._currentFrame == 2) correct = false;
    if (seven._currentFrame == 1) correct = false;
    if (eight._currentFrame == 2) correct = false;
    if (nine._currentFrame == 2) correct = false;
    if (correct) {
        trace("Correct Code!");
    } else {
        trace("Wrong Code!");
    }
}
```

This function checks each of the numeric keys and determines whether the correct code has been entered. In this case, the code is 1, 2, and 7. It starts by setting the local variable `correct` to true, assuming from the start that the code has been entered.

It then checks the `_currentFrame` of each numeric key. If the frame is 2, the user has turned on the key. If it is 1, the key is off. If key 1, 2, or 7 is off, the code must be wrong. If key 0, 3, 4, 5, 6, 8 or 9 is on, the code is wrong as well. If none of these conditions are met, the code is correct because keys 1, 2, and 7 are on, and the rest are off.

Test the movie. Select 1, 2, and 7; then press the pound key. Now try it with 1, 2, 4, and 7. How about 5, 8, and 9?

In this example, the only thing that happens is that a message is placed in the Output window. However, you could place a `stop();` command in the frame script—the same frame script with the two functions. Then have the movie `gotoAndStop` a certain frame if the code is wrong, or `gotoAndStop` another frame if the code is right.

Dragging

Now that you know how to select a movie clip, the next step is to learn how to move it. This is called *dragging*. You can drag files around your operating system's desktop, for instance.

There are two ways to drag a movie clip. You can use Flash's built-in drag commands. These are easy to use but do not allow you many options to modify or monitor the way movie clips are dragged, so we will also look at using some other code to bypass Flash's drag commands.

Basic Dragging

Flash's drag commands are simple: There is a `startDrag` and a `stopDrag` command. You issue the `startDrag` command whenever you want a movie clip to follow the mouse around, and a `stopDrag` when you want the movie clip to stop following the mouse around.

In the example movie 08basicdrag.fla, you can see the following simple script in action:

```
onClipEvent (mouseDown) {
    if (this.hitTest(_root._xmouse, _root._ymouse)) {
        this.startDrag();
    }
}

onClipEvent (mouseUp) {
    if (this.hitTest(_root._xmouse, _root._ymouse)) {
        this.stopDrag();
    }
}
```

The `onClipEvent` handlers look similar to the ones we have been using. They use `hitTest` to make sure that it is the current movie clip that the user is clicking. If so, either the `startDrag` or `stopDrag` command is issued. The first is issued when the `mouseDown` message is sent, and the second when the `mouseUp` message is sent.

In the example movie, you can click and drag either of the two movie clip instances independently. But notice that you can only drag one at a time. Using these drag commands also limits how you can monitor and modify the drag. You will need something a little more flexible if you want to drag movie clips in advanced applications and games.

The `startDrag` command can actually accept up to five additional parameters. The first is a true or false value that determines whether the center of the movie clip locks to the mouse location. The default is false, which is what you usually want. The other four parameters are the left, top, right, and bottom limits of the drag. If you set these, the movie clip can't be dragged beyond these boundaries.

Complex Dragging

If you wanted to drag a movie clip, but couldn't use the `startDrag` and `stopDrag` commands, how would you do it?

You'll need a movie clip script that has four parts to it. The first part, the `onClipEvent(load)` handler, will set a global variable called *`dragging`* to false. When this variable is true, it will signal the movie clip to follow the mouse.

Then, when the user clicks on the movie clip, the *`dragging`* variable will be set to true. The dragging will then take place in the `onClipEvent(enterFrame)` handler. It will simply set the _x and _y properties of the movie clip to the `_root._xmouse` and `_root._ymouse` properties.

Then, when the user lifts up the mouse button, the `dragging` property will be set to false again, and the movie clip will no longer move around to follow the mouse. Here is the complete script:

```
onClipEvent (load) {
    // start out not dragging
    dragging = false;
}

onClipEvent (mouseDown) {
    if (this.hitTest(_root._xmouse, _root._ymouse)) {
        // follow the mouse from now on
        dragging = true;
```

```
    }
}

onClipEvent (enterFrame) {
    if (dragging) {
        // set to location of the mouse
        this._x = _root._xmouse;
        this._y = _root._ymouse;
    }
}

onClipEvent (mouseUp) {
    if (this.hitTest(_root._xmouse, _root._ymouse)) {
        // don't follow the mouse any longer
        dragging = false;
    }
}
```

This script looks long compared to the ones we have been writing so far, but there is really not much to it. Each `onClipEvent` handler really only does one thing. Check the script and make sure that you understand each part.

The example movie 08complexdrag.fla contains two movie clips. Test the movie, but only use the movie clip on the left. This is the one that contains the previous script. Notice how the movie clip locks its center to the mouse location. It makes the movie clip jump immediately after you click it.

Usually, when you want an element to drag around the screen, you don't want it to jump to lock the mouse location with the center of the element. Try dragging files around your desktop. Notice how they drag with the mouse locked to the point of the icon where you initially clicked. This is the same way the `startDrag` command worked too.

To get this functionality, we only need to add a little more to the script. When the user first clicks, we'll get the mouse offset—that is, the distance from the mouse to the center of the movie clip. Then, instead of assigning the mouse location to the center of the movie clip, we'll add this little offset so that the movie clip always appears offset by the same amount as the user drags.

Imagine, for example, that the user clicks five pixels to the right of the center of the movie clip. Then we always want to make sure that the movie clip and the mouse are offset by those same five pixels. This makes it appear as if the user has grabbed that one spot on the movie clip and is dragging it around by that spot. Here is the new script:

```
onClipEvent (load) {
    // start out not dragging
    dragging = false;
}
```

```
onClipEvent (mouseDown) {
    if (this.hitTest(_root._xmouse, _root._ymouse)) {
        // follow the mouse from now on
        dragging = true;

        // get the mouse offset
        xOffset = this._x - _root._xmouse;
        yOffset = this._y - _root._ymouse;
    }
}

onClipEvent (enterFrame) {
    if (dragging) {
        // set to location of the mouse
        this._x = _root._xmouse + xOffset;
        this._y = _root._ymouse + yOffset;
    }
}

onClipEvent (mouseUp) {
    if (this.hitTest(_root._xmouse, _root._ymouse)) {
        // don't follow the mouse any longer
        dragging = false;
    }
}
```

In the same example movie, 08complexdrag.fla, if you drag the movie clip to the right, you will see this new script in action. Notice the different behavior between the two movie clips as you drag them. The difference is more pronounced if you click near the edge of the movie clip instead of the center.

Drag and Drop

Now that you can drag movie clips around the screen, where do you drag them? Chances are that you want to monitor the user's actions and determine where the user placed the movie clip.

Basic Drop Zone

The `hitTest` function can be used to determine when the movie clip is overlapping with another movie clip. In the following script, we'll use the simpler `startDrag` command so that the dragging portion of the script is simple and we can concentrate on the new functionality.

In the following script, the `hitTest` function is used to compare the movie clip that was dragged with another one named `dragZone` that is one level up, at the root level.

```
onClipEvent (mouseDown) {
    if (this.hitTest(_root._xmouse, _root._ymouse)) {
        this.startDrag();
    }
}
onClipEvent (mouseUp) {
    if (this.hitTest(_root._xmouse, _root._ymouse)) {
        this.stopDrag();

        // see if this mc is inside the dropZone mc
        if (this.hitTest(_parent.dropZone)) {
            trace("Dropped in zone");
        } else {
            trace("Dropped outside zone");
        }
    }
}
```

Notice that `hitTest` is not used in the same way as it was before. Instead of giving it an x and y location, we are now giving it another movie clip.

This form of `hitTest` compares the location and area of coverage of two movie clips. In this case, `this` is compared with `_parent.dropZone`. If these two movie clips overlap, `hitTest` returns true. To determine whether an overlap exists, the rectangles of both movie clips are used. So this means that when we use two circles, as in the example movie, the circles themselves don't even have to touch as long as the rectangles of the two movie clips touch.

To illustrate, look at Figure 8.2. Every one of the DRAG ME movie clips is overlapping with the drop zone. The dashed line around the movie clips demonstrates why this is so.

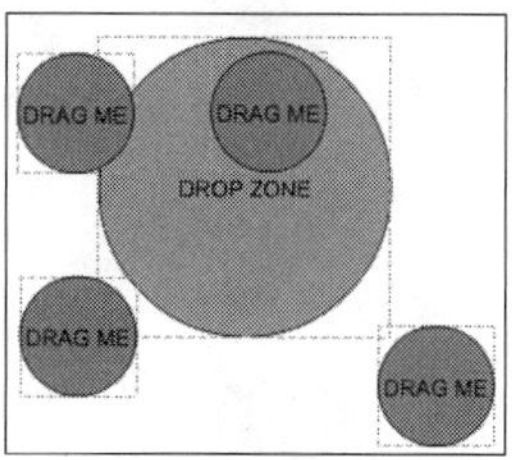

FIGURE 8.2
The dashed lines show the invisible rectangle around all the movie clips that `hitTest` *uses to determine an overlap. All these clips overlap the drop zone.*

For many purposes, the way that `hitTest` determines an overlap is too liberal. There are other ways to use `hitTest`, however. First, we can go back to using it with x and y coordinates. We can use the center point of the draggable movie clips as the x and y location, and then use `dropZone` as the primary movie clip. The line would look like this:

```
if (_parent.dropZone.hitTest(this._x,this._y)) {
```

With this line, instead of the one in the previous example, the draggable movie clip's center must be inside the drop zone's rectangle.

We can go one step further with `hitTest`. By adding a third parameter, we can force `hitTest` to look at the exact shape of the movie clip and determine whether an x and y location is inside it. This third parameter needs to be `true` if you want this behavior. If it is `false`, it will act just like a normal `hitTest` function. Here is the final code:

```
if (_parent.dropZone.hitTest(this._x,this._y,true)) {
```

Now the draggable movie clips behave a little better. If you use the example movie 08drop.fla, the rightmost movie clip will use the original script and will signal an overlap when its rectangle overlaps the drop zone's rectangle. The other movie clip will use the more complex `hitTest` to only overlap when its center is on the drop zone's shape.

Task: Matching Game

Now let's create a movie that has more than one draggable movie clip and more than one drop zone. This will be a little game where the user has to match movie clips on one side of the screen with movie clips on the other side.

Figure 8.3 shows the movie in its starting state. The three movie clips on the left are draggable. The three on the right are drop zones. The three on the right have the names dropZone1, dropZone2, and dropZone3. All six movie clip instances are made from different movie clips in the library. This is because their text contents are different.

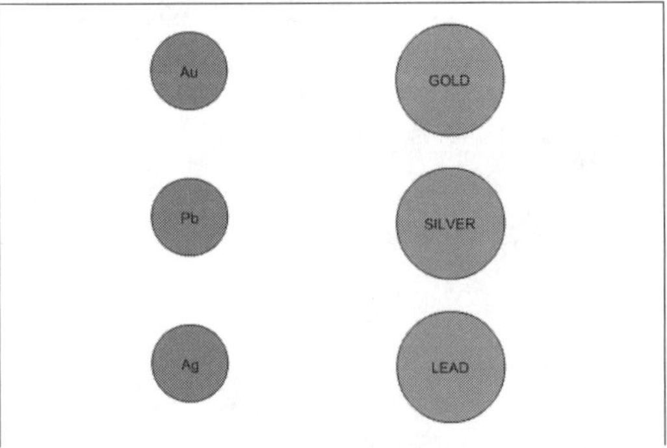

FIGURE 8.3
The starting positions of the movie clips in the matching game.

1. Start with the example movie 08matchinggame-noscripts.fla. Or, you can create your own movie with six similar movie clips. Just make sure that the three drop zones are properly named.

Note that I had to select the drop zones, one by one, and choose Modify, Arrange, Send To Back to make sure that they would all be behind the draggable movie clips when the user moves them into the same space.

2. Notice that the movie clips are arranged out of order. "Au" is "Gold," but "Ag" is "Silver," and "Pb" is "Lead." So the user will have to work a little to get this right.
3. All the code is in the movie clip scripts attached to the movie clips on the left. It is similar to the last example of drag-and-drop code, except for what happens when the drag is over.

   First, the original position of the movie clip is noted and stored in the variables *origX* and *origY*. Then, if the movie clip isn't over the proper drop zone, the _x and _y locations are reset to these values. However, if the movie clip is over the right drop zone, the draggable clip's location is set to the center of the drop zone. Here is the code:

```
onClipEvent (load) {
    origX = this._x;
    origY = this._y;
}

onClipEvent (mouseDown) {
    if (this.hitTest(_root._xmouse, _root._ymouse)) {
        this.startDrag();
    }
}
onClipEvent (mouseUp) {
    if (this.hitTest(_root._xmouse, _root._ymouse)) {
        this.stopDrag();

        // see if the dropZone conatins the center of this mc
        if (_parent.dropZone1.hitTest(this._x,this._y,true)) {

            // center it on the drop zone
            this._x = _parent.dropZone1._x;
            this._y = _parent.dropZone1._y;
        } else {

            // return it to its original location
            this._x = origX;
            this._y = origY;
        }
    }
}
```

The other two movie clips have the same code, except that dropZone1 is replaced with dropZone2 and dropZone3 in all three places that it appears in the code.

Give the movie a try to see how it works. The example movie 08machinggame.fla contains the complete code.

So how do you finish a game like this? The code should check to see whether the user got all the answers right. It is a little early in the book to throw this complexity in, but I have included it in the example movie as a button in case you are curious.

Summary

Selecting, dragging, and dropping elements is a standard way that computer programs allow users to interact with the environment.

To allow a movie clip to be selected, you must first detect a click on it. You can either place a button inside the movie clip, or use `onClipEvent(mouseUp)` along with `hitTest` to determine whether the movie clip has been clicked. You can then send the movie clip to another frame to signify that it has been selected.

To allow for dragging, you can use ActionScript's built-in `startDrag` and `stopDrag` commands, or build your own dragging scripts using `onClipEvent` handlers.

You can use `hitTest` to determine whether one movie clip overlaps with another. You can then determine the result of a user's dragging. You can use this to allow the user to drag elements onto other elements.

Q&A

Q Why can't buttons be made selectable?

A To be selectable, the user should be able to click on the item and change its appearance. A button will change its appearance while it is clicked but will always revert to the up state when the click is complete.

Q Can the third method of using `hitTest`—the one that includes a true as the third parameter so that the shape of the movie clip is taken into account—be used to more accurately determine whether the user has clicked a movie clip?

A Certainly. As a matter of fact, you should use the third parameter so that the click area of a movie clip is defined by its shape rather than its rectangle.

Q Many examples in this hour use nearly identical scripts applied to several movie clips. Is there a better way to do this?

A Yes and no. By the time you finish this book, you will be good enough to use root level functions to take over much of the work done by each movie clip script. But you will usually still need to start with the `onClipEvent` handlers attached to each movie clip. These handlers will then call root level functions that appear once in your movie instead of repeating lines of code in each movie clip script.

Q How can I expand on the matching game?

A You can build up the matching game to become a deep educational or computer-based training game. However, you will probably want to go through the rest of this book first and become more confident at ActionScript programming first.

Workshop

The quiz questions are designed to test your knowledge of the material covered in this hour. The answers to the questions follow.

Quiz

1. When a user clicks, which movie clip gets the `mouseDown` event?
2. How many different ways are there to use `hitTest`?
3. Do the shapes of two movie clips need to touch for `hitTest` to detect an overlap?
4. What unique function does `startDrag` perform that cannot be done any other way in ActionScript?

Quiz Answers

1. All of them. These handlers get triggered in all movie clips rather than just the one clicked on.
2. Three. You can use it with an x and y location; an x and y location and a third parameter, true or false, as to whether the shape instead of the rectangle of the movie clip is used; or you can use it with two movie clips to see whether they overlap.
3. No. If you use `hitTest` with two movie clips, it only matters that the rectangles overlap, regardless of any unusual shape that the movie clip graphics may have.
4. None. The `startDrag` command doesn't do anything that can't be re-created with other ActionScript code.

Part III

Manipulating Information with ActionScript

Hour

HOUR 9

Getting Input from the User

Until now, all the interaction our movies have allowed is through the mouse. However, you can also get user input from the keyboard. You can detect user keystrokes and allow the user to type letters, words, and sentences into text fields.

In this hour, you will:

- Learn how to detect keypresses
- Find out how to use text input fields
- See a variety of string operations and functions
- Create a user input form

Detecting Keypresses

There are three ways to detect a single keypress on the keyboard. The first uses buttons. The second uses the Key object. A third method is new to Flash MX and uses listeners.

Detecting Key Presses Through Buttons

Strangely enough, you can use buttons to detect keyboard key presses. All you need to do is use a special on handler in the script attached to the button. For instance, here is a handler that looks for the "a" key to be pressed:

```
on (keyPress "a") {
    trace("Key 'a' pressed.");
}
```

The example movie 09keybutton.fla has a simple button on the screen with this script and some other examples in it. If you run the movie and press "a" on your keyboard, the message will go to the Output window. If it does not, the test window probably doesn't have focus. Click in the test window to give it focus.

Because the keyboard doesn't have a position on the screen like the mouse does, the question often arises as to what element on the screen do keystrokes get routed to. In many cases, such as Web browsers and other complex applications such as Flash, many elements can accept keyboard input at any one time.

The one element that gets the keystrokes is said to have keyboard focus. For instance, in a Web form, the field being typed into has focus, whereas the other fields do not. When you are finished with a field, you usually press Enter, Return, or Tab to move the focus to the next field.

Windows work the same way. Only one window will have keyboard focus. In this case, we want to make sure that the movie testing window has focus so that the buttons in the movie get the keystrokes. To ensure focus, clicking on the window or field usually does the trick.

The on (keyPress) handler is case sensitive, so one that detects "a" will not detect "A." You'll need to use a separate on (keyPress) handler for the capital "A." Fortunately, button scripts can contain as many on handlers as you want.

If you want to detect other keys, such as the arrow keys, there are special codes for these. For instance, <Left> can be used to detect the left arrow key.

```
on (keyPress "<Left>") {
    trace("Left pressed.");
}
```

Here is a list of other special codes:

`<Left>` `<Right>` `<Up>` `<Down>` `<Home>`
`<End>` `<Insert>` `<Delete>` `<Backspace>` `<Enter>`
`<PageUp>` `<PageDown>` `<Tab>` `<Escape>` `<Space>`

You can also combine events in an `on` statement. For instance, suppose that you want to have a button that has a keyboard shortcut. You would normally just do an `on (release)` handler. However, you can also do a slightly more complex handler that would handle the click and a key press at the same time:

```
on (keyPress "b", release) {
    trace("'b' pressed or button clicked.");
}
```

You can see all these code examples at work in the 09keybutton.fla example movie. Try the "a" key and the "A" key. Try the left arrow key. Also try clicking the button and pressing "b".

The Key Object

Although buttons are useful for getting a single key press, they are no good for detecting whether a key is being held down—for instance, if you want to make a game where the player's character continues to move as long as the arrow keys are pressed.

For this type of functionality, you need the Key object. The Key object is a set of functions and constants built into Flash. You can use these functions and constants to determine whether a key is being pressed. For instance, to see whether the left arrow key is pressed, use this code:

```
if (Key.isDown(Key.LEFT)) {
    trace("The left arrow is down");
}
```

The `Key.isDown` function returns a true or false depending on whether the key listed as a parameter is pressed. The `Key.LEFT` constant represents the left arrow key. So this `if` statement is true when the left arrow key is pressed.

The list of constants like `Key.LEFT` reads just like the previous list of constants understood by buttons. It has a few more keys, such as Control and Shift. It also has different spellings for other keys.

`Key.BACKSPACE`	`Key.ENTER`	`Key.PGDN`
`Key.CAPSLOCK`	`Key.ESCAPE`	`Key.RIGHT`
`Key.CONTROL`	`Key.HOME`	`Key.SHIFT`
`Key.DELETEKEY`	`Key.INSERT`	`Key.SPACE`
`Key.DOWN`	`Key.LEFT`	`Key.TAB`
`Key.END`	`Key.PGUP`	`Key.UP`

But what if you want to detect a normal key such as "a"? You still need to know the code for the key; you can't just use the character "a." The `Key.getCode` function does that. Here is an example:

```
if (Key.isDown(Key.getCode("a")) {
    trace("The left arrow is down");
}
```

The example movie 09keyobject.fla has a movie clip with a script that demonstrates both of the previous examples.

Key Listeners

The problem with the Key object method of detecting key presses is that it cannot detect the initial key press. It just tests, over and over again, for the key to be down.

Consider a slow computer. The `onClipEvent(enterFrame)` handler runs and checks for the "a" key to be down. It isn't. Then the user clicks down on it quickly, before the next time the `onClipEvent(enterFrame)` runs. When the `onClipEvent(enterFrame)` does run, the key is no longer pressed. The key press is never recognized by the handler. So a user can click quickly, and your Flash movie will miss it.

Another problem would occur if you want the user to click multiple times. For instance, pressing space could fire a bullet in a game. The Key object might not be able to tell the difference between one long click and series of quick ones.

In Flash MX, you have a third choice when it comes to listening for key presses. You can create a *listener* to pay attention for the key press event to occur.

A listener has two parts. The first part is its creation. You have to tell the movie that you want it to listen for an event. In this case, you tell it with the following command:

```
Key.addListener(_root);
```

The `Key.addListener` command takes an object, such as the root movie or a movie clip, as its parameter. This is the object that gets a message when the event happens.

In this case, the root level of the movie gets the event. For the root level to respond to this event, it should have a function that has been assigned to handle it.

The key listener can send two different types of messages: `onKeyUp` and `onKeyDown`. To make a function that handles one of these, you write code that looks like this:

```
_root.onKeyUp = function() {
    trace(Key.getAscii());
}
```


You could also use another object, such as a movie clip, in place of `_root`, as long as it was the same object used in the `Key.addListener` command.

The `Key.getAscii()` function returns the ASCII code for the key pressed. ASCII code is a number that corresponds to a character: "A" is 65, "B" is 66, and so on.

Take a look at the movie 09keylistener.fla to see this code in action. Notice that it has absolutely no movie clips in it; it doesn't need any. The script is placed on the first and only frame of the main timeline.

Furthermore, if you want to see real characters rather than ASCII codes, you can use the `String.fromCharCode()` function to convert them. Here is the new line:

```
trace(String.fromCharCode(Key.getAscii()));
```

Movie Clip Key Events

There is actually a fourth way to detect key presses. This is to use the `onClipEvent` handlers `keyDown` and `keyUp`. You then need to use `Key.getAscii()` to determine which key was pressed.

I won't go into this method; it is obsolete now that Flash MX has introduced listeners. However, you should know about it in case you see it in older code examples.

Task: Keyboard-Controlled Movie Clip

Let's use our knowledge of testing the keys on the keyboard to allow the user to move a movie clip around the screen.

1. Start with a new movie.
2. Create a simple movie clip. A simple shape such as a circle will do.

3. Attach this script to it:

```
onClipEvent(enterFrame) {
    if (Key.isDown(Key.LEFT)) this._x -= 5;
    if (Key.isDown(Key.RIGHT)) this._x += 5;
    if (Key.isDown(Key.UP)) this._y -= 5;
    if (Key.isDown(Key.DOWN)) this._y += 5;
}
```

   All that this script does is test each of the four arrow keys and send the movie clip a little in that direction if the key is pressed.

4. Now replace that script with one that is a little more ready for future use. This script stores the starting location of the movie clip in *x* and *y*. It also sets the *speed* variable to 5.

   In Every frame that goes by, it tests the four arrow keys but adjusts the *x* and *y* variables instead of directly adjusting the location of the movie clip. It uses *speed* as its adjustment amount. Then it sets the location to *x* and *y*:

```
onClipEvent(load) {
    x = this._x;
    y = this._y;
    speed = 5;
}

onClipEvent(enterFrame) {
    if (Key.isDown(Key.LEFT)) {
        x -= speed;
    }
        if (Key.isDown(Key.RIGHT)) {
        x += speed;
    }
        if (Key.isDown(Key.UP)) {
        y -= speed;
    }
        if (Key.isDown(Key.DOWN)) {
        y += speed;
    }

    this._x = x;
    this._y = y;
}
```

   This longer script has two advantages. First, because we are adjusting variables rather than the real location, we can test the new location before making the move. This will come in handy in games where you don't want the object to be seen outside a certain area. Second, this script makes it easy to adjust the speed since it is in one place only.

   Because we use *speed* instead of repeating the number 5 four times, we have one central place where we can adjust the speed of the movie clip.

Input Text

In Flash, users can also type in an input text field. You can have them enter a series of characters, and then you can access what they typed with ActionScript.

To allow the user to type, you'll need to create an input text field. This is done the same way as you would create any text in Flash. First, use the Text tool to draw a text area on the screen. Type something in it, such as `input text` so that it doesn't disappear if you use other tools.

Now, with this new text area selected, choose Window, Properties. You can also use the keyboard shortcut Command+F3 on Macs and Ctrl+F3 in Windows. You'll get a panel that looks like Figure 9.1.

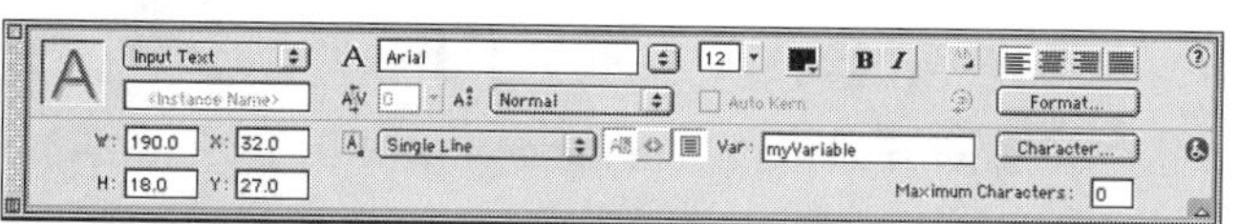

FIGURE 9.1
The Properties panel allows you to see almost every property about a text area. The small triangle allows you to expand or contract the bottom portion.

To make a text area an input text field, you'll need to change its type with the pop-up menu at the upper-left corner of the panel. In Figure 9.1, it is already set to Input Text.

You can use this panel to adjust the font and font settings used by this field. You can also change how the field lays out the text with the pop-up menu item set to Single Line in Figure 9.1. You can also set it to Multiline so that the user can type large amounts of wrapped text into a larger input field. Multiline No Wrap forces the user to press Return between lines. Password hides the letters the user types, using "*" instead of each character.

The third little button to the right of that pop-up menu is also handy. You can select it so that there is a border around the text field.

The most important setting to the ActionScript programmer is the `Var` property. You'll need to set this to the name of a variable that the input text represents. This means that the value of that variable will be the same as the contents of that input text. As the user changes it, the variable changes as well.

The example movie 09input.fla contains a simple input text field and a button. Test the movie, type some text into the input text field, and press the button. The contents of the input text will be sent to the Output window.

The code to do this is simple. First, the input text field is set so that it is linked to the variable *myVariable*. That is how Figure 9.1 is set as well. Then, this code on the button puts the contents of this variable to the Output window.

```
on(release) {
    trace(myVariable);
}
```

That's all it takes to get the value of a text input field. It is so easy that it hardly requires any new ActionScript knowledge at all. You just have to remember to set the `Var` property of the text input field. Also remember that this is a global variable that only exists on the level where the field is located. So if you place it in a movie clip, you will have to refer to the variable as part of the movie clip to access it from the root level.

String Operations and Functions

Now that we can get strings from the user, it will be useful to manipulate them.

Concatenation

To combine two strings, use the + symbol. For instance, if you have a variable named *myVariable* and want to add something to it, just use *myVariable+* and the thing you want to add. Here is an example using the Output window:

```
var myVariable = "Hello";
trace(myVariable+" World.");
```

The resulting output will be "Hello World." The variable still contains just `"Hello"`, but the `trace` command gets the full "Hello World."

You can also add the string to the end of the variable permanently using +=:

```
var myVariable = "Hello";
myVariable += " World.";
trace(myVariable);
```

You can combine the + symbol in all sorts of ways. Here is another example:

```
var myVar1 = "This";
var myVar2 = "and";
var myVar3 = "that";
var myVar4 = myVar1 + " " + myVar2 + " " + myVar3;
trace(myVar4);
```

The resulting output is "This and that."

Substrings

You can also get parts of a string. For instance, if you wanted to get the fourth to seventh letters of a string, you could so this:

```
var myString = "Hello World.";
trace(myString.substring(3,7));
```

The result would be "lo W." But the numbers in the function need some explaining. The function got the fourth to seventh characters, but why was the function fed a 3 and a 7 instead of a 4 and a 7?

Unfortunately, the explanation is a little confusing. First, remember that in ActionScript, counting usually starts at 0. So the first character of the string is character 0. That means that the fourth character is 3. So that explains the 3. But if the first parameter is 3, then wouldn't the second parameter be 6? No, because the second parameter is actually the number of the character to stop *before*. So if you want to stop before character 6, you need to use a 7.

Therefore to get the fourth through seventh characters, we use a 3 and a 7. Just remember to subtract 1 at all times when picking out character placement, but that the second parameter of `substring` needs to have 1 added to it.

There is actually another way to get parts of strings. I think you will like this one better. The `substr` function has a similar name but works differently. Its two parameters are the start character and the length of the substring needed. So you can get four characters, starting at character 3, with this:

```
var myString = "Hello World.";
trace(myString.substr(3,4));
```

The result is the same as the previous example—"lo W."

One more command that you should know is `charAt`. You can use this to get a single character from the string. For instance, this gets character 6, the "W," from the string.

```
var myString = "Hello World.";
trace(myString.charAt(6));
```

String Functions

There are a few miscellaneous string functions that you may want to have in your arsenal of ActionScript functions. You can use `indexOf` to find the position of a string inside another string. For instance, to find the "W," you could do this:

```
var myString = "Hello World.";
trace(myString.indexOf("W",0));
```

This returns a 6, because "W" is the sixth character. You can also find strings longer than one character:

```
var myString = "Hello World.";
trace(myString.indexOf("llo",0));
```

This returns a 2, because the string "llo" starts at character 2. Note that the 0 as the second parameter of these two functions means that the search starts at that point. A 0 starts the search at the beginning of the string. If we used a 2, the search would ignore the first two characters and start at the third character.

If the `indexOf` function doesn't find the search string, it returns a -1.

You can use `lastIndexOf` to find a string starting at the back of the other string. For instance, to find the first "l" and the last "l," you can do this:

```
var myString = "Hello World.";
trace(myString.indexOf("l",0));
trace(myString.lastIndexOf("l"));
```

The results are a 2 and a 9. The 2 represents the first "l" in "Hello," and the 9 represents the "l" in "World."

ActionScript also has useful functions that convert all the letters in a string to uppercase or lowercase. Here is an example:

```
var myString = "Hello World.";
trace(myString.toUpperCase());
trace(myString.toLowerCase());
```

The results in the Output window look like this:

```
HELLO WORLD.
hello world.
```

One more thing you should know about strings is how to get their length. For this, just use the `length` property of the string. Here is an example:

```
var myString = "Hello World.";
trace(myString.length);
```

The answer is 12. Remember that just because we start counting characters at 0 doesn't affect how many characters there are. So the first character is character 0, the last is character 11, and the `length` is 12.

With a good working knowledge of how to manipulate strings, you can create any number of interesting applications in Flash. A simple one would be a user input form, just like the ones used on the Web that are usually in HTML.

Task: User Input Form

Flash is a good alternative to plain HTML forms. For one thing, the text in Flash is smooth and scalable and can use any font you want to embed in the movie. When you have a form in a Flash movie, you can also manipulate the data easily.

1. Open the movie 09form-noscripts.fla. This movie looks like Figure 9.2.

FIGURE 9.2
This Flash input form uses text input fields to gather data.

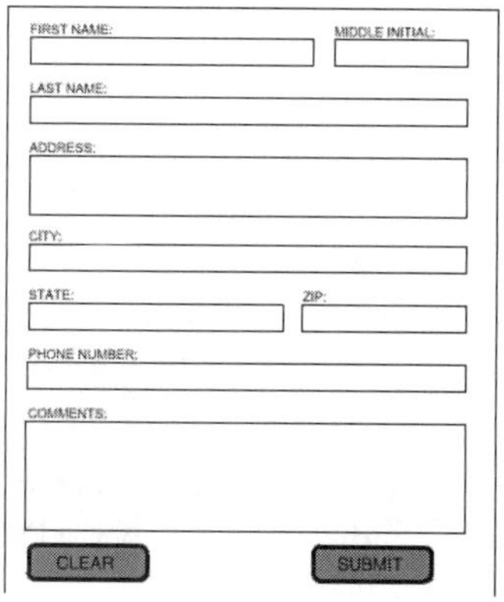

Many static text areas are just decoration. The labels FIRST NAME:, MIDDLE INITIAL:, and so on, play no part in the ActionScript but are necessary so that the user knows what to type in what area.

2. Each of the input text areas needs to be linked to a variable. Click on each one and check to see its name. The name will appear in the Properties panel if it is open. The first input text field is named `firstName`, for instance.
3. Also notice that each input text field has a Maximum Characters setting, which is set to be whatever makes sense for that field. The user can type 64 characters for her last name, for example, but only 1 character for her middle initial.
4. Also check the input field type. Most are Single Line. The address field is Multiline No Wrap, whereas the comments field is Multiline.
5. The two buttons at the bottom of the screen need simple button scripts. The one on the left has this script:

```
on (release) {
    clearForm();
}
```

6. The button on the right has this one:

```
on (release) {
    submitForm();
}
```

7. The functions that the buttons call are located in the first frame of the main timeline. The `clearForm` function simply places an empty string in each variable linked to an input text field. Add this function:

```
function clearForm() {
    firstName = "";
    middleInitial = "";
    lastName = "";
    address = "";
```

```
        city = "";
        state = "";
        zip = "";
        phone = "";
        comments = "";
}
```

8. The `submitForm` function would normally check the data for format and then submit some or all of it to the server. You'll learn about server communication in Hour 18, "Sending Information to the Server."

   For now, the function tests to see whether the user entered any middle initial. If he did, it sends the user's full name, complete with a period after the initial, to the Output window. It does the same if the user did not use a middle initial, but with just the first and last name.

```
function submitForm() {
    if (middleInitial.length == 1) {
        trace("Name: "+firstName+" "+middleInitial+". "+lastName);
    } else {
        trace("Name: "+firstName+" "+lastName);
    }
}
```

As you can see, there is not much to getting input from the user. All you need to do is create the text input fields and link them to variables. Then, the variables are yours to use and manipulate.

Summary

You can detect key presses in many different ways. One way is to use `on (keypress)` handlers attached to a button. You can also write ActionScript code that uses the `Key.isDown` function to check a key at any given time. With listeners, your code can be alerted any time a user presses a key.

To get longer pieces of user input, you can create input text fields. These can be linked to variables so that the contents of the input text can be read by ActionScript. You can use input text areas to get a single character, a word, a line, or many lines of text input.

After you have a string in ActionScript, you can manipulate it in many ways. Operators such as + and += can be used to concatenate strings. You can use `substring` and `substr` to get a portion of a string. You can also use `indexOf` to find the location of one string inside another.

Q&A

Q Why, if I use a button or listener, can I hold down a key and the button or listener will continue to react to the key press? I thought only the `Key.isDown` method could do that.

A Buttons and listeners react to only one key press at a time. However, if you hold down a key on the keyboard, your operating system will automatically repeat that key press over and over again. This is an old-fashioned typewriter repeat function. You can see it if you open a word processor and press and hold down "a." The "a" will type, followed by a delay, followed by a lot of "a's" very quickly. You can adjust this or turn it off in the operating system control panels. Most users will have it turned on by default, but you shouldn't rely on using it for functionality in your movie.

Q What happens if an input text area allows the user to type many characters, but the size of the input text area is small?

A Give it a try. You'll see that the text inside the input text area scrolls from side to side as the user types in it or uses the Backspace or arrow keys. This makes it easy for the user to type a lot of text in a small space.

Q What sort of error checking can Flash do to form input?

A Just about anything. For instance, if the user is supposed to enter an e-mail address, you can use `indexOf` to check for the presence of a the "@" and "." symbols. If they are not present, you know right away that the e-mail address is wrong.

Q Is there any way to get a substring of a string counting from the end of the string?

A You can use `substr` with a negative number as the first parameter. For instance, `*myString*.substr(-7,3)` returns three characters starting seven characters from the end.

Workshop

The quiz questions are designed to test your knowledge of the material covered in this hour. The answers to the questions follow.

Quiz

1. Why is `Key.isDown` not a surefire way to detect whether a key is pressed?
2. How does ActionScript get the value of an input text field?
3. What is character number 7 of the string `"ActionScript"`?
4. What is the result of `("ActionScript").indexOf("c",3)`?

Quiz Answers

1. Because it only checks whether the key is down at that very moment. Even if you are constantly checking, once per frame, the user could still quickly press and release the key between checks.
2. The input text field needs to be linked to a variable. Then ActionScript just accesses that variable.
3. "c." If you answered "S," you forgot that the first character is character number 0.
4. 7. The function is trying to determine the first occurrence of the character "c," skipping the first three characters.

HOUR 10

Creating and Controlling Text

Now that you know how to get and modify text that the user enters, let's look at how to create and modify text in ActionScript. You can place text on the screen in a variety of ways, using different styles and fonts. You can also get text from outside sources, such as the HTML page and external text files.

In this hour, you will:

- Learn about dynamic text
- See how to apply formatting to text
- Find out how to get variables from the HTML page
- Use external text files to store variables
- Make a news ticker
- Build a common Flash text effect

Dynamic Text

You can display text in Flash by using dynamic text fields. These are like the input text fields you learned about in Hour 9, "Getting Input From the User," but they cannot be used for direct user input.

Instead, dynamic text fields can be used to display text with different styling and fonts.

Dynamic Text Options

You create a dynamic text field by using the Text tool just like you would for an input text field. However, instead of choosing "Input Text", choose "Dynamic Text", as shown in Figure 10.1.

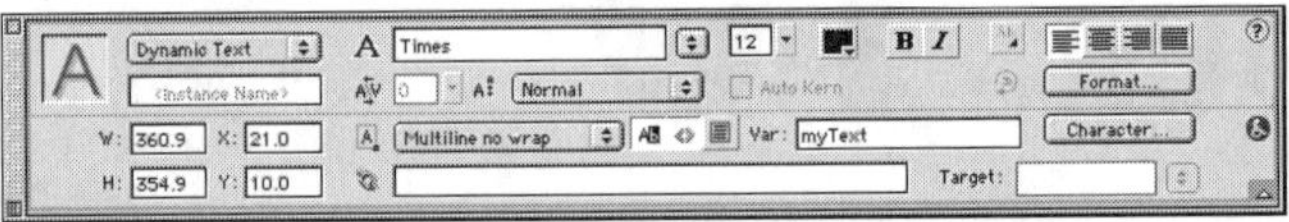

FIGURE 10.1
The Properties panel for a dynamic text field.

The next step is to link this field to a variable, just like you do with input text. In Figure 10.1, you can see that I linked the field with a variable named "`myText`". Now, whenever I change the variable "`myText`", the dynamic text field will change to mirror it.

You can also choose from a variety of other options. You can make it "Single", "Multiline", or "Multiline No Wrap" to reflect how you want the field to handle long lines. For a bit of information that should only take up one line, such as the score in an arcade game, you should use "Single". In most other cases, you should use "Mutliline".

Across the top of the Properties panel, you will see some controls that let you set the font, size, and style of the text in the field. You can also click the Format button to change the indent, line spacing, and margins.

> Although you can change the x and y position of the field in the Properties panel, don't change the width and height. Doing so does not make the text area larger, but instead stretches any text inside it. If you want to change the width and height of a dynamic text field, do so by grabbing the bottom-right corner of the field in the work area and dragging.

In the middle of the Properties panel, you will see three little buttons. The first, which looks like an "Ab" lets you decide whether the user can select the text in the field.

Select this option if the user is supposed to be allowed to select and copy the text. In most cases, you will want it off. The next little button determines whether you can use HTML formatting in the field. We'll look at HTML formatting in the next section. The third button places a border around the field.

The Character button in the Properties panel lets you decide which characters of the font will be saved with the movie when you publish it.

Say that you have a dynamic text field and you want to put "Hello World." into it. First, you need to set the `Var` property in the panel to a variable name, such as *`myText`*. After that is done, don't worry about the field, just set the variable.

```
myText = "Hello World.";
```

It's that easy. But you can do much more with dynamic text fields.

HTML Formatting

The easiest way to add formatting to dynamic text fields is to use HTML. First, you'll need to set the field to accept HTML. You do this by clicking the little Render Text as HTML button in the middle of the Properties panel. It looks like a "<>". When this is turned on, you can use a few select tags to change your text. Here is an example:

```
myText = "This text is <B>bold</B>.<BR>";
myText += "This text is <I>italic</I>.<BR>";
myText += "This text is <U>underlined</U>.<BR>";
myText += "This text is <FONT COLOR='#FF0000'>red</FONT>.<BR>";
myText += "This text is <FONT FACE='Arial Black'>Arial Black</FONT>.<BR>";
myText += "This text is <FONT SIZE='24'>large</FONT>.<BR>";
myText += "This text is <A HREF='link.html'>linked</A>.<BR>";
```

This code builds a string of text that includes some HTML tags. Figure 10.2 shows the result. You can see this example in 10htmltext.fla.

FIGURE 10.2
This styled text was created in ActionScript with HTML-like tags.

Notice that it is not a complete HTML page with a <BODY> tag or anything, so it is not true HTML. However, by using regular tags such as <B>, <I>, and <FONT>, it is easy to learn and remember what works. Here is a complete list of tags that work in Flash 6:

- **<B></B>**: Bold
- **<I></I>**: Italics

- **<U></U>**: Underline
- **<FONT FACE='Arial Black'></FONT>**: Font
- **<FONT SIZE='24'></FONT>**: Set text size
- **<FONT COLOR='#XXXXXX></FONT>**: Color text
- **<A HREF="></A>**: Hypertext link to a Web page
- **<P></P>**: Define a paragraph
- **
**: New line

The hyperlink is the most functional of all the tags. On the one hand, it doesn't display blue and underlined like tags do in browsers, but it does work the same. If you click on a link, the page it refers to will load. If you want to color or style the text, you can apply those tags independently of the <A HREF> tag.

`TextFormat` Object

Another way to set the font, size, and style of dynamic text is to use a `TextFormat` object. To do this, you create a variable and define it as an instance of `TextFormat`. Then, you can set various properties of this variable. In this example, the font is set to Arial Black, the size is set to 26, and the color is set to red. The dynamic text field has been named `textInstance`. We have never named a text field before, but you can see in Figure 10.1 where the name goes.

```
myFormat  = new TextFormat();
myFormat.font = "Arial Black";
myFormat.size = 36;
myFormat.color = 0xFF0000;

textInstance.setTextFormat(myFormat);
```

> You have to use various methods in Flash to define colors. It depends on what part of ActionScript you are using at the time. In this example, `0xFF0000` is used, where the initial `0x` defines this as a hexadecimal color definition. However, in the earlier HTML tag, we used `#FF0000` to define the same color.

You can see this code in action in the example movie 10formattext.fla. The `setTextFormat` command can also accept a second and third parameter to tell it the first and last characters to apply the format to.

You can use text format objects like style sheets in HTML. You can define several of them at the start of your movie and then apply those formats as you need them throughout the movie.

External Variables

Flash allows you to bring external text into a movie by using ActionScript. You can put the external text in the HTML page or in a completely separate file.

Variables from the HTML Page

You can define the initial value of a variable in the HTML page where the Flash movie is embedded. Why would you want to do this? Well, consider an example like a Flash banner that appears on top of a Web page. Instead of making 30 banners for 30 Web pages, you could make one banner and have the different text in the HTML of each page so that the banner displays a different title on each page. One Flash movie works for all 30 pages.

To get some text, or any variable value, from the HTML page, you need to add it to the movie source tags in the HTML. So, first, publish your movie. Then, open the HTML page created. You'll see the combination OBJECT/EMBED tag there.

The OBJECT tag defines the Flash movie for the Internet Explorer browser on Windows machines. The EMBED tag defines it for other browsers, so you'll have to make the change in two places. For instancc, if you want to set the variable *textField*, you need to do this in the OBJECT tag:

```
<PARAM NAME=movie VALUE="10banner.swf?textField=Text from HTML!">
```

Then, later in the EMBED tag, you need to make a similar change:

```
src="10banner.swf?textField=Text from HTML!"
```

Check out the file 10banner.html in a text editor such as SimpleText or WordPad to see exactly where the changes go.

The result is that when the movie loads, the variable is created and set to this value. Check the movie 10banner.fla to see a movie that is set up to use this type of thing. Drag and drop the 10banner.html file onto your favorite browser to see what happens.

You can set more than one variable by placing a `&` character after each variable declaration and then starting a new declaration. Here is an example:

```
<PARAM NAME=movie VALUE="10banner.swf?textField=Text from HTML!&myNum=7">
```

Variables from External Files

You can also get variables from an external text file. Why would you want to do this? Well, suppose that you make a movie that displays some dynamic information, such as a weather report. You can make the movie once and then change a text file on the server to update the text. Someone who doesn't even use Flash can then update the contents of the movie.

To do this, you'll need a single command inside the Flash movie. The file 10external.fla has an example. It loads the variables from the file 10external.txt.

```
loadVariables ("10external.txt",_root);
```

If you run the movie, the text in the dynamic field *textField* is replaced with text from the text file. Here are the contents of the text file:

```
textField=Weather today:
Sunny, with a high of 72.
Chance of showers tonight.
```

An external text file works the same as the extra information in the HTML tag. You can define as many variables as you want, separated by `&`. Line breaks don't matter, which is why all three lines of text get assigned to the *textField* variable.

Task: News Ticker

A simple example that we can build using string functions and a dynamic text member is a scrolling text ticker. This looks like the old-fashioned news tickers that appeared on the sides of buildings announcing news and stock prices.

The idea is to have one line of text, which gradually scrolls to the left, revealing more characters to the right while characters disappear from the left.

Figure 10.3 shows the ticker, but it is difficult to get the idea with a static image. Instead, open the example movie, 10ticker.fla and test it to see the movie in action.

News Alert: Stock prices shoot up sharply with goo

FIGURE 10.3
The scrolling news ticker is much more exciting live than as a static image.

1. Start with a blank movie.
2. Create a dynamic text field that is only one line high but stretches the entire width of the work area. You can place anything in the text field, such as "Text goes here."
3. Link this text field to the variable *text*.
4. Adjust the font to use a monospaced font, such as Courier New.
5. Select the text area and choose Insert, Convert To Symbol. Choose Movie Clip as the type of symbol and name it anything you want. The text field is now the only component of a movie clip.

Using monospaced fonts is an important part of many text effects. Monospaced fonts are different from normal fonts in that each character is the exact same width. This makes it easier to predict the width of text lines and to line up columns of text. Examples of monospaced fonts are Courier New and Monaco.

6. The script attached to the movie clip starts by initializing a variable called *tickerText* that will hold the complete text to be displayed. The script also initializes *firstChar* to 0, which will be the first character displayed in the text field, and *lineLength* to 50, which will be the number of characters displayed at one time.

   Then, the handler places a number of spaces at the start of *tickerText*. This is to make the text start with all spaces and then gradually come in from the right.

```
onClipEvent(load) {
    // full text
    tickerText = "News Alert: ";
    tickerText += ➥
"Stock prices shoot up sharply with good earnings reports. ";
    tickerText += ➥
"The first manned flight to Mars prepares to leave Earth orbit. ";
    tickerText += "Your favorite sports team wins championship. ";
    tickerText += "Scientists find cure for major diseases. ";


    firstChar = 0; // start at character 0
    lineLength = 50; // show this many characters

    // put spaces before text
    for(var i=0;i<lineLength;i++) {
        tickerText = " " + tickerText;
    }

}
```

7. The `enterFrame` handler takes the first 50 characters from *tickerText* and places them in *text*. The first 50 characters will be spaces because we placed them there at the end of the `load` handler.

   Then, *firstChar* is moved over by one. In the next frame, instead of characters 0 through 49 being displayed, characters 1 through 50 will. Then 2 through 51. This is how the text appears to scroll.

   The `enterFrame` handler also tests *firstChar* to see whether it is beyond the end of the string length. If it is, it sets *firstChar* back to 0, so the whole thing starts over again.

10

```
onClipEvent(enterFrame) {
    // set the text to this segment
    text = tickerText.substr(firstChar,lineLength);

    // move segment by one character
    firstChar++;

    // if all text used, then start over again
    if (firstChar > tickerText.length) {
        firstChar = 0;
    }
}
```

8. Using the movie you created, or the example movie 10ticker.fla, try changing the text in `tickerText` and the `lineLength` to see the effect.

   This example would be a good place to use external text rather than hard-coded text. You can use either the HTML or external text file technique to read in text from an external source to populate `tickerText`.

   Note that this might take some adjustment because you need to remember that the `tickerText` variable is in the movie clip, not the root level. So if you define a variable in the URL, or you load one using `loadVariables` at the root level, you will need to refer to `_root.tickerText` rather than `tickerText`.

Although this example is a great way to learn dynamic text field and string functionality, it is not the best way to create a ticker effect. Instead, you can create a wide dynamic text field, mask its left and right sides, and have it slide slowly to the left. This creates a smoother ticker and allows you to use non-monospaced fonts.

Task: Flashy Text

Another common Flash effect is to have text zoom in, letter by letter. Figure 10.4 shows this effect in progress. You can try the movie 10textanimation.fla to see it in action.

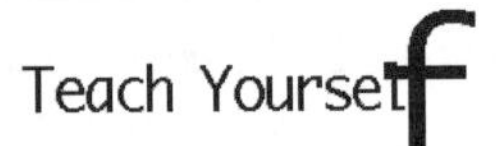

FIGURE 10.4
In this standard text effect, the letters start out huge and shrink into position and size one by one.

The general idea is to create each of the letters of the line of text as individual movie clips. Then have each movie clip start off at many times its normal scale but in the right position. As each frame passes, the scale of the movie clip shrinks until the letter reaches normal size. Then the next letter starts.

1. Start with a new movie.
2. Create a small dynamic text field and place a single letter, such as "a," in it. Set the font and size for this letter. Link the text field to the variable *`letterText`*.
3. Select the dynamic text field you just created and choose Insert, Convert To Movie Clip. Set it to Movie Clip and name it Letter.
4. Find this new movie clip in the Library. Select it and use the pop-up menu in the Library panel to choose Linkage. Set the link name to Letter and select the options Export for ActionScript and Export in First Frame. This ensures that the movie clip is included when you publish, even though the movie clip does not appear to be used in the timeline. The name Letter is used in your ActionScript to refer to the library element.
5. Delete the movie clip from the work area. Leave it in the library, though.
6. Create a simple shape, such as a circle. Move it outside the main work area outside the viewable area. Select it and choose Insert, Convert To Movie Clip. Name this movie clip Actions.

   Making an Actions movie clip is a common practice in Flash movies. This one clip uses `load` and `enterFrame` events to choreograph the changes and movements of other movie clips.
7. The Actions movie clip should now be the only thing in your work area, but the movie clip should be outside the viewable area. Select that movie clip and place the following script on it:

```
onClipEvent(load) {
    // constants
    text = "Teach Yourself ActionScript!";
    letterSpacing = 16; // how far apart the letters are
    startX = 50; // horizontal position of leftmost letter
    startY = 200; // vertical position of letters
    startScale = 600; // how big the letters start
    scaleStep = 50; // how much the letters shrink per frame

    // create all movie clips
    for (i=0;i<text.length;i++) {
         _parent.attachMovie("Letter","Letter"+i,i);

        // fill with letter
        _parent["letter"+i].letterText = text.charAt(i);
```

```
        // move off screen
        _parent["letter"+i]._x = -100;
    }

    // init variables
    letterNum = -1;
    scale = 100;
}
```

All the variables have comments after them to describe what they do. You can adjust any one of them to modify the effect.

The loop in the middle of the handler creates one movie clip instance for every letter in the text. The `attachMovie` handler creates these new movie clip instances from a library element that has its linkage properties set as in step 4. You need to assign each new movie clip instance a unique name and a unique level. Levels are used to determine which movie clip appears on top. In this case, it doesn't matter too much, but movie clips can't share a level number, so each one must have a unique number.

After the movie clip is created, the appropriate character is placed in the *`letterText`* variable inside it. This makes it appear in the dynamic text field. Then the movie clip instance is moved off the visible area until it is needed.

Also notice that the references to these new movie clips are done with the `_parent` prefix. This is because the new movie clips should be at the root level, not inside the Actions movie clip.

The `load` event ends by setting *`letterNum`* and *`scale`*. These are the two variables that change as the animation proceeds.

8. Continue building the Action movie clip script with the `enterFrame` action:

```
onClipEvent(enterFrame) {
    // if scale is 100, then time for next character
    if (scale == 100) {
        letterNum++;

        // set position of next character
        _parent["letter"+letterNum]._x = startX + letterNum*letterSpacing;
        _parent["letter"+letterNum]._y = startY;

        // set to largest size
        scale = startScale;
    }

    // make a little smaller
    scale -= scaleStep;
    _parent["letter"+letterNum]._xscale = scale;
    _parent["letter"+letterNum]._yscale = scale;
}
```

The `enterFrame` handler starts by checking the *`scale`*. If it is 100, the current letter is at its normal size, and it is time to go to the next letter. This also happens at the start of the animation because we set *`scale`* to 100 in the `load` handler.

When it is time to go to the next letter, the *`letterNum`* variable is increased. Then that letter's movie clip is moved into position. The *`scale`* variable is set to its initial value.

Next, the handler decreases the scale by one *`scaleStep`*. It then sets the `_xscale` and `_yscale` properties to that new value. This happens over and over again until the *`scale`* reaches 100 and the next letter goes into action.

This is by far the most complex task you have undertaken so far. Take the time to review it and look at the example movie 10textanimation.fla. In particular, the `attachMovie` process is an important one that we have not covered so far.

Extra Credit: If you look on the CD-ROM, you'll see a movie named 10textanimation2.fla. This is a slight variation on this movie; it animates more than one letter at a time. The result is a little nicer than the script we just built. If you are up to it, you can take a look at this movie to see how it works.

Summary

You can place text in Flash movies with ActionScript by using dynamic text fields. Each field is linked to an ActionScript variable. New text in a text field takes on the font, size, and style of the text field. However, you can customize how text looks using simple HTML tags or a `TextFormat` object.

You can easily get text and other variable contents from external sources in two ways. The first method involves adding a variable declaration to the URL in the movie's HTML page. The second method uses an external text file.

You can create new movie clips with the `attachMovie` command. You can make as many copies of the same movie clip as you want, which allows you to create interesting special effects even if few movie clips are on the screen before the movie starts.

Q&A

Q What happens if I use a font in a dynamic text field that is not on the end user's machine?

A Flash will adapt as best it can, but you want to avoid this. You can embed fonts in your Flash movie. You should do so in any well-designed movie. Then only use these fonts in your text fields.

Q Why does a dynamic text field have both a name and a variable name?

A The variable name is its link to an ActionScript variable. The regular name of the field is used for other references, such as text formatting. Think of the regular name as a reference to the whole text object, whereas the variable name is just a reference to the text in the object.

Q How can I include characters such as ? and & in my variable declarations in the URL and external text files?

A You need to use escape character sequences, which are often used in HTML to represent difficult characters. For instance, %3F is a question mark, %3D is an equals symbol, and %26 is an ampersand. You can find a list of these if you search the Web.

Q Is there any other way, besides `attachMovie`, to create a new movie clip?

A Yes. You can use `duplicateMovieClip` to make a copy of a movie clip instance that is already on the screen.

Workshop

The quiz questions are designed to test your knowledge of the material covered in this hour. The answers to the questions follow.

Quiz

1. How do you put new text into a dynamic text field?
2. How are hyperlinks in dynamic text fields styled?
3. In what tag do you have to put variable declarations to define ActionScript variables in the HTML page?
4. What do you have to do to a movie clip library element to enable it to be used in an `attachMovie` command?

Quiz Answers

1. You need to first link the field to a variable by naming the variable in the field's Properties panel. Then just set that variable to the new text in your code.
2. They aren't. However, you can add additional styling if you want.
3. You have to place the declaration in two tags: the `movie` parameter of the OBJECT tag and the `src` attribute of the EMBED tag. The first is for Internet Explorer in Windows, and the second is for all other browsers.
4. You need to set its Linkage properties so that it exports with the movie. You also need to give it a Linkage name, which will be used by the `attachMovie` command.

HOUR 11

Working with Numbers

We have spent the preceding two chapters dealing with text and strings. In this chapter, we'll focus on numbers. You can manipulate numbers in ActionScript in many ways, and you'll need to understand how to use numbers to write complex ActionScript code.

In this hour, you will:

- Learn about numerical operators and functions
- Find out about trigonometry functions
- Convert numbers to strings and strings to numbers
- Use random numbers
- Create a simple calculator
- Put together an orbiting planets animation
- Make a snowflake animation

Numerical Operators and Functions

In Hour 2, "Using the Script Editing Window," and Hour 3, "Learning to Program," you learned how variables can hold numbers. They can hold integers, such as 7, and floating point numbers, such as 1.3574.

Basic Operators

You also learned about basic numerical operators. Let's review them. The `+` and `-` symbols allow you to add and subtract numbers. The `*` symbol is for multiplication. The `/` symbol is for division.

You can also use `+=`, `-=`, `*=`, and `/=` to simplify your code. For instance, the following two lines perform the same operation. In both cases, 7 is added to "a":

```
a = a + 7;
a += 7;
```

Comparison Operators

You can compare two numbers with the == symbol to see whether they are equal. You can also use the < or > symbols as less than or greater than. The <= and >= symbols are for less than or equal to and greater than or equal to.

In ActionScript, you can freely compare integers and floating point numbers. For instance, a variable containing 7.2 would be greater than a variable containing 7.

`Math.abs`

The `Math` object is a collection of functions that work with numbers. For instance, the `Math.abs` function returns the absolute value of a number. This is simply the number without the positive or negative sign. So -7 returns 7, and 7 returns 7. Here is an example:

```
trace(Math.abs(-7));
```

`Math.round`

If you are using floating point numbers, but want to display them to the user, you may decide to display them as integers instead of with the part of the number after the decimal point.

The most straightforward function for this is `Math.round`, which rounds a floating number up or down to the nearest integer. So 7.2 becomes 7, and 7.8 becomes 8.

```
trace(Math.round(7.2));
trace(Math.round(7.8));
```

Math.ceil, Math.floor

Two other functions that convert floating point numbers to integers are `Math.ceil` and `Math.floor`. The first rounds a number up to the nearest integer, and the second rounds a number down. So the result of both these examples is 7:

```
trace(Math.ceil(6.1));
trace(Math.floor(7.9));
```

Math.min, Math.max

You can compare two numbers and get the smallest or largest of the two using `Math.min` and `Math.max`. For instance, if "a" is 5, and "b" is 4, `Math.min(a,b)` returns 4, and `Math.max(a,b)` returns 5.

Math.pow

If you ever need to raise a number by a power, you can do so with the `Math.pow` function. The first parameter is the number, and the second is the power. So to get 4 to the third power, you can do this:

```
trace(Math.pow(4,3));
```


Math.sqrt

You can also use numbers less than 1 as the power in `Math.pow`. This means that you can use `Math.pow(x,.5)` to get the square root of x. Or, you could use the shortcut function `Math.sqrt`.

```
trace(Math.sqrt(4));
```

Trigonometry Functions

Most of the previous `Math` functions are easy to understand and use. However, you may not remember how to use the trigonometry functions such as sine and cosine.

Although it would be easy to just skip these functions, they are incredibly useful for creating animated effects. So I'll try to explain how they work.

The sine and cosine functions, referred to in ActionScript as `Math.sin` and `Math.cos`, represent the relationship between a straight line and the curve of a circle's circumference.

Figure 11.1 shows a circle with several points marked with letters. Imagine the center of the circle is at point 0,0. The radius of the circle is 1, so the top point is 0,1, and the rightmost point is 0,1.

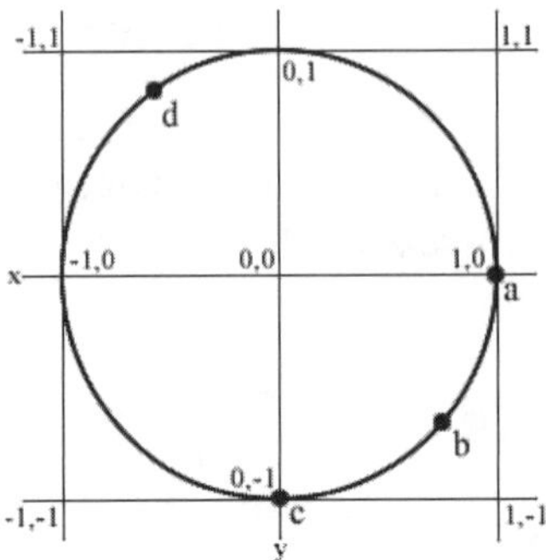

FIGURE 11.1
This diagram shows a circle of radius 1 and several reference points on its circumference.

Imagine the circle as a line. It starts at point 1,0, labeled with an "a" in Figure 11.1. The line curves along to 0,-1, then to -1,0, then to 0,1, and finally back to 1,0. It is a long curved line.

In Flash, and just about any other computer program, we position things according to x and y coordinates. So being able to convert a point on the line of a circle into x and y coordinates can be useful.

This is what sine and cosine do. For instance, if you consider point "a" to be the beginning of the circle's line, you can plug 0 into cosine and sine functions to get the x and y coordinates of point "a." Sure enough, `Math.cos(0)` returns 1, and `Math.sin(0)` returns 0. That corresponds to the 1,0 location of point "a."

So where along the circumference of a circle is point "c"? Well, the line around a circle turns out to be 6.28 times its radius. So because its radius is 1, the line should be 6.28. This is where the magic number *pi* comes from. Pi is 3.14, which is half the distance around a circle.

So if 6.28 is the total distance around the circle, 1.57 should be a quarter of the total distance. That should correspond to point "c," which is a quarter of the way around the circle. `Math.cos(1.57)` is a very small number, pretty close to 0. `Math.sin(1.57)` is a number very close to -1. The reason they are very close, but not right on, is because pi is not exactly 3.14—it is just a close approximation.

So if point "a" is point 0 along the circle, and point "c" is 1.57 along the circle, then point "b" looks like it is about .785 along the circle, or halfway between points "a" and "c." So where is this in terms of x and y screen coordinates? Just plug.785 into `Math.cos` and `Math.sin` to get the answer. The result is .71,-.71, so it is .71 over to the right of center, and .71 down from center.

You can translate any point along the circle into x and y coordinates with this. Point "d" in Figure 11.1 is about 4.2 along the circle. This puts it at -.49 x and -.87 y, which looks about right according to Figure 11.1.

So how is this useful? Well, suppose that you want to make a movie clip fly around the screen in a circle. How would you do that? You could make dozens or hundreds of frames of animation. Or you could use `Math.cos` and `Math.sin` functions to calculate the x and y coordinates as the object moves around the circumference of the circle.

In the following script from example movie 11circle.fla, the movie clip moves along a circle of radius 100. The center of the circle is at 150,150.

As "n" increases, the movie clip moves along the circumference of the circle. `Math.cos` calculates the corresponding x coordinate, and `Math.sin` calculates the y coordinate. They are each multiplied by *`radius`* to make a bigger circle. The variables *`centerX`* and *`centerY`* are added to the coordinates so that the center of the circle is at 150,50 rather than 0,0.

```
onClipEvent(load) {
    n = 0;
    radius = 100;
    centerX = 150;
    centerY = 150;
}

onClipEvent(enterFrame) {
    n += .1;
    this._x = Math.cos(n) * radius + centerX;
    this._y = Math.sin(n) * radius + centerY;
}
```

Notice that as "n" gets bigger, it passes 6.28, the total length of the line around the circle. This is okay because the `Math.cos` and `Math.sin` functions will handle the larger numbers. So 7.28, which is about 1 past the total circumference, will give the same results as 1.

Strings and Numbers

You can convert between strings and numbers and numbers and strings in a variety of ways. For instance, suppose that you have the user type in a number using an input field. Then you want to add 1 to that number. If `num` is the variable linked to that input field, you could try it like this:

```
b = num + 1;
```

If `num` contained “42”, would the resulting value of “b” be 43? No. It would be “421.” This is because “42” is a string with the characters “4” and “2” in it, not the number 42.

To make Flash see the “42” as a number, you use one of two functions to convert strings to numbers. The `parseInt` function takes a string and converts it to an integer. The `parseFloat` function takes a string and converts it into a floating point number.

So `parseInt("42")` returns the number 42. This function doesn’t round, however, so `parseInt("42.9")` also resolves to 42. It just cuts the number off at the first non-digit.

If you use `parseFloat("42.9")`, you get 42.9. So, to round correctly, you could use `Math.round(parseFloat("42.9"))`. The `parseFloat` function also keeps the number as an integer if no floating point portion is needed. So `parseFloat("42")` resolves to 42. Unless you are strictly using integers, you might want to use `parseFloat` as your main conversion function.

One cool feature of `parseInt` is that you can convert numbers that use other bases. For instance, if you wanted to convert hexadecimal numbers, base 16, to decimal numbers, just use 16 as the second parameter. So `parseInt("FF",16)` returns 255.

If you want to convert a number to a string, you need to use the `toString` function. This works a little differently than the parse functions because it is an operation performed on a number variable using dot syntax. Here is an example:

```
a = 325;
trace(a.toString() + 1);
```

The result is “3251” as you might expect.

You can use `toString` to convert a decimal number to a number of another base. This is the opposite of what the `parseInt` function can do, mentioned in the previous tip. If you supply a parameter with the base, you will get the appropriate results. So, `(255).toString(16)` returns “ff”.

The semi-obsolete but convenient functions `Number` and `String` can also be used for conversions. These can be used to convert strings to numbers and vice versa. However, they are mostly present in Flash 6 as a backward compatibility measure for updating older Flash movies.

Random Numbers

Random numbers are a crucial part of games and some animations. Without them, the movie would play out in exactly the same fashion every time.

To make a random number, all you need to do is use the `Math.random` function. This returns a number between 0.0 and 1.0, but never exactly 1.0.

So, if you try this out, you will get a random number sent to the Output window:

```
trace(Math.random());
```

The number might look something like 0.023268056102097, but it will be different each time you run the movie.

A more common task might be to produce a number between 1 and 10. To do this, simply multiply the result by the range and add the starting point. For instance, the range of 1 to 10 is 10. This gives you a number between 0.0 and 10.0, but never 10.0:

```
trace(Math.random()*10);
```

Because you want a number between 1 and 10, not 0 and 10, just add 1:

```
trace(Math.random()*10+1);
```

Now the range of values will be from 1.0 to 11.0, but never 11.0. So use the `Math.floor` function to round it down:

```
trace(Math.floor(Math.Random()*10+1));
```

Random numbers in computers are not really random. There are no dice to roll inside the microprocessor. Instead, a seed number, which could be anything, such as the time of day, is fed into a complex mathematical formula. This formula is so complex, that it is difficult to predict the outcome, so the result looks random to us. The result is then fed back into the function as the seed number of the next time a random number is needed.

If you think about it, random numbers in the physical world are not random either. If you hold the dice exactly the same way and throw them exactly the same way each time, you should get the same results. You'll have to take into account all sorts of things such as wind and slight tremors in the Earth, but it is possible to re-create the same throw over and over again.

There is also something called the law of averages. If you toss a coin 100 times, chances are that about 50 of them will be heads, and 50 will be tails. However, if you toss a coin nine times in a row, and get heads every time, what are the chances that the next one will be tails? Although it seems like the next throw would be more likely to be tails, so that things will start to even out, that is not the case. It is still a 50/50 chance on the next throw.

Let's say that you want a random number from 3 to 7. This is the formula you would end up with:

```
trace(Math.floor(Math.Random()*5+3));
```

The range is from 3 to 7, which is 5. This makes sense because there are five possible outcomes: 3, 4, 5, 6, or 7. How about a random number from 50 to 100?

```
trace(Math.floor(Math.Random()*51+50));
```

The range is 51 because it includes the numbers 50 to 100. If you wanted a random number from 51 to 100, then the range would be 50.

One way to test your random number formulas is to plug in the minimum and maximum values. Taking the preceding example, the smallest value that `Math.random` would return is 0. That would make the formula `Math.floor(0*51+50)`, which is `Math.floor(50)`, which is 50. The largest value is not quite 1.0, so let's say 0.9999. So, plugging in 0.999, we get `Math.floor(.9999*51+50)`, which is `Math.floor(100.995)`, which is 100. So the range is clearly 50 to 100.

Here is the code from the simple movie 11random.fla, where the movie clip moves to a new random location every frame.

```
onClipEvent(enterFrame) {
    this._x = Math.random()*550;
    this._y = Math.random()*400;
}
```

Task: Simple Calculator

The example movie 11calculator.fla re-creates a basic calculator like one you might buy at the store for a few dollars or the one that comes as an accessory program on your computer.

Now, let's re-create this movie by adding the scripts one at a time.

1. Start with the example movie 11calculator-noscripts.fla. This looks like Figure 11.2. There are the 10 digit keys, one key for each operation, an = key, and a decimal point. There is also a C key for clearing the calculator. The characters are superimposed on top of the keys, which are all instances of the same movie clip. A large dynamic text field at the top is linked to the variable *`display`*.
2. Inside each movie clip is a single button. This button is the only other element in the library. The button should have a script attached to it. To do this, edit the Key movie clip and select the button. Now, add this script:

```
on (release) {
    _parent.keyPressed(this._name);
}
```

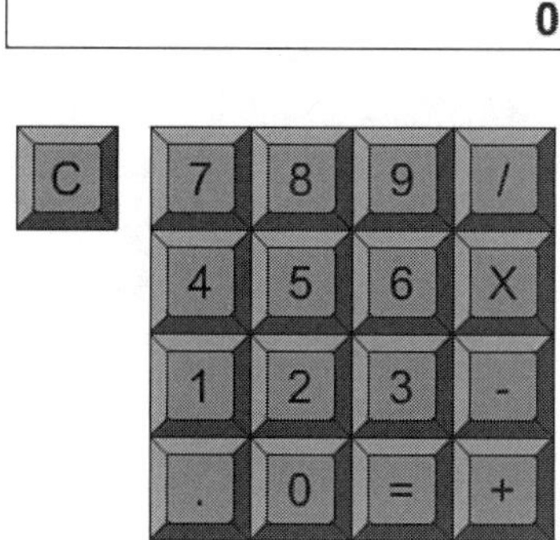

FIGURE 11.2
This simple calculator comes alive with ActionScript.

Whenever the button is pressed, the function `keyPressed` is called one level up, which is the root level. It is sent the name of the movie clip, so if the button is in an instance of a movie clip named Lucy, Lucy gets passed into `keyPressed`.

3. Back at the root level, each movie clip should have a unique name. Note that all the number keys are named after the digit they represent, so the 5 key is named 5. The same is true for the "." key. The rest of the movie clips are named plus, minus, multiply, divide, equals, and clear.

4. The rest of the scripts belong in the main movie frame. The first function clears out the display variable and sets many other variables. This function is also called immediately when the movie first runs. You will see that as the first line of the script:

```
// start by clearing the display and variables
clearAll();

function clearAll() {
    display = "0"; // the visible display
    memory = 0; // the buffer
    operation = "none"; // what operation is happening
    newNum = true; // whether to start a new number
}
```

The *`display`* variable is a string linked to what the user sees. It starts off with a "0" in it because typical calculators display that when they are turned on.

The *`memory`* variable holds the previous contents of the display window. If you think about how a calculator works, you will see why this is necessary. If you type **7**, then **+**, and then **5**, 7 disappears to be replaced by the 5. The 7 is held in memory as the user completes the next portion of the operation.

The operation also needs to be held in memory. If the user presses **7**, then **+**, and then **5**, the operation does not yet take effect. Then the user presses = or perhaps +

again. At this point, the calculator must recall the first + and perform the operation between the 7 in memory and the 5 in the display.

The `newNum` flag is used to determine when the user's next keystroke starts a new number. For instance, if you type **7**, then **+**, then **5**, and then **=**, the answer, 12, displays. The next number you type, such as a 3, starts a new calculation.

5. The next portion of the program is the function that each button calls when it is pressed.

   This function uses a `switch` structure in place of a series of `if, then, else` statements. It works the same way, but the variable is presented in the `switch` command, and the alternate values for the variable are presented in subsequent `case` statements. Each `case` segment must end in a `break` command. A catchall `default` statement is last and executes if none of the values match.

```
// function called by buttons
function keyPressed(keyName) {

    // do something different for different keys
    switch (keyName) {
    case "clear" : // for clear key, start over
        clearAll();
        break;

    case "plus" : // for any operation, go to operate function
        operate(keyName);
        break;
    case "minus" :
        operate(keyName);
        break;
    case "multiply" :
        operate(keyName);
        break;
    case "divide" :
        operate(keyName);
        break;
    case "equals" :
        operate(keyName);
        break;

    default : // all others are added as part of the number
        if (newNum) { // new numbers replace the display
            display = keyName;
            newNum = false;
            if (display == "0") newNum = true; // don't allow leading 0s
        } else {
            display += keyName; // append a digit
        }
        break;
    }
}
```

If the user presses the C key, the `clearAll` function is called to reset the calculator. If the user presses any operation key, the function `operate` is called. We'll get to that function next.

If the user presses any other key, such as a digit or the "." key, the digit either replaces the *`display`* variable or is appended to the end of it.

6. The `operate` function performs the actual calculations. It looks at the operation previously requested and performs that between the previous number and the current one. it uses `parseFloat` to convert the string in `display` to a number.

   The `none` operation happens when the first number is entered after a clear. In this case, the *`memory`*" is simply replaced by the `display`. The four normal operations use += structures to perform the operations; *`memory`* now holds the result.

   The *`operation`* variable remembers the new operation for next time. If it is `equals`, the `none` operation is stored.

   Finally, the *`memory`* variable, which holds the result, is displayed. The `newNum` flag is set to true so that if the user starts typing a new number, it replaces the current display instead of appending itself to the end of it.

```
// perform operation and prepare for next operation
function operate(keyName) {
    switch (operation) {
    case "none" : // this is the first number
        memory = parseFloat(display); // set memory to that number
        break;

    case "plus" : // perform operation with memory and new number
        memory += parseFloat(display);
        break;
    case "minus" :
        memory -= parseFloat(display);
        break;
   case "multiply" :
        memory *= parseFloat(display);
        break;
    case "divide" :
        memory /= parseFloat(display);
        break;
    }

    // equals operation is like a clear, but results are displayed
    if (keyName == "equals") {
        operation = "none";
    } else {
        operation = keyName; // remember this operation for next time
    }

    display = memory.toString(); // display result
```

11

```
        newNum = true; // prepare for next number
    }
```

This calculator program has some tricky parts to it. If you are having trouble, try playing computer. Walk through the code in a typical sequence of key presses such as 1+2-7= to see how *memory*, `display`, and `operate` change.

Task: Orbiting Planets

In the trigonometry example earlier this hour, you learned how to make a movie clip go around in a circle. Let's carry that concept even further by making a movie showing four planets orbiting the sun. In addition, the third planet will have a moon orbiting it.

1. Create a new movie.

   Make six movie clips from simple circles. Name them sun, mercury, venus, earth, mars, and moon. Give them the same instance names as their library names. You can make them different sizes, relative to each other. They should all be fairly small. See the example movie 11planets.fla to get the idea of their sizes.

3. Position the sun movie clip in the center of the screen. All the planets will orbit around the center of this movie clip. The positions of the other movie clips don't matter because we will take control of their positions with ActionScript right away.

4. Attach this script to the mercury movie clip:

```
onClipEvent(load) {
    speed = .4;
    radius = 40;
    orbit = 0;
}

onClipEvent(enterFrame) {
    orbit += speed;
    this._x = Math.cos(orbit) * radius + _root.sun._x;
    this._y = Math.sin(orbit) * radius + _root.sun._y;
}
```

   The `load` event sets the speed of the planet and the distance it remains from the sun. The speed determines how much of the circumference of the circle the planet travels in each frame. A speed of 6.28 would mean that the planet would move completely around the sun in one frame. A speed of .4 would mean that it would take 15.7 frames (6.28/.4) to orbit the sun.

   Every `enterFrame`, the orbital position is increased by *speed*, and the new position is calculated. Both x and y positions are adjusted by the location of the sun so that the planet's orbit is centered on the sun.

5. Test the movie. All the movie clips except mercury should remain in place; mercury should quickly orbit the sun. If the orbit looks lopsided, you may have to edit the movie clips to make sure that the planets and sun graphics are centered in their own movie clips.
6. Attach the same script to the venus, earth, and mars movie clips. However, use different numbers for the *speed* and *radius* variables. Each planet should get farther from the sun and should have a slower *speed* so that it takes longer to complete an orbit. In the movie 11planets.fla, the speeds of mercury, venus, earth, and mars are .4, .2, .1, and .05. Likewise, the *radius* for the orbit of each planet is set to 40, 90, 150, and 210.
7. Test the movie again. All four planets should now orbit. The farther the planet is from the sun, the longer it should take for it to complete an orbit. The moon hasn't been programmed yet, so it will remain in place.
8. Use this script for the moon. It has a fast speed and a small orbital radius. It also orbits the earth rather than the sun, so the `enterFrame` handler modifies the new location using the location of the earth rather than the sun.

```
onClipEvent(load) {
    speed = .5;
    radius = 15;
    orbit = 0;
}

onClipEvent(enterFrame) {
    orbit += speed;
    this._x = Math.cos(orbit) * radius + _root.earth._x;
    this._y = Math.sin(orbit) * radius + _root.earth._y;
}
```

9. Test the movie again. It should all work now, with one exception. The moon orbits slightly off-center from the earth. Why? Well, the moon's location changes first because it is in front of the earth in the movie's layering. So the moon's position is set relative to the location of the earth, and then the earth moves slightly. We need to make the earth move first and then the moon. To do this, select the moon movie clip and choose Modify, Arrange, Send to Back.

11

Task: Random Snowflakes

A good example of the usefulness of random numbers is a snowflake animation. You can create such an animation without ActionScript, but that would mean making as many as 100 snowflake instances, each with its own tweened path.

With ActionScript and random numbers, you can position a snowflake randomly on the screen, give it a random speed and spin, and even move the snowflake back to the top of the screen when it hits the ground so that the snow continues to fall.

1. Create a new movie.
2. Draw a snowflake. Make it a movie clip named Snowflake and name the instance of this movie clip on the screen snowflake.
3. Attach this script to it. This will assign it a random position when the movie starts. It will also have a random vertical speed, horizontal drift, and spin.

```
onClipEvent(load) {
    this._x = Math.random()*550; // 0 to 550
    this._y = Math.random()*400; // 0 to 400
    speed = Math.random()*3+3; // 3 to 6
    drift = Math.random()*2-1; // -1 to 1
    rotate = Math.random()*6-3; // -3 to 3
}

onClipEvent(enterFrame) {
    this._y += speed;
    this._x += drift;
    this._rotation += rotate;

    // bring back to top
    if (this._y > 400) this._y = 0;

    // one side to another
    if (this._x < 0) this._x = 550;
    if (this._x > 550) this._x = 0;
}
```

   When the `enterFrame` handler runs, it moves the snowflake down by *`speed`* and horizontally by *`drift`*. It also rotates the snowflake by *`rotate`*.

   It checks to see whether the snowflake has passed the bottom of the screen and recycles it back to the top if it has.

   If the snowflake drifts off the right side of the screen, it is moved to the left side of the screen and vice versa.

4. Test the movie. The snowflake appears somewhere randomly and drifts down. When it hits the bottom, it appears back at the top.
5. Now let's make it really snow. Place this script in the frame on the main timeline:

```
// create 50 additional snowflakes
for(var i=0;i<50;i++) {
    snowflake.duplicateMovieClip("snowflake"+i,i);
}
```

The `duplicateMovieClip` function works like the `attachMovie` function to make a new movie clip while the movie is running. The difference is that it uses an existing movie clip instance and makes an exact copy of it, code and all. You need to give that movie clip a unique name and level.

When you run the movie now, 50 copies of the snowflake are made. Each has its own copy of the same script. Each snowflake, however, generates its own starting location, speed, drift, and rotation. So you end up with a field of random snowflakes.

You can check the movie 11snowflakes.fla to see this movie in action. It looks something like Figure 11.3.

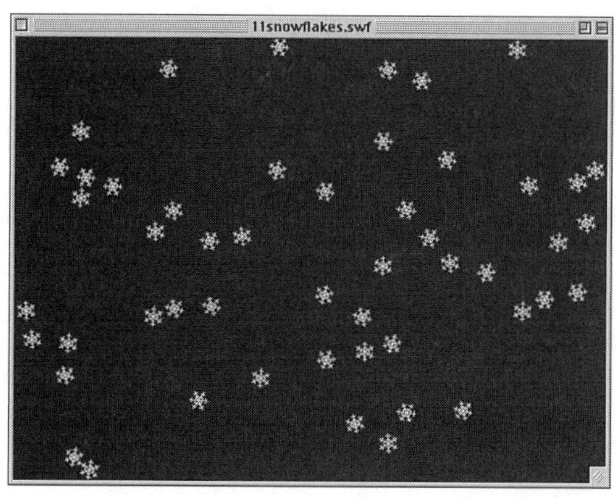

FIGURE 11.3
A field of 51 random snowflakes.

Summary

Numbers are an important part of complex ActionScript programs. You can use the `Math` object to perform standard mathematical functions on numbers. You can convert numbers to strings and strings to numbers.

Trigonometry functions such as sine and cosine can be used to convert a point along the circumference of a circle into an x and y coordinate.

Random numbers can be created with the `Math.random()` function. You must perform additional operations on the result to get a random number that fits the range you need.

The `duplicateMovieClip` function can make an exact copy of an existing movie clip instance.

Q&A

Q What is the largest number that you can represent in ActionScript?

A It's a pretty big number. Using the ActionScript `Number.MAX_VALUE` constant, you can find out that it is 1.79769313486231e+308. The "e+308" means that you can move the decimal point over 308 places to the right!

Q What if I want to use the real value of pi, rather than approximations such as 3.14?

A Use the constant `Math.PI`. It resolves to 3.14159265358979, which is still an estimation, but it is much more accurate than 3.14.

Q What is `Math.round(0.5)`?

A This rounds up to 1.

Q Do I have to convert a number into a string before I place it into a text field?

A No. This conversion is not needed. A text field displays a number just as easily as a string.

Q When should I use `attachMovie` and when should I use `duplicateMovieClip`?

A Because `duplicateMovieClip` leaves its original in place, it usually works out that you want to use `attachMovie` instead. Otherwise, you will always have the first movie clip to deal with in some way. However, `duplicateMovieClip` comes in handy when you want to have a movie clip script attached to each new instance that you create.

Workshop

The quiz questions are designed to test your knowledge of the material covered in this hour. The answers to the questions follow.

Quiz

1. What is the result of `Math.min(10,Math.max(5,a))` when a is equal to 12? What is the purpose of such a statement?
2. If a movie clip is halfway around a circle, how do you get its horizontal position on the screen?
3. What is the largest possible value returned by `Math.random()*7`?
4. If you use `duplicateMovieClip` to create a copy of a movie clip instance, what happens to the original instance?

Quiz Answers

1. The answer is 10. `Math.max(5,a)` resolves to 12; then `Math.min(10,12)` resolves to 10. The purpose of code like this is to make sure that the variable stays between two numbers. In this case, the result will never be less than 5 or greater than 10, no matter what "a" is.
2. Use `Math.cos` with a value of 3.14, or `Math.PI`. `Math.cos` returns the horizontal position of a point on a circle. A complete circle is 6.28, or two times pi, so halfway would be 3.14 or pi. You also need to multiply the result by the radius of the circle.
3. The largest value of `Math.random` is slightly less than 1.0. So the largest possible value of `Math.random()*7` is slightly less than 7.0.
4. Nothing. It is still there and any script assigned to it is still active.

HOUR 12

Objects and Arrays

Until now, all variable data has been stored individually, one bit of data per variable. This works fine for most simple applications, but you soon end up with a lot of variables. You can also find yourself faced with difficult situations where you need to store a lot of data, and single variables are just not able to do it easily.

ActionScript can use two methods to store a lot of data. The first method we will look at is custom objects. You can use these to group pieces of data together. The second method is arrays, which is a fundamental part of any advanced programming language.

In this hour, you will:

- Find out how to make custom variable objects
- See how to use built-in ActionScript objects such as colors and dates
- Learn about arrays
- Build a word server animation
- Teach movie clips to form a trail behind the mouse

Custom Variable Objects

When working with movie clip screen positions, you always have two components: x and y. Wouldn't it be nice to be able to organize them a little better? For instance, you could name your variables *positionX* and *positionY* instead of just *x* and *y*.

But these are still just totally different variables. The names just look similar.

You can use custom variable objects to better organize your variables. For instance, you could store the x and y position of your movie clip like this:

```
pos = {x:10, y:20};
```

By using the curly brackets, you are creating an object. In this case, the object has two parts: *x* and *y*, with values 10 and 20. You can access the parts like this:

```
trace(pos.x);
```

You can also modify the parts with operators and such, just like a normal variable. In this example, you would just use *pos.x* instead of *x*.

Imagine a more complex structure such as a record in a database. The object could be *record*, and the properties of it could be things such as *name*, *address*, *phone*, and so on. You would access them with syntax like *pos.name*.

You can create an object gradually, placing new properties in it as you need them. Here is an example:

```
record = new Object();
record.name = "Gary";
record.age = 32;
record.state = "Colorado";
trace(record.name);
```

In addition to making data easier to organize, custom objects are similar to built-in Flash objects. Two examples of built-in objects are the Color object and the Date object.

Color Objects

You can use ActionScript to change the color of a movie clip. The easiest way to do this is to use the `setRGB` command. However, you cannot apply this directly to the movie clip instance. Instead, you first ask Flash for a reference to the movie clip's Color object. Do this with a `new Color()` function. Then you can use `setRGB` to set the color.

Here is a simple example. A reference to the color of the movie clip circle is placed in the variable *circleColor*. Then, the `setRGB` command changes this color to 0xFF0000, which is the hexidecimal value for red.

```
circleColor = new Color("circle");
circleColor.setRGB(0xFF0000);
```

You can also get the color of a movie clip. This is usually just 0 (0x000000 or "000000"). But if you use the Advanced Effect dialog to change it, you can get a different value. Figure 12.1 shows the Advanced Effect dialog.

You use `getRGB` to get the color of a movie clip. However, this needs a `toString(16)` function to convert it to the hexadecimal value. The `toString(16)` tells it to convert the number to a string in base 16 rather than base 10:

```
circleColor = new Color("circle");
trace(circleColor.getRGB(0xFF0000).toString(16));
```

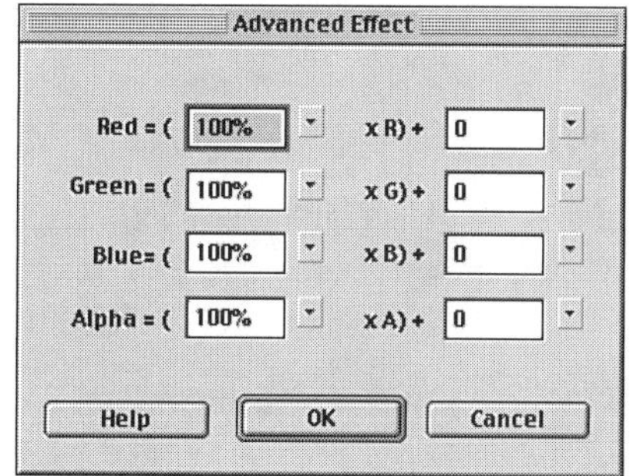

FIGURE 12.1
The Advanced Effect color settings dialog allows you to modify the color and transparency of a movie clip. It corresponds to capabilities of the `setTransform` *ActionScript command.*

There is another way to change the color of a movie clip. You can create a color transform object that corresponds to the eight entries shown in Figure 12.1.

To do this, first make a standard custom variable object. Then, assign to it the properties `ra`, `ga`, `ba`, `aa`, `rb`, `gb`, `bb`, and `ab`. These correspond to the eight entries in Figure 12.1. The first letters—*r*, *b*, *g* and *a*—refer to red, green, blue, and alpha. The second letters—*a* and *b*—refer to the left and right columns.

Then, instead of using `setRGB`, use `setTransform`, with this object as the parameter. Here is an example:

```
circleColor = new Color("circle");
myObject = new Object();
myObject = {ra:100, rb:255, ga:0, gb:0, ba:0, bb: 0, aa: 100, ab: 0};
circleColor.setTransform(myObject);
```

The `setTransform` command gives you pretty much complete control over the color of a movie clip.

Date Objects

Another type of object that is built in to Flash is the `Date` object. It helps to think of the `Date` object as a different type of variable altogether, like numbers and strings. `Date` objects represent a point in time.

The `Date` object is broken into seven parts: year, month, date, hour, minute, second, and millisecond. You can create a new date object by supplying all these elements:

```
myDate = new Date(2002,3,29,10,30,15,500);
```

If you want to examine the contents of `myDate` with a `trace` command, you will get a string in the Output window that looks like this:

```
Mon Apr 29 10:30:15 GMT
```

This is easy to read and understand, but one odd thing sticks out: the month is `Apr`. But in the previous line, the month was set to 3. Shouldn't that be March?

`Date` objects in Flash work like `Date` objects in other computer languages. Most of them share the idiosyncrasy that months are numbered 0 to 11. This is strange because days of the month are numbered 1 to 31. It is just something you have to get used to.

You can get the components of a `Date` object by using one of a whole list of `Date` object functions. For instance, to get the year, you can use `myDate.getYear()`.

If you want to get the current time, all you need to do is create a blank `Date` object. The current time will be inserted. Try this in a frame of a blank movie:

```
myDate = new Date();
trace(myDate);
```

Flash gets the current date from the clock in the user's machine. It is always a mistake to assume that this time is correct. Many users do not have their clocks set correctly. You can use this time and date for normal movies, but nothing critical like e-commerce or account transactions.

Arrays

The last major aspect of programming that we need to cover is arrays. You'll find arrays in almost every programming language; they are almost indispensable tools for complex programming.

An *array* is a list of data. Usually, the data is all of the same type, such as a list of names or a list of movie clip positions.

Making Arrays

Here is an example of an array. You need to use square brackets and commas to build one from scratch:

```
myArray = [36,23,63,71,25];
```

This array has five elements, all integers. To get an element of the array, use code like this:

```
trace(myArray[0]);
```

The first item in an array is always item number 0. So this example array has five items in it, item 0 being the number 36 and item 4 being the number 25.

Another way to create a new array is with the `new Array()` construct. You can use this to make a global variable or a local variable when you start the line off with `var`.

```
myArray = new Array();
```

When you want to add an item to the end of an array, use the `push` command. Here is a sequence of lines that create a new array with the same contents as the one before:

```
myArray = new Array();
myArray.push(36);
myArray.push(23);
myArray.push(63);
myArray.push(71);
myArray.push(25);
```

Manipulating Arrays

You can do a number of things with the array after you have it. To get the length of the array, use the `length` property of the array variable. For instance, this tells you that the array has five items in it:

```
myArray = [36,23,63,71,25];
trace(myArray.length);
```

You can get the last item in the array, and remove it from the array at the same time, with the `pop` command. Here is an example:

```
myArray = [36,23,63,71,25];
trace(myArray);
a = myArray.pop();
trace(a);
trace(myArray);
```

You first get the starting list of items, showing that there are five items in the array. Then you get a 25 as the value of `a`. Finally, you get the new list of items, showing you that the array now has only four items, because `pop` removed the last one.

Using push and pop creates a last-in-first-out system, sometimes called a *stack*. Think of a stack of pancakes. As the cook makes the pancakes, they pile higher. The top pancake is the one made most recently. When someone takes a pancake, he takes from the top. The last pancake to be eaten is the first one made.

The opposite of pop is shift. This removes the first element from the array. So the following code performs the same as the previous code, but the number 36 is put into a instead:

```
myArray = [36,23,63,71,25];
trace(myArray);
a = myArray.pop();
trace(a);
trace(myArray);
```

The opposite of pop is unshift. This puts a new item at the beginning of the array.

To get a portion of an array, use the slice command. The arguments are the first and last items to be taken:

```
myArray = [36,23,63,71,25]
trace(myArray.slice(1,3));
```

This returns 23,63 because the third item is actually not included. If you omit the second argument altogether, you will get all the items until the end of the array.

The Swiss Army knife of array commands is splice. The first parameter of splice is the position of the array where the operation should begin. The second parameter is the number of items to delete. This can be 0 if you don't want to delete any items. The rest of the parameters are items to insert. You cannot list any items if there are none to insert.

Here is an example where the 23 and 63 are removed, and a 17 is inserted in their place:

```
myArray = [36,23,63,71,25];
myArray.splice(1,2,17);
trace(myArray);
```

Sorting Arrays

You can also sort an array with the sort command. The following code returns the array in numerical order:

```
myArray = [36,23,63,71,25];
myArray.sort();
trace(myArray);
```

The sort command also sorts a list of strings into alphabetical order:

```
myArray = ["Gary","Will","Jay","Brian"];
myArray.sort();
trace(myArray);
```

Looking to sort an array in some other way besides numerical or alphabetical? You can modify the `sort` command to do almost anything you want. Such an advanced topic is beyond this book, but if you really need it, you can refer to the documentation for `sort` to see how to make a specialized `sort` function.

The `reverse` command takes an array and reverses the order of the items in it. For instance:

```
myArray = ["Gary","Will","Jay","Brian"];
myArray.reverse();
trace(myArray);
```

Want to sort an array in descending order? Just use a `sort` command and then a `reverse` command to get the job done.

You can combine two arrays with the `concat` function. This works a little differently because it does not alter either array. Instead, it creates a new one:

```
myArray = [36,23,63,71,25]
otherArray = [58,97,16];
newArray = myArray.concat(otherArray);
trace(newArray);
```

Converting Between Strings and Arrays

If you want to convert an array to a string, use the `join` command. It takes one argument, which would be the character to place between the items. If you don't supply it, it will use a comma. This returns the string 36:23:63:71:25.


```
myArray = [36,23,63,71,25]
myString = myArray.join(":");
trace(myString);
```

Whereas the `join` command is marginally useful, the `split` command is very valuable. It converts a string to an array. For instance, this takes the string "36,23,63,71,25" and converts it to the example array we have been using:

```
myString = "36,23,63,71,25";
myArray = myString.split(",");
trace(myArray);
```

Suppose that you have a sentence, and you want to break up each word into the items of an array. Here's how you do it:

```
myString = "This is a test";
myArray = myString.split(" ");
trace(myArray);
```

Now let's look at some examples of arrays in movies.

Task: Word Animation

In this example, the entire Flash movie is one large text field that displays a message one word at a time. It gets the words from a sentence defined in ActionScript and changes to the next word every so many frames.

1. Start with a blank Flash movie.
2. Create a dynamic text field. Use a large font, such as 64 point. Place it in the middle of the screen and set the alignment of the text so that it is centered. Link this text field to the variable *`text`*.
3. Create a small movie clip by drawing a shape and then choosing Insert, Convert to Movie Clip. Name the instance of this movie clip Actions. Move the movie clip outside the visible area.
4. Place the following script on the movie clip. It starts off by using `split` to divide a sentence into an array of words. It then sets three other variables. The *`wordNum`* variable is which word is to be displayed next. The *`frameDelay`* variable is the number of frames that need to pass until the word changes. The *`frameCount`* variable keeps track of the frames as they go by.

```
onClipEvent(load) {
    // get the words
    wordList = ("Imagination is more important than knowledge").split(" ");

    // set up variables
    wordNum = 0;
    frameDelay = 6;
    frameCount = frameDelay; // prime for first word
}
```

The `enterFrame` handler checks to see whether *`frameCount`* equals *`frameDelay`*. If they are equal, it is time for another word. The new word is placed in the text field, which is at the root level. Then *`wordNum`* is increased to prepare for the next word. If there are no more words, then *`wordNum`* is set back to 0. The handler ends by increasing *`frameCount`* by 1, which it does every frame.

```
onClipEvent(enterFrame) {
    // time for new word
    if (frameCount == frameDelay) {
        _root.text = wordList[wordNum]; // display word
        wordNum++; // next word
        if (wordNum >= wordList.length) wordNum = 0;
        frameCount = 0;
    }
    frameCount++;
}
```

5. Test your movie or look at 11wordserver.fla. You can color up the movie with some background elements. The example has a short message, but this type of movie could be an effective introduction to a larger presentation.

Task: Dragging with Trails

In this next example, we'll store a series of locations in an array. As the mouse moves, we'll `push` the current location onto the array and `shift` the oldest location off of the array. That way, we'll maintain a list of the 10 most recent positions of the cursor.

We'll use this information to set the locations of 10 movie clips. The result will be a trail of movie clips that follow the cursor around.

1. Start with a new movie.
2. Create a small movie clip that will be an element of the tail. It can be just a very small circle. Leave this movie clip in the Library, but delete it from the screen. Set its Linkage properties so that it exports with the movie and uses the linkage name Cursor.
3. Create an Actions movie clip to hold the scripts, as in the previous task. Place it off the visible area of the workspace.
4. Attach this script to the Actions movie clip. It starts by creating 10 instances of the Cursor movie clip. Then it makes an array named `trail`.

```
onClipEvent(load) {
    // create 10 cursor followers
    for(var i=0;i<10;i++) {
        _root.attachMovie("cursor","cursor"+i,i);
    }

   // start the array
    trail = new Array();
}
```

With every frame that passes, the new location of the mouse will be put into a simple custom object. This object will have *x* and *y* properties with values that correspond to the `_root._xmouse` and `_root._ymouse` properties of the movie.

This new object will be pushed onto the array. This means that the value goes on the end of the array. If more than 10 items are in the array, the first and oldest item is removed.

The array now holds the last 10 locations of the mouse, in order from oldest to most recent. It sets each one of the 10 movie clips to one of these locations. The `_alpha` of each movie clip also changes to reflect the age of the location. Its oldest location will be at 10 percent, whereas the most recent will be at 100 percent.

```
onClipEvent(enterFrame) {
    // mark the mouse location
    cursorLoc = {x:_root._xmouse, y:_root._ymouse};

    // add the new location to the array
    trail.push(cursorLoc);

    // delete the oldest location
    if (trail.length > 10) trail.shift();

    // change the positions of all cursor followers
    for(var i=0;i<trail.length;i++) {
        _root["cursor"+i]._x = trail[i].x;
        _root["cursor"+i]._y = trail[i].y;
        _root["cursor"+i]._alpha = i*10; // change blend too
    }
}
```

5. Test the movie, or try 11cursortrail.fla to see it in action. As you move the cursor around, you will see the little movie clips follow it. Figure 12.2 shows what this should look like. You can make the trail closer by increasing the frame rate of the movie. You can also try to see what happens when you use 20, or even 100 movie clips rather than 10.

FIGURE 12.2
These small movie clips follow the cursor around.

Summary

By creating custom variable objects, you can better organize your variable values and pass along large amounts of information more easily.

You can also use built-in objects like the `Color` object and `Date` object. The `Color` object allows you to change the color of a movie clip. The `Date` object allows you to get the current time and access different aspects of a moment of time.

Arrays are a powerful part of programming that allow you to store large lists of similar data. You can manipulate arrays with all sorts of ActionScript commands, such as `push` to add a new item and `pop` to get the last item. You can also modify and sort arrays.

Q&A

Q What if I have a variable named the same thing as a movie clip? How do I differentiate between them in my code?

A You can't. For example, if you have a movie clip instance at the root level named mine and you create a variable at the root level named mine, you will not be able to access that movie clip instance. Always use different names for movie clip instances and variables.

Q If I have a movie clip that uses all sorts of colors, how does setting the `Color` object of the movie clip affect it?

A It changes each color depending on how it relates to the `Color` object. It is difficult to predict unless you are very good with colors. However, you can test the changes by choosing Advanced color in the Properties panel and then clicking the Settings button. You can then adjust the numbers and see the changes live.

Q If I can't trust the user's computer time, how can I get a time that I trust?

A Only server time is trustworthy, and then only if you trust your server. In most cases, for instance, in an e-commerce application, you don't need to trust the time on the client's machine because the server will apply its own time when the transaction is made. However, you can always set up your server to pass the time to the Flash movie via one of the external data methods discussed in Hour 10, "Creating and Controlling Text."

Q Can arrays store items of different types? Can an array contain numbers and strings?

A Yes, an array can store data of mixed types. For instance, suppose that you had an array that stored mouse location and clicks. Most of the elements might be x and y locations, but some might be the string "click" to signify that a click was made at that point. You just have to make sure that the code that reads the array can handle what comes.

Workshop

The quiz questions are designed to test your knowledge of the material covered in this hour. The answers to the questions follow.

Quiz

1. If you set the month of a `Date` object to 6, which month is that?
2. What are the two commands that can change the color of a movie clip?

3. How many ways can an element be removed from an array?
4. What is the difference between `push` and `unshift`?

Quiz Answers

1. July. Months are numbered starting with 0, so month 6 is the seventh month.
2. The `setRGB` command can apply a color to a movie clip's `Color` object. The `setTransform` command can apply a complex color alteration to the movie clip `Color` object.
3. Four. The `pop`, `shift`, and `splice` commands all remove items from an array.
4. The `push` command adds an item to the end of an array. The `unshift` command inserts an item at the start of the array.

Part IV
User Interface Elements

Hour

HOUR 13

Rollovers

Some common interface elements are used throughout computer applications. In the next few chapters, we will look at things such as scrolling text fields and pop-up menus. In this chapter, we will look at simpler interface elements: the cursor and the rollover.

In this hour, you will:

- Learn how to create a custom cursor
- Learn how to create rollovers
- Build a quick reference application with rollovers

Creating Custom Cursors

In Hour 7, "Moving and Changing Movie Clips," you learned how to set a movie clip's location to the location of the mouse with the `_xmouse` and `_ymouse` properties. While the movie clip remains at the location of the cursor, it is not useful as a cursor because the real cursor stays visible. We can change this, however, by getting rid of the cursor altogether with the `Mouse.hide()` function.

By first using `Mouse.hide()` and then making a movie clip follow the cursor location, you can effectively create a custom cursor.

This cursor can be anything you want: your own stylized arrow, a hand, or something that fits the movie you are working on.

Figure 13.1 shows an example of a movie clip that will be used as a cursor. It is just a simple arrow. Notice that the graphic is positioned so that the crosshairs that signify the center of the movie clip are at the tip of the arrow. When we set the location of the movie clip, this spot will be placed at the position we specify. This is often called the *hotspot* of the cursor.

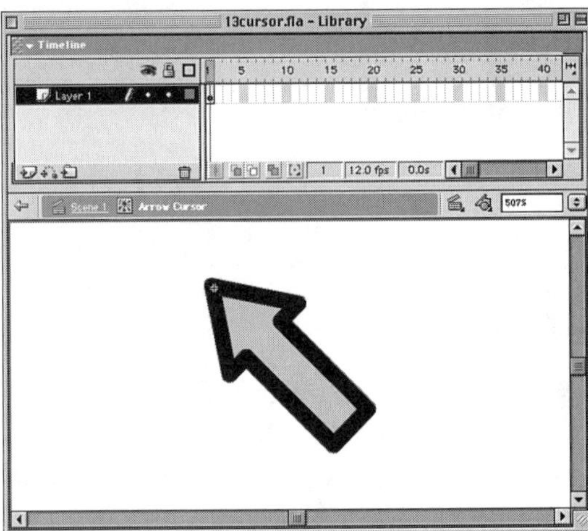

IGURE **13.1**
An example of a cursor movie clip.

If you want to switch from using a custom cursor back to the regular cursor, all you need to do is to use the `Mouse.show()` command to make the regular cursor visible again.

How about an animated cursor? This is just as easy to create; you simply need to place the animation across multiple frames of the movie clip. No additional ActionScript is needed. Using an animated movie clip is just as easy as using a static one.

One last step in creating a custom cursor is to make sure that it appears on top of all the other movie clips. To switch the level of a movie clip, you can choose Modify, Arrange, Bring to Front. However, this only moves the movie clip above all other static movie clips on that layer. It does not move it above movie clips on other layers. Even if you placed the cursor movie clip in the top layer, it could still be behind movie clips created with ActionScript using the `duplicateMovieClip` and `attachMovie` commands.

To ensure that the movie clip is above all else, you will want to use the `swapDepths` command to bring the movie clip the very front.

The `swapDepths` command takes a movie clip and places it at a new level. A level can be any integer: 0, 1, 10, 9999, anything. If anything was at that level previously, it will now be at the former level of the other movie clip.

When you use the `duplicateMovieClip` or `attachMovie` commands, you specify a level for the new movie clip to reside. As long as these numbers are less than the level of the cursor movie clip, the cursor will always be on top. For instance, this command virtually ensures that the cursor movie clip stays on top:

```
cursor.swapDepths(99999);
```

Task: Full-Time Custom Cursor

So what if you want to replace the cursor throughout the entire Flash movie. This is the easiest case. All you need to do is place a cursor movie clip across all the frames of your movie and attach a script to it.

1. Start with a new Flash movie.
2. Create a movie clip to replace the cursor. You can use a simple arrow. Be sure to position the arrow within the movie clip so that the crosshairs are at the tip as shown in Figure 13.1.
3. Back at the root level, start building a script for the movie clip. This begins with code to hide the real cursor and move this movie clip to the front:

```
onClipEvent(load) {
    // hide the real cursor
    Mouse.hide();

    // bring this movie clip to the front
    this.swapDepths(99999);
}
```

4. The script continues with the main `enterFrame` handler. This positions the movie clip to where the cursor would have been:

```
onClipEvent(enterFrame) {
    // follow the mouse
    this._x = _root._xmouse;
    this._y = _root._ymouse;
}
```

13

5. The last part of the movie clip script restores the real cursor when the movie clip ends. If your movie truly uses the custom cursor during the entire movie, you will never need this. However, if you only place the cursor movie clip on some of the frames, this is necessary or you will leave the user without any cursor at all.

```
onClipEvent(unload) {
    // show the real cursor again
    Mouse.show();
}
```

6. Test your movie or look at 13fulltimecursor.fla.

Task: Rollover Custom Cursor

The custom cursor in the preceding task has one major flaw: It does not change when it rolls over a button like a real cursor does. We can fix this easily enough:

1. Start with the movie you completed from the previous task, or use 13fulltimecursor.fla.
2. Create a button at the root level. You should give the button different over and down states. See 13rollovercursor.fla for an example.
3. In the cursor movie clip, make a few changes. First, add a second key frame to the movie clip. This should be similar to how the first key frame looks but with some sort of indicator to the user that the cursor is over a button. Figure 13.2 shows an example.

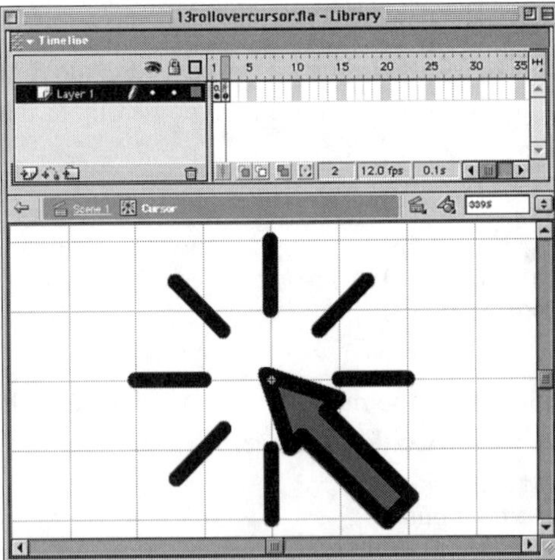

FIGURE 13.2
The second frame of the movie clip is used when the cursor is over a button.

4. Name the two frames of the movie clip **normal** and **over button**.

5. Place a `stop();` command in the first frame of the movie clip to prevent it from animating between the two frames when the movie starts.
6. At the root level, name the movie clip **cursor**.
7. Place a script on the button that tells the cursor to change when it is over the button:

```
on (rollOver) {
    cursor.gotoAndStop("over button");
}

on (rollOut) {
    cursor.gotoAndStop("normal");
}
```

8. Test the movie or use 13rollovercursor.fla.

Figure 13.3 shows the cursor right next to the button, in its normal state. It also shows the cursor moved just over the button, now in its over button state.

FIGURE 13.3
On the left is the custom cursor not quite over the button. On the right is the cursor in its other state while it is over the button.

You can place more than one extra frame in the cursor movie clip. For instance, you can have over choice button, over menu button, and over quit button key frames, each with a slightly different graphic. A common method extra would be to have an over inactive button graphic that the cursor changes to when it rolls over a button that can't be used on the current frame.

Information Rollovers

A common technique in applications that need to display large amounts of information is to use rollovers to bring up information instead of requiring the user to click on buttons.

The general idea is to allow the user to quickly roll over various hotspots. Each hotspot triggers a different piece of information that appears in another part of the screen.

Figure 13.4 shows an example. The nine hotspots, each with the name of a planet, appear on the left. The user has moved the cursor over a hotspot, which triggers another movie clip to display information to the right. When the user moves the cursor off that hotspot, the information disappears.

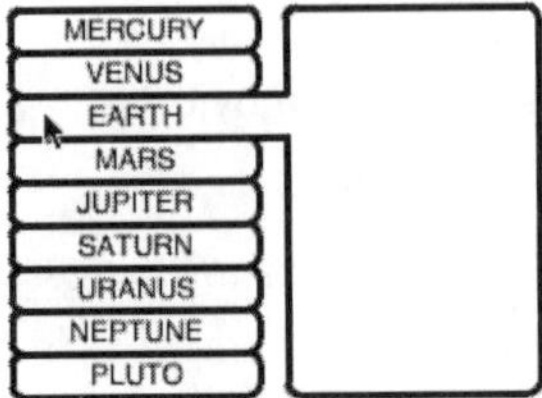

FIGURE 13.4
This rollover example has nine hotspots. Each brings up different information.

You can create rollovers with ActionScript in many different ways. Let's take a look at a few of them.

Rollovers Using Buttons

Earlier in this chapter, you saw the `on (rollOver)` and `on (rollOut)` handlers used with buttons. You can use these for rollovers in a similar way. In fact, the second cursor task basically turned the cursor into a rollover. The code is the same.

The following code is an example of using buttons to create rollovers. When the button is rolled over, another movie clip is sent to a specific frame. Check out 13buttonrollover.fla to see it in action.

```
on (rollOver) {
    information.gotoAndStop("information 1");
}

on (rollOut) {
    information.gotoAndStop("none");
}
```

Buttons make good choices as rollover hotspots because you can also easily attach a script to an `on (release)` handler that performs another action. So rolling over the Mercury button brings up a summary of the section on the planet, and clicking on the button goes to that section.

Rollovers Using Movie Clips

You can also detect when a mouse enters and leaves a movie clip. However, you have to use a little more code to do this. There is no such thing as a `onClipEvent(mouseOver)` handler, so you have to use another method.

The `hitTest` function tells you whether the cursor is over the movie clip. So you could do this:

```
onClipEvent (enterFrame) {
    if (this.hitTest(_root._xmouse,_root._ymouse, true)) {
        _root.information.gotoAndStop("information 1");
```

```
        } else {
            _root.information.gotoAndStop("none");
        }
}
```

This works, but it presents a few problems. First, it continually sets the frame of the information movie clip over and over. Every frame that goes by, a `gotoAndStop` is executed.

In addition, consider whether there is more than one rollover. The first one might send the information movie clip to frame none, whereas the other one will send it to mercury. They will constantly be sending conflicting messages to the information movie clip.

A better way to handle this is to make the script remember whether the cursor is currently over the movie clip. If it is, it should only act if the cursor leaves the movie clip. If it is not, it should only act if the cursor enters the movie clip.

To do that, we'll use a variable, called *over* in the following script, to hold a true or false depending on where the cursor is. Then once per frame, the script uses `hitTest` to see whether the cursor is really over the movie clip. Only if this conflicts with *over*, then a change is made.

```
onClipEvent (load) {
    over = false;
}

onClipEvent (enterFrame) {
    // if the cursor over it right now?
    testOver = (this.hitTest(_root._xmouse,_root._ymouse, true));

    // if it is over it, but wasn't last time
    if (testOver and !over) {
        _root.information.gotoAndStop("information 1");
        over = true;

    // if it isn't over it, but was last time
    } else if (!testOver and over) {
        _root.information.gotoAndStop("none");
        over = false;
    }
}
```

Check out 13mcrollover.fla to see this script in action.

Rollovers Using Frames

As I mentioned at the start of this section, there are many ways to create informational rollovers. I want to show at least one variation here.

Instead of using a single movie clip to hold all the information in the rollovers, you could use the main timeline. The first frame of the main timeline could be the none frame, and each one after that could hold information relating to each of the hotspots.

Figure 13.5 shows the main Flash window for the movie 13framerollover.fla. You can see that the buttons are stretched over all three frames of the movie, whereas the information layer has different elements for each frame.

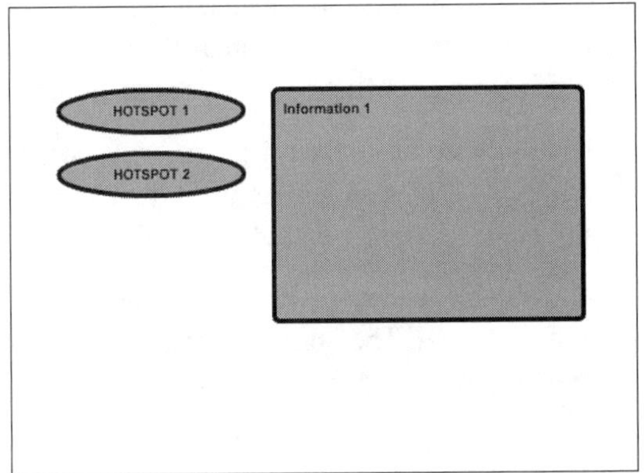

FIGURE 13.5
This method of doing rollovers adds more frames to the movie but doesn't require an additional movie clip.

This example uses buttons for the hotspots. However, you could also use movie clips with `onClipEvent(enterFrame)` handlers.

The scripts look similar to the script from the button rollovers. However, instead of addressing the `gotoAndStop` command to the information movie clip, it just goes to the main timeline, which is at the same level as the buttons themselves:

```
on (rollOver) {
    gotoAndStop("information 1");
}

on (rollOut) {
    gotoAndStop("none");
}
```

The advantage of doing it this way is that it makes it easier to edit the information on each frame. You don't have to dig inside a movie clip. If you are used to editing many frames in your Flash movie, this is probably a better solution than the one in 13button-rollover.fla.

Notice that the results of all three rollover examples are identical. The button method, movie clip method, and frame method all produce the same results. This shows how

ActionScript programming is largely based on your own personal style that you will develop as you learn.

Task: Quick Reference Application

Now let's use our knowledge of cursors and rollovers to create a complete application. This application acts as a quick reference information guide on a topic, in this case the planets.

The movie has nine hotspots, each triggering a rollover information box to appear. These hotspots also are buttons that the user can click to go to a particular frame of the movie with more information.

One key element of this movie is that the rollovers work across all the frames. For instance, the user could click on Saturn to see the details about Saturn. Then, the user can roll over Jupiter to see Jupiter's rollover at the same time. Therefore rollover will be independent of the current frame. You can see this in Figure 13.6.

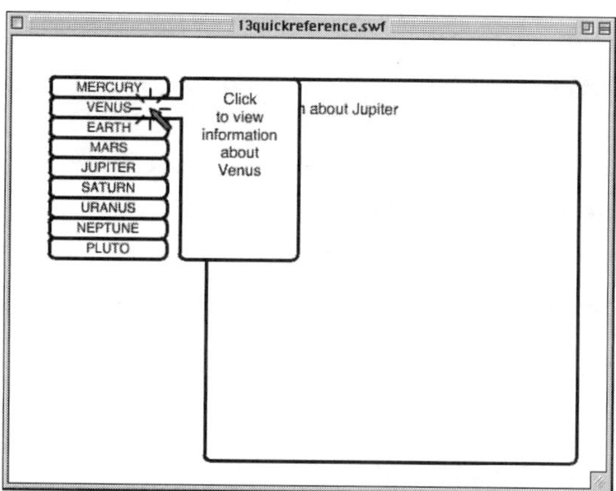

FIGURE 13.6
This complete application allows the user to see rollovers even while viewing other information.

Start with the movie 13quickreference-noscripts.fla. This movie includes 10 frames. Frames 2 through 10 have information about each of the nine planets. In frame 1, labeled none, the information area is blank.

Nine buttons on the left, one for each planet. A summary movie clip appears when one of the buttons is rolled over. This movie clip also has 10 frames: a blank one and one about each planet.

Note that the layering of these elements is important. In the movie 13quickreference-noscripts.fla, I spread out the elements over three layers so that the summary movie clip appears on top of the others.

2. Place `stop();` scripts in the first frame of the main timeline. Also place one in the first frame of the summary movie clip. This prevents the main movie and the movie clip from animating when playback begins.

3. Let's get the rollover working first. The hotspots are buttons, so we'll use the button rollover script. Here is the one for the Mercury button:

```
on (rollOver) {
    summary.gotoAndStop("mercury");
}

on (rollOut) {
    summary.gotoAndStop("none");
}
```

4. These buttons take the user to the frame of the movie that relates to the planet. This happens in the `on (release)` handler:

```
on (release) {
    gotoAndStop("mercury");
}
```

   Note that now two frames are named mercury: one on the main timeline and one in the movie clip summary.

   With these two small scripts, the main portion of our functionality works. The rollovers appear, and the buttons work. Now, let's add a changing cursor.

5. The 13quickreference-noscripts.fla movie has a cursor movie clip placed slightly off the screen. Inside this clip is a normal frame and an over button frame. You'll need to add a `stop();` command to the first frame.

6. Add this script to the cursor movie clip so that it follows the location of the cursor:

```
onClipEvent(load) {
    // hide the real cursor
    Mouse.hide();

    // bring this movie clip to the front
    this.swapDepths(99999);
}

onClipEvent(enterFrame) {
    // follow the mouse
    this._x = _root._xmouse;
    this._y = _root._ymouse;
}

onClipEvent(unload) {
    // show the real cursor again
```

```
        Mouse.show();
    }
```

7. Next, let's make the cursor change to its over button state when it moves over any of the buttons. We'll add some code to the button scripts to do this. Here is the next complete button script:

```
on (rollOver) {
    summary.gotoAndStop("mercury");
    cursor.gotoAndStop("over button");
}

on (rollOut) {
    summary.gotoAndStop("none");
    cursor.gotoAndStop("normal");
}

on (release) {
    gotoAndStop("mercury");
}
```

8. Don't forget that you need to put scripts similar to the preceding button script on each button. The only difference is that the word "mercury" needs to be replaced with "venus," "earth," and so on. This corresponds to the names of the frames in the main timeline and the names of the frames in the summary movie clip.

This completes the scripts needed for the quick reference movie. You can test it with the movie you made, or use 13quickreference.fla.

This example is just one way to make a quick reference movie. You can get much more creative with your buttons, rollovers, and information areas. A movie like this could comprise the complete contents of a small Web site.

Summary

Custom cursors are created in three steps. First, you create a movie clip that follows the cursor around the screen. Second, you use `Mouse.hide()` to hide the real cursor. Third, you make sure that the cursor is on top of all other movie clips.

You can detect when the mouse rolls over a button or movie clip in a variety of ways. Buttons have special `on` handlers, whereas movie clips need more complex scripts.

Because you know when the cursor enters and leaves a button or movie clip, you can use this to trigger rollovers that appear in such cases. This can lead to a variety of information display and quick reference applications.

Q&A

Q If I hide the cursor and the user moves the mouse outside the Flash movie, what happens?

A The cursor is only hidden when the mouse is over the movie. When the user moves away from it, the cursor reappears.

Q How do I get an odd-shaped rollover area rather than a square or circular one?

A If you use buttons, the fourth frame of the button symbol defines the hit area of the button, which affects when the `on (rollOver)` and `on (rollOut)` handlers are called. If you use movie clips, you should set the last parameter of `hitTest` to true so that the function uses the exact shape of the movie clip.

Workshop

The quiz questions are designed to test your knowledge of the material covered in this hour. The answers to the questions follow.

Quiz

1. What properties return the location of the mouse in the movie?
2. What movie clip handler tells you when the cursor enters the movie clip?
3. What does the command `myMovieClip.swapDepths(99999)`do?
4. What ActionScript do you need to make animated custom cursors?

Quiz Answers

1. To answer just `_xmouse` and `_ymouse` is not enough. This would return the location relative to the movie clip if the code is inside a movie clip. However, `_root._xmouse` and `_root._ymouse` give you the location relative to the movie.
2. There is none. You have to constantly check for it yourself using variables and `hitTest`.
3. This places the movie clip myMovieClip at level 99999. If nothing is above that level, the movie clip appears on top of everything else. If something is already at level 999999, it will now be at the previous level of the movie clip.
4. You need the same ActionScript that you would need to make a static custom cursor. However, the movie clip with the cursor would need to be more than one frame with an animation.

Hour 14

Scrolling

Another common user interface element, and one seen in just about every type of modern program, is the scrollbar. This is usually used to allow the user to scroll through large amounts of text.

In this hour, you will:

- Read about the elements of a scrollbar
- Learn how to make a text field that scrolls
- Create a full-featured scrollbar
- Use a scrollbar to scroll an image

Scrollbar Elements

Although scrollbars are all over the Mac and Windows operating systems and in Web browsers and other applications, few people really understand the individual elements or how they work. This is mainly because the scrollbar is an intuitive interface element, requiring no instructions. People just use it—they don't think about it.

As a result, when it comes time for Flash developers to make their own scrollbars, they often fail to implement the elements correctly. So let's go over each of the four parts of a scrollbar and define what it does.

Figure 14.1 shows a scrollbar. There are four parts: the up arrow, the down arrow, the slider, and the bar itself.

FIGURE 14.1
A plain-looking scrollbar.

The Slider

The slider, also called the thumb, serves several purposes. First, its position along the bar shows the user where he is along the full body of text. If the slider is at the top, the user is seeing the first lines of text. If the slider is at the bottom, the user is seeing the last lines of text.

The slider can also be gripped and moved along the bar. When this happens, the text immediately adjusts to show the appropriate portion. So if the user clicks and drags the slider to the middle, the text scrolls immediately to the middle.

Recently, scrollbars have begun to add a new feature. The slider, instead of being of fixed height, resizes itself depending on how much of the text is shown. The result is that the top of the slider indicates the position of the first visible line of text, and the bottom of the slider indicates the position of the last visible line of text. A scrolling text field that shows 10 lines out of 100 will then have a slider that is 10 percent of the height of the bar. We won't add this complexity to our scrollbars here; they are already complex enough for someone just learning ActionScript.

The Bar

The bar is mainly used as a background for the slider. The slider's position along the bar indicates the portion of text being shown.

However, the bar also serves a purpose of its own. If the user clicks on the bar, the text scrolls up one page at a time. If the click is above the slider, the text scrolls toward the beginning. If the click is below the slider, the text scrolls toward the end. Either way, the page-by-page scrolling stops when the slider reaches the position of the click. So, for instance, if the slider is at the bottom of the bar, and you click at the middle of the bar, the slider moves up, one page at a time, until the slider is in the middle.

The Arrows

The arrows at the top and bottom of the scrollbar are the simplest elements. They allow the user to scroll up and down by one line. The slider needs to be updated after an arrow is pressed so that it will reflect the new position.

Universal Properties

There are some universal properties of scrollbar elements that we should consider. First, the elements should act once when the element is clicked, but then act again and again until the element is released. For instance, if the user clicks and holds the down arrow button, the text field should scroll, line by line, until the user releases the button.

Another common factor is that the slider needs to be updated every time an element is used. So when the up arrow, down arrow, and bar are clicked, the slider needs to be updated. It should always show the exact position of the visible text within the full text.

Now that you know about the different elements of scrollbars, let's look at how dynamic text fields can be controlled by them.

Dynamic Text Scrolling

If you bring up the Properties panel and select a dynamic text field, you will see that you can name the text field in addition to assigning it to a variable. In Figure 14.2, the dynamic text field is named scrollText.

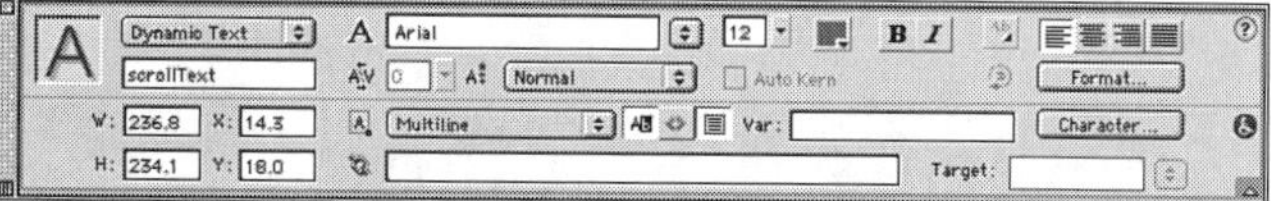

FIGURE 14.2
You must name your text fields to control them with ActionScript. This one is named scrollText.

After you name a text field, you can refer to it in your ActionScript code and get and set its properties. But before you do that, you need to change the text field to allow it to scroll.

If you select a field, you can grab and drag the white box at the bottom-right corner of the field to change its size. However, the field always remains big enough so that all the text is visible. You cannot shrink it so that some of the text is not visible.

Instead of dragging this white box, you need to first change the text field so that it has a black box at the bottom right. To do this, hold down the Shift key and click on the white box; it should change to a solid black box. Now you can drag it so that the text field is smaller than the text it holds.

Now that you have changed the text field to make it scrollable, several properties of a text field relate to scrolling.

The `scroll` property tells you what line is the first one visible on the screen. If `scroll` is 1, the first line is visible. If `scroll` is 2, the first line is hidden, and the second line of the text is the first line visible.

The `maxscroll` property tells you what the largest possible value for `scroll` is, given the size of the field and the text in it. So if the field is actually 20 lines long, but only 10 lines are visible at a time, `maxscroll` will be 11. Why? Because when `scroll` is equal to 11, lines 11 through 20 are in the visible area, line 20 being the last line. You can't scroll to line 12, because that would attempt to make lines 12 through 21 visible, and there is no line 21.

The `scroll` and `bottomScroll` properties of the field tell you precisely which line is at the top and which is at the bottom. So if you subtract 1 from the other and add 1, you get the total number of visible lines in the field.

To make a scrolling field move up and down, all we need to do is increase or decrease `scroll`. We don't even need to check for this value going below 1 or above the `maxscroll` because Flash just does not allow it. For instance, if you set the `scroll` property of a field to 0, Flash simply adjusts it to 1.

Task: Simple Text Scrolling

It is actually easy to create a simple scrolling text field. If you throw out the complexities of a full scrollbar, and just keep the up and down arrow keys, you can make it with only a few lines of code.

In this example, we'll build a movie with a dynamic text field and two buttons. You can see what it could look like in Figure 14.3.

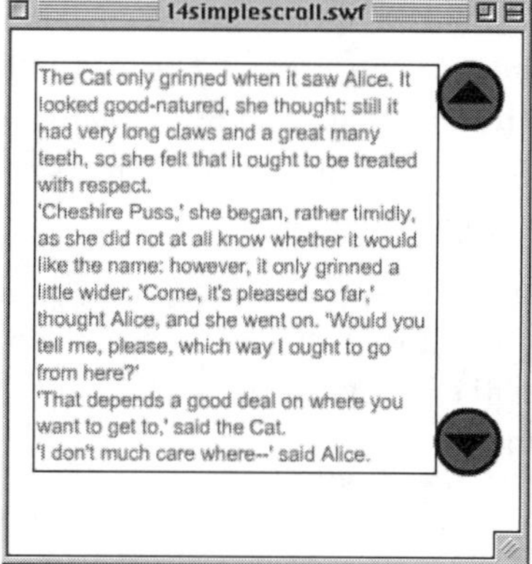

FIGURE 14.3
This simple scrolling example has only two buttons.

1. Find some text to paste into a text field. Make it at least 20 lines long, with paragraphs that are longer than one line so that it looks like text you would find in a book.
2. Start a new Flash movie.
3. Create a dynamic text field by using the Text tool.
4. Bring up the properties dialog and name this text field **scrollText**. Make sure you give it the name scrollText, which is different than linking it to a variable named scrollText. Set it to Multiline and select Show Border Around Text.
5. Paste the text you have selected in step 1 into the text field.
6. Create two buttons, an Up button and a Down button.
7. Attach this script to the Up button. It will scroll the text field back up by one line:

```
on (press) {
    scrollText.scroll--;
}
```

8. Attach this script to the Down button. It will scroll the text field down by one line:

```
on (press) {
    scrollText.scroll++;
}
```

9. Test the movie. You should be able to scroll up and down using these two buttons. Check out 14simplescroll.fla to see another example.

Task: Full-Featured Text Scrolling

Now let's go all out and create a full scrollbar. This would include the four elements mentioned earlier in this chapter.

A script this big needs some planning before we get into building the movie step-by-step. First, we'll want to figure out how the movie is put together. In this case, all four scrollbar elements will be buttons. All these buttons will be grouped together in a single movie clip named scrollBarMovieClip. The dynamic text field, however, will remain at the root level. It will be identical to the field used in the last task.

This time you need to create four buttons. These look like the four parts of the scrollbar from Figure 14.1. The two arrow buttons will have an up and down state, but no rollover state. The other two elements will only have an up state, so they will not change as the user rolls over them or clicks them.

Figure 14.4 shows the complete scrollbar with the text. You can see this in the movie 14complexscroll.fla.

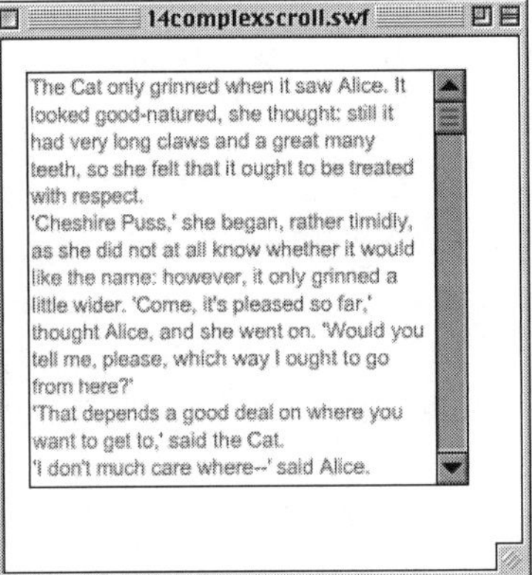

FIGURE 14.4
The complete scrollbar solution.

So where will the scripts go? Certainly some scripts need to be on the buttons. A script should also be on the movie clip itself so that `enterFrame` events can be used to trigger scrolling while the user is holding down the mouse over a button.

However, button scripts and movie clip scripts can all call functions in the timeline. By placing the core code in functions in the timeline, we can keep all of our more difficult code together. This code will not be on the main timeline but also on the first and only frame of the scrollBarMovieClip timeline.

This is the most complex movie in this book. If you would rather not go into so much detail right now, just open 14complexscroll.fla and follow along by looking at where all the scripts go. Try to understand the basic concepts, but don't worry too much about the specific calculations.

1. Open the movie 14complexscroll-noscripts.fla. This movie contains some text and the scrollbar elements.
2. Take a tour of the scrollbar elements. First, open the movie clip scrollBarMovieClip. Look at the four buttons inside it. They are named upArrow, downArrow, slider, and bar. I've placed a single comment in the scripts for each that simply states that a script must go here. There is also such a comment in the first frame of this movie clip.

   Back at the root level, notice that the text field is named scrollText. The scrollBarMovieClip also has a single-line comment where the script should go.
3. Start adding the scripts. On the scrollBarMovieClip, you'll need this script. It simply calls a function inside the movie clip each and every frame.

   ```
   onClipEvent(enterFrame) {
       sbFrame();
   }
   ```

   That is all that is needed at the root level, although technically a movie clip script is not at the root level, but one level down. The rest of the scripts are inside the scrollBarMovieClip.
4. Let's start with the upArrow button script. It calls a function named *pressArrow* when the button is first pressed, and then *releaseArrow* when the mouse is released. It calls *releaseArrow* regardless of whether the mouse is released inside or outside the button.

   ```
   on (press) {
       pressArrow(-1);
   }

   on (release, releaseOutside) {
       releaseArrow();
   }
   ```
5. The script on the downArrow button is nearly the same, except that a 1 instead of a -1 is passed into the *pressArrow* function. This number is used to determine the direction of the scroll.
6. The slider has a similar script on it. It calls *pressSlider* and *releaseSlider* when it is clicked.

   ```
   on (press) {
       pressSlider();
   }

   on (release, releaseOutside) {
       releaseSlider();
   }
   ```

7. The bar has another script like these that calls `pressBar` and `releaseBar`.

```
on (press) {
    pressBar();
}

on (release, releaseOutside) {
    releaseBar();
}
```

8. That takes care of all the buttons. Now all that is left is to build the functions that handle the button actions. This will all be put into the frame script on the first and only frame inside the scrollBarMovieClip; they are at the same level as the buttons.

   The first function is `pressArrow`. In the preceding task, this function simply increased or decreased `scroll`. However, this time we want to allow the user to click and hold down the button to scroll several lines.

   To do this, we will set a variable `mode` to a string that indicates that scrolling is taking place. Then, every frame that goes by, one line will scroll. When the user releases the arrow button, the `mode` is changed so that scrolling no longer takes place.

```
// start line-by-line scrolling
function pressArrow(d) {
    mode = "scroll";

    // remember direction
    amount = d;

   // do it at least once
    sbFrame();
}

// stop scrolling
function releaseArrow(d) {
    mode = "none";
}
```

   Notice a few more things. The parameter `d` is the -1 or 1 that we pass into the function from the upArrow and downArrow buttons. We'll record that in the variable `amount` so that the scrolling goes in the desired direction.

   The actual scrolling does not take place here but in the `sbFrame` function. This function looks at the `mode` variable and determines what needs to be done at that moment.

   Notice that the `pressArrow` function calls the `sbFrame` as well. This is to force the action to take place one time immediately.

9. The *pressBar* function is similar to the *pressArrow* function except that the *amount* variable is not set to -1 or 1, but instead to the number of lines visible in the text field—a page of lines. It is set to negative if the scrolling is to be up rather than down. This is determined by whether the click takes place above or below the slider.

   A variable called *limit* is set to the exact line indicated by where the user clicked on the bar. This is done with a function named *getSlider*, which we will look at later.

```
// start page-by-page scrolling
function pressBar() {
    mode = "page";

    // remember location of click and compute limit of paging
    clickLoc = _ymouse;
    limit = getSlider(_ymouse);

    // compute number of lines in page
    amount = (_parent.scrollText.bottomScroll - _parent.scrollText.scroll);

    // scroll the other way?
    if (clickLoc < slider._y) amount *= -1;

    // do it at least once
    sbFrame();
}

// stop paging
function releaseBar() {
    mode = "none";
}
```

10. The *pressSlider* and *releaseSlider* functions are the simplest because all the work is done in the *sbFrame* function. Only the *mode* needs to be set so that the *sbFrame* function knows what to do.

```
// signal to follow slider
function pressSlider() {
    mode = "slide";
}

// stop following slider
function releaseSlider() {
    mode = "none";
}
```

11. Finally, here is the much-talked-about *sbFrame* function. What it does depends on the value of *mode*: either `"scroll"`, `"slide"`, or `"page"`.

If "scroll", the scroll property of the scrollText field is changed by *amount*, which is either -1 or 1. Then a function named *setSlider* is called to change the position of the slider to reflect the text now visible.

The "page" is similar to the "scroll" mode, except that the *amount* variable will be a larger number. In addition, the new value of scroll is checked to see whether it has passed the *limit* variable set in pressBar. If it has, the *mode* is changed, and scroll is set to exactly *limit*.

```
// code to perform once per frame
function sbFrame() {
    if (mode == "scroll") {
        // scroll one line
        _parent.scrollText.scroll += amount;
        setSlider();

    } else if (mode == "slide") {
        // compute new line and scroll to it
        line = getSlider(_ymouse);
        _parent.scrollText.scroll = line;
        setSlider();

    } else if (mode == "page") {
        // scroll by page
        _parent.scrollText.scroll += amount;

        // stop scrollng when limit reached
        if (((amount > 0) and (_parent.scrollText.scroll > limit)) ➥
 or ((amount < 0) and
 (_parent.scrollText.scroll < limit))) {
            mode = "none";
            _parent.scrollText.scroll = limit;
        }
        setSlider();
    }
}
```

12. Now we have the *setSlider* function. This sets the vertical position of the slider button to the position along the bar that represents where the reader is in the text. It computes the height of the bar, minus the height of the slider, to get the total available area of the bar. Then it compares scroll with maxscroll to get the amount along the body of text that the visible portion represents. Finally, it sets the vertical location of the slider.

```
// set the slider position according to the scroll
function setSlider() {
    sbHeight = bar._height - slider._height;
    sbAmount = (_parent.scrollText.scroll-1)/ ➥
(_parent.scrollText.maxscroll-1);
```

```
        slider._y = bar._y + sbHeight*sbAmount;
    }
```

13. The *getSlider* function is the opposite of *setSlider*. It uses the vertical position of the slider to compute the line of the text that should be at the top of the field. It does this by calculating *pos* as the percentage along the bar that the slider is located. It then applies this percentage to the total number of lines. Some adjustments are needed to get it just right—such as subtracting half the height of the slider and subtracting 1 from `maxscroll`.

```
// get the scroll according to the slider position
function getSlider(y) {
    sbHeight = bar._height - slider._height;
    pos = (y-bar._y-slider._height/2)/sbHeight;
    line = Math.ceil(pos*(_parent.scrollText.maxscroll-1));
    return(line);
}
```

This completes the scrolling bar scripts, the most complex script in this book. You can use the 14complexscroll.fla file to see it all in action. Even if you don't build this entire movie from scratch, you'll want to make sure that you understand how each part works.

Summary

Scrollbars contain up and down arrow buttons, a slider, and a bar. You can create your own set of elements and make them work with ActionScript.

Text fields can be set to scroll by Shift+clicking on the hollow white box at the bottom-right corner to change it to a solid black box. When a field is set to scroll, you can place as much text in it as you want without it automatically growing to fit the text.

The text field property of `scroll` can be tested and set to control the first visible line of text in a field. You can get the total number of lines with `maxscroll`.

Building simple scrolling buttons only requires that you increase or decrease `scroll`. You can create a complex scrollbar with more elements by following user interface standards and using text field properties.

Q&A

Q What about the scrollbar component that comes with Flash MX? Wouldn't it be easier to use that instead of writing my own scripts?

A Yes. You don't have to learn how to drive if the bus can take you where you want to go. But if you want to learn how to make your own custom ActionScript scrollbar, you'll need to learn these things. However, if the component scrollbar works in a particular situation, you can use that.

Q Can I create a horizontal scrollbar with this method?

A Definitely! All you have to do is find the corresponding horizontal properties of the text field and make some changes to the code. Most of what you need is in this chapter if you understand the concepts.

Q How about images? Can I use this to make scrolling images?

A Yes, but it is not as easy. You can't use `scroll` or `maxscroll`, but instead need to modify the location of the movie clip. You will also have to mask the portion of the scrolling movie clip that you don't want seen. It is not an easy task, and a bit beyond the scope of this book, but you now have the basic building blocks.

Workshop

The quiz questions are designed to test your knowledge of the material covered in this hour. The answers to the questions follow.

Quiz

1. How many different ways are there to move text with a scrollbar?
2. If a text field has eight visible lines, and there are a total of nine lines in the text, what would `maxscroll` return?
3. What do you need to do to a button to be able to change its location before setting the _x or _y properties of the button?
4. How can you find the total number of visible lines in a text field?

Quiz Answers

1. Five. You can use the up arrow button, the down arrow button, click on the bar above the slider, click on the bar below the slider, or click and drag the slider.
2. It would return 2. If `scroll` was set to 2, lines 2 through 9 would be visible. That is the maximum possible because there are only nine lines.
3. Name it. The button must have a unique name so that you can refer to it in ActionScript.
4. Subtract `scroll` from `bottomScroll` and add 1. For instance, if `scroll` is 7 and `bottomScroll` is 9, then 9-7+1=3. Lines 7, 8, and 9 are visible.

HOUR 15

User Input Elements

You can create many other user input elements with ActionScript. You can see most of these in HTML as part of the <FORM> tag. You'll see how to use ActionScript to create check boxes and radio buttons. You'll also learn how to control tabbing between fields and restrict what the user can type in those fields.

In this hour, you will:

- Learn how to make check boxes
- Learn how to make radio buttons
- Control the tab order of text fields
- Restrict user input in text fields

Check Boxes

In Hour 8, "Selecting and Dragging," I showed you two methods for making a movie clip selectable. Check boxes are basically selectable movie clips that resemble the standard check box design used in Mac and Windows operating systems.

To create a basic check box, you need two buttons and a movie clip. The first button represents the check box while it is off. This means that it is usually an empty box. The second button represents the check box in its on state, which means that it is the same box, but filled with a check mark or X.

The movie 15checkboxes.fla features such buttons. You can see them in the Library. The up and down states of the buttons differ only in that the white fill of the buttons changes to gray when the user presses down on the button.

Figure 15.1 shows three check boxes. The first one is on. The second is off. The third one is off, but the user is in the process of clicking it to turn it on. If you look closely, you will see that the third box has a grayish fill.

FIGURE 15.1
Three check boxes. The text next to them is separate.

The way these check boxes are assembled is simple. The off state button is converted into a movie clip. A second frame is added to the movie clip by pressing F6, which copies the first key frame. Then the button on the second frame is swapped for the on state button. So you have two frames: one with the off state button and one with the on state button. The two frames are named off and on.

A `stop();` command is placed in the first frame of the movie clip so that the movie clip does not animate. Each of the buttons gets this script, which simply calls a function in the movie clip's timeline:

```
on (release) {
    pressButton();
}
```

The first frame of the movie clip contains a little more than just the `stop()` command. It also contains a function and a variable declaration. The *`state`* variable represents whether the check box is on or off. When a button is clicked, the *`pressButton`* function toggles the *`state`* variable and then goes to the appropriate frame so that the appearance of the movie clip matches *`state`*.

```
state = false;

function pressButton() {
    state = !state;
    if (state) {
        gotoAndStop("on");
    } else {
```

```
        gotoAndStop("off");
    }
}
```

Now the user can click on the button in the movie clip and move it between frames 1 and 2. The `state` variable also changes to reflect the state of the check box.

To get the state of the check box, refer to the variable `state` in the movie clip. If your check box movie clip is named checkBox1, you can use this to get its state:

```
trace(checkBox1.state);
```

The sample movie 15checkboxes.fla includes a button that sends the states of all three check boxes to the Output window. Open and test this movie to see it in action.

Radio Buttons

Radio buttons are a little more complex than check boxes. All the radio buttons in a group are related.

Whereas check boxes are used when the user needs to choose options that are not exclusive, radio buttons are used when options are exclusive. At any one time, only one radio button in a group can be on. The rest in the group are off.

Figure 15.2 shows a group of radio buttons. The first one is on, but the user is in the process of selecting the second one. When the selection is complete, the first radio button turns off automatically.

FIGURE 15.2
These four radio buttons are all part of one group, so only one can be on at a time.

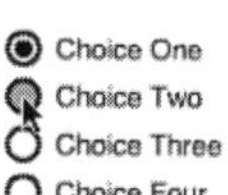

The basic radio button is the same as a check box. There is an on state and an off state represented by the two frames of the movie clip. Each frame contains its own button. The first button has an empty circle, whereas the second button has a circle with a dot inside it.

Check boxes make sense, but what are radio buttons? That name comes from old-fashioned car radios. Before digital tuners, you used to need to turn a dial to change the station. To have memory buttons on the radio, they had to be mechanical. You would press one, and it would move the dial

> to that station. On some radios, it would stay pressed until you pressed another one. Either way, only one button—or option—could be selected at a time.
>
> Modern car radios work in basically the same way, except that the buttons don't stay pressed. However, the ideas that all the buttons are related and that only one option can be active at any one time still applies.

The major difference between check boxes and radio buttons is the script. Radio buttons need a much longer one because they need to act together as a group.

The first part of the script runs on the first frame of the radio button movie clip. It runs outside a function, which means that it gets executed as soon as the movie clip loads.

It checks to see whether there is an array named `radioButtons` one level up. If there is not, this must be the first radio button to load. The array is created. In addition, because this is the first radio button loaded, it is turned on. All other radio buttons will be turned off.

The `radioButtons` array sits one level up, usually at the root level. It holds a reference to each radio button movie clip created. The script uses `push` to place a reference to itself into the array.

```
// don't animate
stop();

// see if this is the first radio button
if (_parent.radioButtons == undefined) {
    // create array
    _parent.radioButtons = new Array();

    // turn this first one on
    gotoAndStop("on");
    state = true;
} else {
    // if not first, then off
    state = false;
}

// add this button to array one level up
_parent.radioButtons.push(this);
```

When a user clicks the button, the `turnOn` function is called. The first thing this does is loop through all the radio buttons using the `radioButtons` array. The function `turnOff` is called in each of these movie clips. The result is that all the radio buttons are turned off.

Then, the current button is turned on. This ensures that only one will be on at a time.

```
// button pressed
function turnOn() {
    // use array to turn all buttons off
    for(var i=0;i<_parent.radioButtons.length;i++) {
        _parent.radioButtons[i].turnOff();
    }

    // turn this one back on
    gotoAndStop("on");
    state = true;
}
```

Next is the `turnoff` function. It sets the *`state`* variable and moves the movie clip to the proper frame.

```
// told to turn off
function turnOff() {
    gotoAndStop("off");
    state = false;
}
```

This is all that is needed to get the radio buttons working. You can now make as many copies of the radio button movie clip as you need. They will all act as a group.

One last function in all of them is the `getValue` function. This is used by other scripts to determine which radio button is pressed. You can call it using any of the movie clips. It loops through the `radioButtons` array and looks for one with *`state`* set to true. It returns the name of the movie clip that is turned on.

```
// asked for value
function getValue() {
    // use array to loop through all buttons
    for(var i=0;i<_parent.radioButtons.length;i++) {
        // if this one is on, then return its name
        if (_parent.radioButtons[i].state) {
            return(_parent.radioButtons[i]._name);
        }
    }

    // if no button is on, return empty string -- should never happen
    return "";
}
```

Here is how you use the `getValue` function. You simply use any one of the radio button instances:

```
trace(radio1.getValue());
```

The value returned will be `radio1` if that movie clip is the one turned on, or the name of another movie clip if another is turned on.

Task: Simple Survey

Now let's use check boxes and radio buttons to make a simple application. Each frame of the movie 15survey.fla is a different question in a survey.

The first frame, shown in Figure 15.3, has a question that can be answered by a series of check boxes. Here's how to set it up:

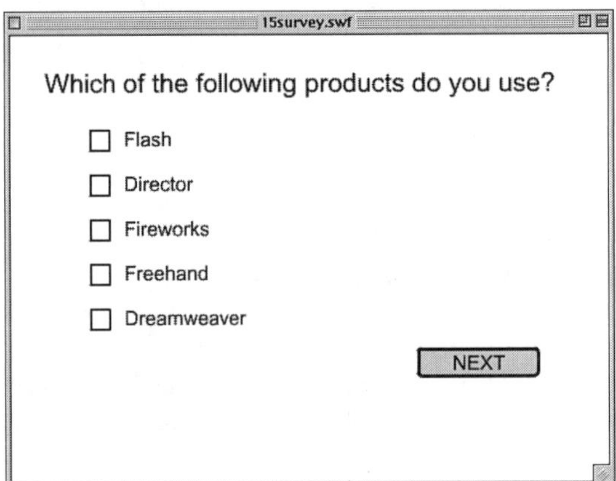

FIGURE 15.3
This survey question can be answered using check boxes.

1. Start with a blank movie.
2. Make a check box button, like the one described earlier this hour. This should have two buttons, one on each frame, and the script described earlier. You can copy the check box movie clip from 15checkboxes.fla.
3. Place five copies of the movie clip on the Stage. Name each one differently: **Flash**, **Director**, **Fireworks**, **Freehand**, and **Dreamweaver**.
4. Create the title text and the static text to appear next to each check box. The result should look like Figure 15.3.
5. Create a Next button as shown in Figure 15.3. In the example movie 15survey.fla, I have placed the buttons, text, and Next button on three separate layers to make it easier to edit them.
6. A short script needs to be placed on the first frame of the movie. It creates an array to hold the results of the survey and also stops the movie on the first frame.

```
results = new Array();
stop();
```

7. The Next button needs to tally the results of the check boxes and store them in the `results` array.

```
on (release) {
    if (Flash.state) results.push("Flash");
    if (Director.state) results.push("Director");
    if (Fireworks.state) results.push("Fireworks");
    if (Freehand.state) results.push("Freehand");
    if (Dreamweaver.state) results.push("Dreamweaver");
    nextFrame();
}
```

8. Now on to the second frame of the movie. This one uses radio buttons. The question asked has only one possible answer, so radio buttons are appropriate.

   Figure 15.4 shows frame 2 of the example movie. Insert a new frame after the first one. Do this for each layer if you are using more than one.

   Copy the radio button from the 15radiobuttons.fla movie. Place three copies of it with the names **Windows**, **Macintosh**, and **Linux**.

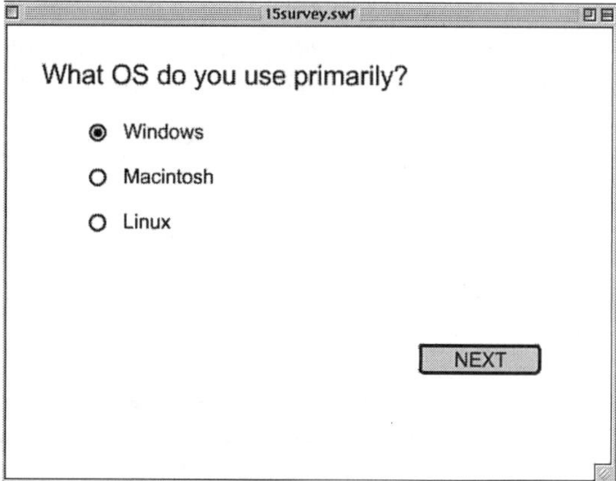

FIGURE 15.4
This survey question uses radio buttons.

9. Add the title and static text to the frame as shown in Figure 15.4.

10. Copy the Next button onto this frame as well but attach a different script to it. This one calls the `getValue` function in one of the radio buttons to determine which one is on.

```
on (release) {
    results.push(Windows.getValue());
    nextFrame();
}
```

11. I'll leave it up to you to continue to add more questions to the survey. Each question should either use a series of check boxes or radio buttons. All the names of these elements should be unique.

    At the end of the survey, you can use `trace` to send the contents of `results` to the Output window. This will show the results of the survey.

In Hour 18, "Sending Information to the Server," you'll learn how to send this information back to your Web server to be recorded.

Input Text Tab Order

In Flash 5, one of the biggest complaints that developers had was that they could not set the Tab order of input fields. Tab order refers to the automatic movement of the cursor between input fields when the user presses the Tab key. This happens in all professional applications such as Web browsers. Users have come to expect that when they press Tab, the cursor will move to the next logical field.

However, Flash's choice for the next logical field is not always correct. After all, Flash can only assume so much based on the position of the fields. For instance, in Figure 15.5, Flash assumes that the field after the first one is the field under it, not across from it.

FIELD 1 FIELD 2
FIELD3 FIELD 4

FIGURE 15.5
These fields are not laid out in the obvious Tab order.

Fortunately, you can override Flash's automatic Tab order with the `tabIndex` property of a text field. So if the field variables range from *`text1`* to *`text4`*, you could use this to set Flash straight:

```
text1.tabIndex = 1;
text2.tabIndex = 2;
text3.tabIndex = 3;
text4.tabIndex = 4;
```

When using `tabIndex`, take care to label all the text fields, leaving none undefined. Also avoid using the same number twice. This will confuse Flash.

One thing that neither the default Tab ordering nor the use of `tabIndex` does is to automatically set the focus on the first field. To do that, you have to use a command in the Selection object to specifically tell Flash that you want the cursor to appear there.

```
Selection.setFocus(text1);
```

This command can be used at any time in any way you want. It makes the cursor jump to any field you want. However, its most obvious use is to start the cursor off in a field instead of requiring the user to click in it before typing.

You can also use `Selection.getFocus()` if you need to know where the cursor is located. If you want to know when the focus has been changed, you can set a listener to watch for it. Here is an example:

```
Selection.addListener(this);
this.onSetFocus = function(oldFocus, newFocus) {
    trace(oldFocus+","+newFocus);
}
```

You can see this script active in the movie 14taborder.fla. Every time you Tab to a different field, references to the previous field and the current field are sent to the Output window.

You could use a listener like this to monitor the progress of a user entering data into a form. If the user Tabs away from a field, you could check the data in that field to see whether the user entered enough characters or entered the right sort of characters. We'll look at an example at the end of this hour.

Restricting Text Input

When a user is entering data into a field, it is often a good idea to only allow him to type characters that make sense. For instance, if the user is asked what year he was born, he should only need the number keys to answer. There is never a need to type letters or other characters.

You restrict which characters can be typed into an input field by using the `restrict` property of that field. If you don't set this property at all, any character would be allowed in the field. However, if you set it to a string, only characters in that string are allowed.

Here is how you would set the input field *text1* to only accept number characters:

```
text1.restrict = "01234567890";
```

Suppose that you have a field where the user is supposed to type her e-mail address. E-mail addresses can only have the basic letters and numbers in them, plus the special characters "@" and ".". In addition, dashes and underscores are allowed in e-mail addresses. This is how you would restrict the user to only these characters:

```
text2.restrict = "abcdefghijklmnopqrstuvwxyz0123456789@.-_";
```

The preceding line leaves one question: Will the input field accept both upper- and lowercase letters? Yes, it will accept both, so the `restrict` property ignores case.

You can also limit the number of characters allowed in an input field. This can be done without ActionScript because there is a Maximum Characters option in the Properties panel. If you set this to 32, only 32 characters would be allowed in the field. You can also set this property with ActionScript using the `maxChars` property. For instance, if you wanted to limit a field to only accept years, you would want it to only accept digits, and only four of them:

```
text1.restrict = "01234567890";
text1.maxChars = 4;
```

The example movie 15restrict.fla contains the preceding code and sample input field for you to try out.

Task: Checking for a Valid Input

Next, let's build a simple user input form that checks the user's input as the user types. It asks for the user's name, year of birth, and e-mail address. It checks to make sure that each entry fits certain criteria.

The name, for instance, should be at least three characters long. The date of birth should be four digits and be sometime in the last 100 years. E-mail address should be at least seven characters long and be of the format *a@b.c*, where *a* and *b* can be anything, but *c* must be at least three characters long. The "@" and period must be present.

1. Start with a new movie.
2. Create three input fields, one for the user's name, one for the user's year of birth, and one for the user's e-mail address. Name these fields **userName**, **userYear**, and **userEmail**. Link these three fields to the variables *`userNameText`*, *`userYearText`*, and *`userEmailText`*. You'll also need to create a dynamic text field linked to the *`feedback`* variable. In addition, create a Submit button. Your final movie should look something like Figure 15.6. You can examine the example movie 15inputmonitor.fla as well.

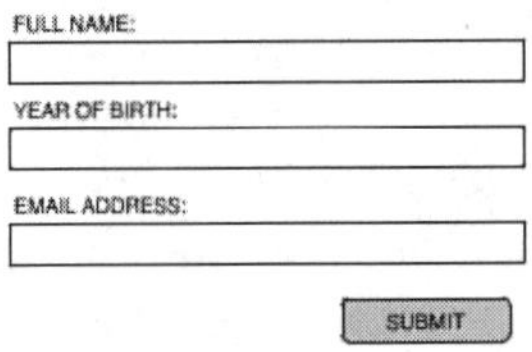

FIGURE 15.6
This movie checks all three fields to make sure that the input is appropriate.

FULL NAME:
YEAR OF BIRTH:
EMAIL ADDRESS:
SUBMIT

3. The main part of the code goes on the frame. It starts with the `stop()` command so that the movie doesn't continue past the first frame. Then, the `restrict` and `maxChars` properties are set for each field.

```
stop();

// restrict name to 64 characters
userName.maxChars = 64;

// restrict year to 4 digits
userYear.restrict = "01234567890";
userYear.maxChars = 4;

// restrict email address characters
userEmail.restrict = "abcdefghijklmnopqrstuvwxyz0123456789@.-_";
userEmail.maxChars = 128;
```

4. Next, we'll force the movie to start with the keyboard focus on the first field.

```
Selection.setFocus(userName);
```

5. To recognize when a user is finished with a field, we'll monitor the focus of the keyboard with a Selection object listener. This alerts us whenever the `onSetFocus` event occurs.

```
Selection.addListener(this);
```

6. Next, we'll set a variable named *`ignoreSetFocus`* to false. We'll use this variable later in the script.

```
ignoreSetFocus = false;
```

7. The function that deals with the `onSetFocus` event gets two parameters passed to it. The first is a reference to the field that was the previously focused text field, and the second is the currently focused text field.

   We'll use the *`oldFocus`* parameter to determine which field was just completed. But first, the variable *`ignoreSetFocus`* is checked. If it is true, it is set to false for next time. The function exits immediately by using the `return` command.

   Then the *`oldFocus`* variable is compared to the three text fields. If it matches one of them, one of three functions is called. The result of this function is placed in *`ret`*.

   The variable *`ret`* is set to false by one of these functions if the value of the field is not appropriate. In that case, *`ignoreSetFocus`* is set to true, and the focus is changed back to the previous field. The purpose of *`ignoreSetFocus`* is to prevent the function from being called a second time when the focus is changed by the code.

```
this.onSetFocus = function(oldFocus, newFocus) {
    // this is a focus reset, so ignore
    if (ignoreSetFocus) {
        ignoreSetFocus = false;
        return(0);
    }
```

```
        // use the appropriate check function
        if (oldFocus == userName) {
            ret = checkUserName();
        } else if (oldFocus == userYear) {
            ret = checkUserYear();
        } else if (oldFocus == userEmail) {
            ret = checkUserEmail();
        }

        if (!ret) {
            // ignore this focus change and go back
            ignoreSetFocus = true;
            Selection.setFocus(oldFocus);
        }
    }
```

8. The *checkUserName* function examines the length of the *userNameText* to make sure that it is at least three characters. If it is not, a message is placed in the text field linked to the *feedback* variable. The function returns a false as well. Otherwise, the *feedback* variable is cleared, and a true is returned.

```
// make sure that the use name is at least three characters
function checkUserName() {
    if (userNameText.length < 3) {
        feedback = "You must enter more than 3 characters for your name."
        return(false);
    }

    // reset feedback field
    feedback = "";
    return(true);
}
```

9. The next function checks the *userYearText* variable. It makes sure that there is a value there, and then it compares the value to the current year. It gets the current year from the user's system clock. It makes sure that the year is at least 100 years ago and no more than this year.

```
// make sure the year is one of the last 100
function checkUserYear() {
    // get this year
    today = new Date();
    thisYear = 1900+today.getYear();

    // check to make sure something was entered
    if (parseInt(userYearText) == Math.NaN) {
        feedback = "You must enter year.";
        return(false);

    // check to make sure that the year is not too early
    } else if (parseInt(userYearText) < thisYear-100) {
```

```
        feedback = "You must enter a more recent year.";
        return(false);

    // check to make sure that the year is not past this year
    } else if (parseInt(userYearText) > thisYear) {
    feedback = "You must enter a year earlier than this year.";
    return(false);
    }

    // reset feedback field
    feedback = "";
    return(true);
}
```

10. This last function checks the *userEmailText* to make sure that it is at least seven characters long, that it contains a "@" and a dot, that at least two characters are after the dot, and that the "@" comes before the dot.

```
// check the email address
function checkUserEmail() {
    if (userEmailText.length < 7) {
        feedback = "Email address too short.";
        return(false);
    } else if (userEmailText.indexOf("@") == -1) {
        feedback = "Missing @.";
        return(false);
    } else if (userEmailText.indexOf(".") == -1) {
        feedback = "Missing the dot.";
        return(false);
    } else if (userEmailText.indexOf("@") > userEmailText.indexOf(".")) {
        feedback = "@ and dot in wrong order.";
        return(false);
    } else if (userEmailText.lastIndexOf(".") > userEmailText.length-3) {
        feedback = "Not a valid domain extension."
        return(false);
    }

    // reset feedback field
    feedback = "";
    return(true);
}
```

11. Now all the fields are checked as the user Tabs through them. However, we'll want to perform a complete check when the user clicks the Submit button. This calls the same three functions, one-by-one, until it hits one that is not true. If all are true, then it returns a true.

```
function checkAll() {
    if (!checkUserName()) {
        return(false);
    } else if (!checkUserYear()) {
```

```
            return(false);
        } else if (!checkUserEmail()) {
            return(false);
        }

        return(true);
    }
```

12. It is up to the button script to call the `checkAll` function. If it gets a true from the `checkAll` function, it can move the movie to the next frame, where there is a "Thank You" message.

    ```
    on (release) {
        if (checkAll()) {
            nextFrame();
        }
    }
    ```

    In a complete movie, you will probably want to submit the information to your server. You will find out how to do that in Hour 18.

You could simplify this movie a great deal by removing the listener. Instead, just check for the correct input when the user clicks the Submit button.

Summary

Check boxes and radio buttons are common interface elements that can be created with ActionScript. Check boxes have an on and off state and are independent of each other. Radio buttons also have on and off states, but they are related to each other so that only one radio button is on at any given time.

Text input fields can be modified to only accept certain characters. You can restrict text input to what is appropriate to that field. You can also restrict the input length of a field.

Using the `tabIndex` property of a field, you can change the order in which the fields receive keyboard focus when the user Tabs between them. You can also be notified when a Tab occurs by using the `onSetFocus` listener event.

Q&A

Q Radio button and check box components come with Flash MX. Would it be easier to use them instead of writing my own code?

A In many cases, yes. But you can customize your own code in ways that the components cannot. Plus, you have more control over how your movie looks and how it performs.

Q How can I have more than one group of radio buttons on the screen at the same time?

A You could simply place all the radio buttons in a group together in their own movie clip. If you do that, you'll need to refer to the movie clip to use the `getValue` function: `group1.myRadioButton.getValue()`.

Q Is there a way to restrict user input to only upper- or lowercase letters?

A No, but you can use `String.toUpperCase` or `String.toLowerCase` to convert the results of their input when they are finished.

Workshop

The quiz questions are designed to test your knowledge of the material covered in this hour. The answers to the questions follow.

Quiz

1. If you have five check boxes on a screen, how many of them can be turned on at one time?
2. If you have five radio buttons on a screen, how many of them can be turned on at one time?
3. If you want the cursor to immediately appear in an input text, what do you need to do?
4. How do you prevent the user from entering any non-numbers into a text field?

Quiz Answers

1. All of them. Check boxes are independent of each other, so any combination of check boxes can be on or off.
2. Only one radio button in a group can be on at a time. Radio buttons represent a situation where the choice is exclusive.
3. First, set a name for the text field. Then use `Selection.setFocus()` to place the cursor there.
4. Set its `restrict` property to "0123456789".

HOUR 16

Pull-Down Menus and Dynamic Buttons

Menu systems are seen in almost every computer application. Both your operating system and Flash put pull-down menus at the top of your screen. They are a great way to offer many options to the user without taking up too much screen real estate.

In this hour, you will:

- See how to make simple Flash pull-down menus
- Use pull-down menus in a simple Flash movie
- Make pull-down menus that require a button click to expand
- Find out how to create buttons dynamically
- Use dynamic buttons in a simple Flash movie

Simple Pull-Down Menus

Beginning ActionScript programmers always want to learn how to make pull-down menus. They are actually simple to make using ActionScript that we have already learned.

The basic idea is to have a title button and then several buttons that appear below the title when the user rolls over it. Figure 16.1 shows the title button by itself and then what happens when the user moves the cursor over the title button.

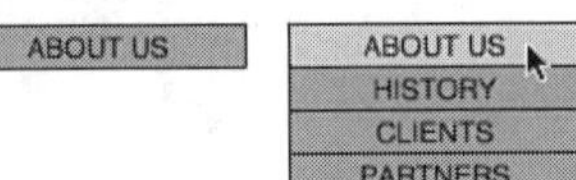

FIGURE 16.1
When a user moves the mouse over a title button, the other three buttons appear.

The entire pull-down menu appears in one movie clip that contains all four buttons. There are two frames to this movie clip. The first frame contains only the title button, which also stretches on its layer across to the second frame. The second frame, in addition, contains the other three buttons.

When the user rolls over the movie clip, which is waiting on the first frame, it goes to the second frame. It stays there until the user rolls off the movie clip.

The script to do this looks something like the scripts from Hour 13, "Rollovers." It uses `hitTest` to determine whether the cursor is over the movie clip. It keeps track of that fact and monitors any changes. When a change occurs, the movie clip goes to the first or second frame depending on whether the cursor is entering or leaving the movie clip.

```
onClipEvent(load) {
    previouslyOver = false;
}

onClipEvent(enterFrame) {
    // is the cursor over the movie clip
    currentlyOver = this.hitTest(_root._xmouse,_root._ymouse,true);

    // if there is a change, go to another frame
    if (!previouslyOver and currentlyOver) {
        previouslyOver = true;
        this.gotoAndStop("on");
    } else if (previouslyOver and !currentlyOver) {
        previouslyOver = false;
        this.gotoAndStop("off");
    }
}
```

This controls the appearance of the pull-down menu but does nothing for its functionality. Instead, you need to put normal button scripts on each button. They could take the user to another frame if clicked, or perhaps to another page. No script should be on the title button, so this need not actually be a button at all. However, I like having it as a button because you can use the over state of a button symbol as an easy way to give the user feedback when she rolls over it.

> If you are using ActionScript to control other elements on the same frames as the pull-down menus, you will probably want to use `swapDepths` to ensure that the pull-down menus appear over any other screen content.

The example movie 16dropmenu.fla contains the example shown in Figure 16.1 along with the script. No script is attached to the buttons. Examine it to make sure that you understand how it works.

Task: Using Pull-Down Menus

Now let's build a simple movie that uses this pull-down menu script. We'll pretend that it is a small Web site made up entirely of a single Flash movie. The pull-down menus are used for navigation.

There are three sets of menus: About Us, Products, and Store. Each of these three menus has between three and five choices.

1. Start with a new movie.
2. Create a simple button. It shouldn't have any text on it, but leave a space for a text overlay to label the button. Make sure that you use a nice over state, but the down state doesn't need to be anything special.
3. Create a new movie clip. Name it **About Us Menu**. Make two layers in the movie clip named **Label** and **Buttons**.
4. On the Label layer, place a copy of your button. On top of it, place the static text **About Us**.
5. Make the Label layer stretch across two frames. However, the Buttons layer should have two separate key frames on each frame. Name the two key frames **off** and **on**.
6. On the second frame of the Buttons layer, add three copies of the button symbol. Place them vertically right under the button in the Label layer. Add text on top of them to read **History**, **Clients**, and **Partners**. The finished movie clip should look like Figure 16.2. You'll also need to place a `stop()` command on the first frame.

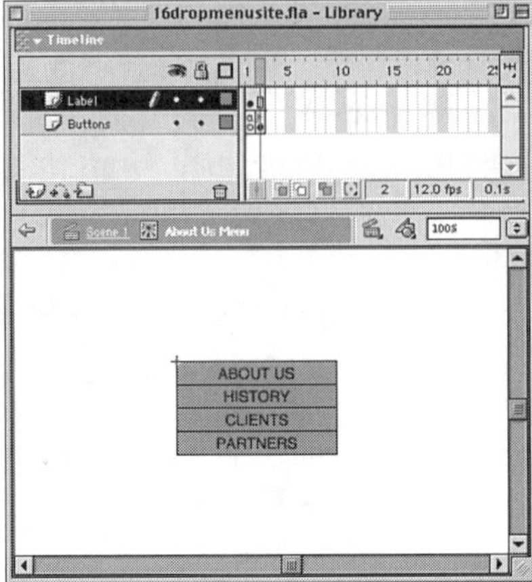

FIGURE 16.2
This movie clip contains a title button across both frames and other buttons only on the second frame.

7. Back at the root level, drag the About Us Menu movie clip from the Library to the Stage. Name the movie clip **aboutUsMenu** and attach this script to it:

```
onClipEvent(load) {
    previouslyOver = FALSE;
}

onClipEvent(enterFrame) {
    // is the cursor over the movie clip
    currentlyOver = this.hitTest(_root._xmouse,_root._ymouse,true);

    // if there is a change, go to another frame
    if (!previouslyOver and currentlyOver) {
        previouslyOver = true;
        this.gotoAndStop("on");
    } else if (previouslyOver and !currentlyOver) {
        previouslyOver = false;
        this.gotoAndStop("off");
    }
}
```

   This gives the movie clip the menu functionality mentioned in the previous section.

8. Test the movie. You should be able to roll over the About Us button and see the other buttons appear. You can then roll over those other buttons without any of them disappearing. When you move completely away from the buttons, the pull-down menu collapses, leaving only the title button.

9. Repeat steps 3 through 8, but name the new movie clip **Products Menu**. The title button should be **Products** and the three buttons under it **Widgets**, **Toys**, and **Power Tools**. At the root level, name the movie clip **productsMenu**. Test the movie again to make sure that this one works.

Alternatively, you could duplicate the About Us Menu movie clip in the library, make changes to the text inside it, and drag the new movie clip to the Stage. Remember to apply the same script to it.

10. Repeat steps 3 through 8, but name the new movie clip **Store Menu**. The title button should be **Store**, and this menu should have five buttons under it: **Order Online**, **Find a Store**, **Order Catalog**, **Track Shipment**, and **Return Item**. At the root level, name the movie clip **productsMenu**. Test the movie again to make sure that this one works.

You can see my finished example at 16pulldownsite.fla. No scripts are attached to the buttons, but that is the easy part. You could make each button go to another frame in the movie, but stretch the layer with all the menus across the entire movie. This way, the menus act as the navigation solution for the movie.

Push Pull-Down Menus

There are many different ways to program a pull-down menu. There are also many alternate ways that a pull-down menu can work. For instance, in the preceding example, all the user has to do is roll over the title button and the menu appears. I like this way because the user can easily figure out where the pull-down menus are by just moving the mouse around.

However, pull-down menus commonly work in another way: The user clicks on the title button for the menu to appear. Then the user must hold down the mouse button, move the cursor down to the selection, and release the mouse button at that point.

The example movie 16pushmenu.fla demonstrates this variation of the pull-down menu. The menu elements are the same: a two-frame movie clip with a title button on both frames and the menu buttons on the second frame only. However, the scripts are completely different.

No scripts are on the movie clip. They are all inside the movie clip on the frame, or attached to the buttons.

The title button has the following script. It calls the function `expandMenu` when the button is clicked. If the mouse is released over the title button, or anywhere outside the buttons, `collapseMenu` is called:

```
on (press) {
    expandMenu();
}

on (release, releaseOutside) {
```

```
    collapseMenu();
}
```

In addition, the script continues with `on (dragOver)` and `on (dragOut)` handlers. These are like `on (rollOver)` and `on (rollOut)` handlers, but the mouse button needs to be clicked while the cursor moves.

```
on (dragOver) {
    rollOverMenu();
}

on (dragOut) {
    rollOutMenu();
}
```

The four functions defined in the title button handlers are all in the frame script. The `expandMenu` function sets a variable named *expanded* to true and then goes to the second frame of the movie clip:

```
function expandMenu() {
    expanded = true;
    gotoAndStop("on");
}
```

The `collapseMenu` function does the opposite:

```
function collapseMenu() {
    expanded = false;
    gotoAndStop("off");
}
```

The `rollOverMenu` and `rollOutMenu` functions check *expanded* and change the frame if the menu is currently expanded. This means that the user can click on the title button, hold down the button, and move out from and back over the menu to see it collapse and expand. This is a minor feature of the menus, but a nice touch.

```
function rollOverMenu() {
    if (expanded) {
        gotoAndStop("on");
    }
}

function rollOutMenu() {
    if (expanded) {
        gotoAndStop("off");
    }
}
```

The scripts in the three buttons of the menu use an `on (release)` handler to catch the user choosing that menu option. It calls `collapseMenu` and then performs its function—which is just a `trace` command in this example.

The `on (dragOver)` and `on (dragOut)` handlers keep the menu expanded when the mouse moves over the buttons and also collapses the menus when the cursor moves completely off all menu buttons:

```
on (release) {
    collapseMenu();
    trace("History Button Pressed");
}

on (dragOut) {
    rollOutMenu();
}
```


One last thing needs to be done for this to work. The buttons need to have a property change. The Track as Button setting seen in the button's Property panel needs to be changed to Track as Menu Item. This allows the button to get mouse events such as `release` without first getting a `press` event.

Give the example movie 16pushmenu.fla a try. It is interesting to see a similar functionality to the previous example but with completely different code.

There are also many more pull-down menu variations and script variations to go with them. It depends on the exact functionality you are looking for and which ActionScript commands you feel the most comfortable with.

Dynamic Buttons

Another way to make pull-down menus and similar things is with dynamic buttons. If you open the example movie 16dynamicbuttons.fla, you can examine the Stage and observe that nothing at all is on it—not a single movie clip or button.

However, when you run the movie, three buttons appear. If you roll over one of the buttons, several more appear below them.

These buttons were all created dynamically by ActionScript. All that is in the Library is a movie clip and a button. This movie clip is used as the template for all the buttons created by ActionScript at runtime.

To use this technique, you first need to make your button template. I started off with a simple button, including an over and down state.

Next, place this button inside a movie clip. The movie clip should contain two elements: the button and a dynamic text field floating above it. The dynamic text field should be linked to the variable *buttonLabel*.

Select this movie clip in the Library and set its Linkage properties to Export for ActionScript and its Linkage name to **buttonMovieClip**.

Now you have a button template that can be used by ActionScript to create new buttons. Creating a new button is just a matter of using `attachMovie` to create a new instance of the movie clip, setting *buttonLabel* in the movie clip to change the text on the button, and positioning the movie clip by setting its _x and _y properties.

Here is a handler that does all this. It makes a copy of the movie clip in the Library, sets its label and location, and then returns a reference to that movie clip:

```
function createButton(buttonLabel, x, y) {
    this.attachMovie("buttonMovieClip","button"+buttonLevels,buttonLevels);
    bmc = this["button"+buttonLevels];
    bmc.buttonLabel = buttonLabel;
    bmc._x = x;
    bmc._y = y;
    buttonLevels++;
    return(bmc);
}
```

You can test this script in the movie 16dynamicbuttontest.fla. The code there creates one button with the label Test Button.

You can create a whole series of buttons by using multiple calls to `createButton`. Or you can store the names of buttons in an array and use a `for` loop to call `createButton` with the name of each button. We'll look at that technique in the next task.

Another problem that needs to be dealt with is how to get different buttons to react differently. The script in each movie clip's button must be the same, so placing a `gotoAndStop` command in there means that all the buttons act the same. However, if you have the button call a function at the root level, that function can figure out which button called it and perform an action specific to that button.

Task: Using Dynamic Buttons

Let's create a complete system of buttons using what we just learned.

1. Start with the movie 16dynamicbuttontest.fla.
2. Notice that inside the movie clip is a script attached to the button that looks like this:

```
on (rollOver) {
    _parent.buttonRolloverAction(thisAction,buttonLabel);
}

on (release) {
    _parent.buttonClickAction(thisAction,buttonLabel);
}
```

This basically calls the functions `buttonRolloverAction` and `buttonClickAction` whenever the button is rolled over or clicked. It is up to these functions to figure out what to do based on which button was clicked.

To help these two functions determine which button was clicked, two variables are passed back to the functions. You know that *`buttonLabel`* is the visible label on the button. The variable *`thisAction`*, which is not linked to a dynamic field, will be set when the button is created.

3. Here is a new `createButton` function. It looks just like the previous one, except that a new parameter `buttonAction` is used to set the variable *`thisAction`*. All that is done with *`thisAction`* is to send it along on calls to the two functions in step 2. An example of a *`thisAction`* value might be something like `"goto"` to signify that the buttons are supposed to perform a `gotoAndStop` command. It can be anything you want as long as the two functions mentioned in step 2 know how to interpret it.

> This example's script is long and has many parts. You may want to open the movie 16dynamicbuttons.fla and refer to its script to see how the parts fit together.

```
function createButton(buttonLabel, x, y, buttonAction) {

this.attachMovie("buttonMovieClip","button"+buttonLevels,buttonLevels);
    bmc = this["button"+buttonLevels];
    bmc.buttonLabel = buttonLabel;
    bmc._x = x;
    bmc._y = y;
    bmc.thisAction = buttonAction;
    buttonLevels++;
    return(bmc);
}
```

4. Here's a function that takes an array of button values and creates an entire set of buttons. It uses the `direction` parameter to determine whether to space the buttons across or down.

For this function to work, it needs to get an array passed in as the parameter `buttonList`. This array will have custom variable objects with the properties *`label`* and *`action`*. You'll see an example of these in the next step.

When each button is created, a new property of each object in the array is added. This property is called `mc` and is a reference to the movie clip created. So the array starts off containing the labels and actions of each button, but after `createButtonList` is done, each object in the array also has an `mc` property.

```
function createButtonList(buttonList, x, y, direction) {
    for (var i=0;i<buttonList.length;i++) {
        ret = createButton(buttonList[i].label,x,y, buttonList[i].action);
        buttons[i].mc = ret;
        if (direction == "down") {
            y += 20;
        } else if (direction == "across") {
            x += 100;
        }
    }
}
```

How did I get the numbers 20 and 100 in the preceding script? These are simply good distances to use according to the size of the buttons in my example movie. Larger buttons may require larger spacing, and smaller buttons may require smaller spacing. I got these values with a little trial and error. I also wanted to make sure that the vertical spacing was just right so that when the buttons are drawn in a vertical strip, they barely touch each other with no gap.

5. Next is an example of a list of buttons. Each element of the array is a variable object that contains *`label`* and *`action`* properties:

   ```
   mainButtonList = new Array();
   mainButtonList.push({label:"About Us", action:"aboutUsButtonList"});
   mainButtonList.push({label:"Products", action:"productsButtonList"});
   mainButtonList.push({label:"Store", action:"storeButtonList"});
   ```

6. After you have a button list, you can create the buttons by calling *`createButtonList`*:

   ```
   buttonLevels = 1;
   createButtonList(mainButtonList,100,100,"across");
   ```

7. If you run the movie now, it will create three buttons. However, those buttons will do nothing if rolled over or clicked. So let's create the `buttonRolloverAction`

function. This performs a slightly different function depending on which of the three buttons is rolled over.

```
function buttonRolloverAction(thisAction,thisLabel) {
    if (thisAction == "aboutUsButtonList") {
        deleteAllButtonLists();
        createButtonList(aboutUsButtonList,100,120,"down");
    } else if (thisAction == "productsButtonList") {
        deleteAllButtonLists();
        createButtonList(productsButtonList,200,120,"down");
    } else if (thisAction == "storeButtonList") {
        deleteAllButtonLists();
        createButtonList(storeButtonList,300,120,"down");
    }
}
```


I'll explain the `deleteAllButtonLists` function in step 9.

8. The `buttonRolloverAction` function calls `createButtonList` with one of three different arrays and locations. The locations are planned so that the list of buttons appears under the button that is being rolled over.

   The three arrays are defined earlier in the code:

```
aboutUsButtonList = new Array();
aboutUsButtonList.push({label:"History", action:"goto"});
aboutUsButtonList.push({label:"Clients", action:"goto"});
aboutUsButtonList.push({label:"Partners", action:"goto"});

productsButtonList = new Array();
productsButtonList.push({label:"Widgets", action:"goto"});
productsButtonList.push({label:"Toys", action:"goto"});
productsButtonList.push({label:"Power Tools", action:"goto"});

storeButtonList = new Array();
storeButtonList.push({label:"Order Online", action:"goto"});
storeButtonList.push({label:"Find a Store", action:"goto"});
storeButtonList.push({label:"Request Catalog", action:"goto"});
storeButtonList.push({label:"Track Shipment", action:"goto"});
storeButtonList.push({label:"Return Item", action:"goto"});
```

9. The `deleteAllButtonLists` function makes all the three button lists defined in step 8 disappear. The result is that all three lists disappear, but the one list linked to the button being rolled over then reappears. So only one of these three lists is visible at a time.

   The first step is to make an array that holds references to the three arrays of button lists.

```
allButtonLists = new Array();
allButtonLists = [aboutUsButtonList,productsButtonList,storeButtonList];
```

Next, we'll need a function that takes a list of buttons and removes all the movie clips, based on the mc property of each button created when the button was created.

```
function deleteButtonList(buttons) {
    for (var i=0;i<buttons.length;i++) {
        buttons[i].mc.removeMovieClip();
    }
}
```

Finally, here is the deleteAllButtons function that loops through the allButtonLists array and calls deleteButtonList with each one.

```
function deleteAllButtonLists() {
    for(var i=0;i<allButtonLists.length;i++) {
        deleteButtonList(allButtonLists[i]);
    }
}
```

10. Notice that when all the buttons for the three lists in step 8 were created, "goto" was assigned at the thisAction property. This will come in to play with the buttonClickAction function. If the thisAction property is "goto", the thisLabel property passed in will be used to determine which frame of the movie should be jumped to. In the case of our example movie, however, there is only a simple trace command used to demonstrate that the button does work.

```
function buttonClickAction(thisAction,thisLabel) {
    deleteAllButtonLists();
    if (thisAction == "goto") {
        trace("Goto: "+thisLabel);
    }
}
```

Although this example contains a long script, it is not very complex. There is only some manipulation of movie clips, arrays, and variable objects, so there is a lot of code, but not much complexity.

Check out the movie 16dyanmicbuttons.fla if you haven't yet done so. Try changing the labels of the buttons and try adding and removing buttons to see the effect. Get to know how the functions work.

Summary

Pull-down menus allow you to include many user options without taking up much space on the screen. You can implement pull-down menus in many different ways. Pull-down menus use a combination of button rollovers and clicks to expand and collapse lists of other buttons.

One way to make pull-down menus is to use a movie clip where the first frame represents the collapsed menu, and the second frame represents the expanded menu.

You can also create buttons on-the-fly by using the `attachMovie` and `removeMovieClip` commands. This enables you to create a whole system of buttons by only modifying ActionScript code.

Q&A

Q What about submenus? Can a button in a pull-down menu then bring about another pull-down menu?

A Yes. You often see this in programs nowadays. You can simply place another pull-down movie clip inside your main pull-down movie clip. The new buttons will probably need to be shifted over to the right to avoid covering the buttons of the main pull-down menu. You can go many levels deep this way.

Q Can you have the pull-down menus slide in?

A Yes. Instead of having just two frames, you can use `gotoAndPlay` and have a series of movements along several frames and a `stop()` command at the end. You might want to use a mask layer to hide the buttons as they slide under the title. Or, you could have them dissolve in slowly.

Q Do pull-down menus always have to pull *down*?

A No. The buttons on a pull-down menu can actually expand up, to the side, or in any direction. But some scripts require that the buttons all touch so that the user can move the cursor from one to the other without ever leaving the movie clip.

Workshop

The quiz questions are designed to test your knowledge of the material covered in this hour. The answers to the questions follow.

Quiz

1. What element *must* be present on the Stage to create dynamic buttons?
2. How do you ensure that a pull-down menu will be on top of all other elements on the screen?
3. How does the `dragOver` event differ from `rollOver`?
4. How many names does a movie clip instance have?

Quiz Answers

1. Trick question—no element needs to be present. Scripts can create buttons and menus from elements in the Library.
2. Use the `swapDepths` command with a large number to ensure that the movie clip is higher than any other element.
3. The mouse button must already be clicked.
4. A movie clip instance has only one name. But the original movie clip in the Library also has a name that can be different from the instance name. In addition, the Library element also has a Linkage name set in the Linkage properties dialog. This is the name used by `attachMovie`.

Part V

Controlling External Events with ActionScript

Hour

HOUR 17

Browser Navigation and Communication

You can do two things with a Flash movie: embed it into a Web page or make a standalone application. If you embed it into a Web page, the movie can communicate with the browser, telling it what to do as well as the other way around.

In this hour, you will:

- Learn how to load new Web pages
- Find out how to communicate with JavaScript
- Open a new window from your movie
- Make JavaScript send messages to the movie
- Save user data as JavaScript cookies
- Create a playback controller in JavaScript
- Use special commands for standalone applications

Loading Browser Pages

Flash movies are often used as a substitute for HTML on Web sites. A Flash movie can be a front door to a Web site or a navigation bar that appears throughout the Web site. Either way, there are times when the movie will have to trigger the browser to load a new Web page.

Simple Loading

You can easily replace the Web page that the Flash movie is on. All it takes is a `getURL` command. Think of it as the equivalent to the <A HREF> tag in HTML. Here is a button that replaces the current page with another one:

```
on (release) {
    getURL("anotherpage.html");
}
```

You can use a relative URL, as in the preceding example, or a complete absolute URL to direct the user to another Web site.

You also can direct the user to another Web site by using hypertext links in text fields. These work just like <A HREF> tags—they actually are <A HREF> tags. They don't require any ActionScript code at all.

Targeted Loading

You can use a second form of the `getURL` tag to target a frame or window in the browser. If you have never used frames or windows in your HTML code, you probably don't need them. However, if you have used them, you know that frames and windows all have names. You can refer to a named frame or window by using a second parameter in the `getURL` command.

So if you are using frames and have the movie in a frame named Navigation and the content in a frame named Main, you could tell the frame Main to load the page summary.html with a button like this:

```
on (release) {
    getURL("summary.html","Main");
}
```

You could do the same to target a window if it was named Main.

There are also four special targets that tell the browser to do special things. Here is a list:

- `_blank`—Creates a new window and loads the page there. The default window settings for a new window in the browser are be used.
- `_parent`—Loads the page in the parent frame of the current frame.

- `_top`—Loads the page in the current window, regardless of whether the movie is in a frame in the current window. It replaces the entire window contents—all frames.
- `_self`—Essentially the default behavior, with the contents of the current frame or window being replaced.

What if you want to create a new browser window that is not the default size and settings? You'll need to use JavaScript to do that. I'll explain later this hour.

Task: Navigation Bar

Now you know all the ActionScript you need to make a Flash movie navigation bar. However, you'll also need to be familiar with HTML, at least to the point of knowing how to make frames.

Our navigation bar runs in a frame to the left side of the browser window. The right side of the browser window is another frame that contains the content.

The Flash movie consists of various buttons that use `getURL` to load a new HTML page in the other frame.

1. First, we'll need to create an HTML page with frames. Here is the code of the main HTML page, which defines the two frames:

```
<HTML><HEAD>
<TITLE>Flash Navigation Example</TITLE>
</HEAD>
<BODY BGCOLOR="#FFFFFF">

<FRAMESET cols="120,*">
<FRAME name="navigation" src="navbar.html" scrolling="no">
<FRAME name="content" src="content1.html" scrolling="auto">
</FRAMESET>

</BODY>
</HTML>
```

2. Now, we need to create the HTML pages for the two frames. We won't worry about the left frame now because that will just be taken from the HTML page created when we publish the Flash movie. The right frame, however, should have several variations.

   Let's create three simple HTML pages named content1.html, content2.html, and content3.html. They will all look basically like this, except that the text inside will reflect which page it is:

```
<HTML><HEAD>
<TITLE>Content 1</TITLE>
```

```
</HEAD>
<BODY BGCOLOR="#FFFFFF">
Content 1
</BODY>
</HTML>
```

3. Next comes the Flash movie. it should be 100 pixels wide by 400 high to fit in the frame allotted for it.

   This will be a simple movie with three buttons in it. The buttons can look like anything you want. Here is the script for the first button:

   ```
   on (release) {
       getURL("content1.html","content");
   }
   ```

   The other two buttons will be the same, except that they will go to pages 2 and 3.
4. Save the Flash movie as navbar.fla.
5. Publish the Flash movie, making sure that the Publish settings are set so that an HTML file, navbar.html, is also exported.
6. Combine all the pages and the Flash movie into one folder. You should have the following: navigation.html, content1.html, content2.html, content3.html, navbar.html, and navbar.swf.
7. Open the file navigation.html with your standard Web browser. You should see something like Figure 17.1.

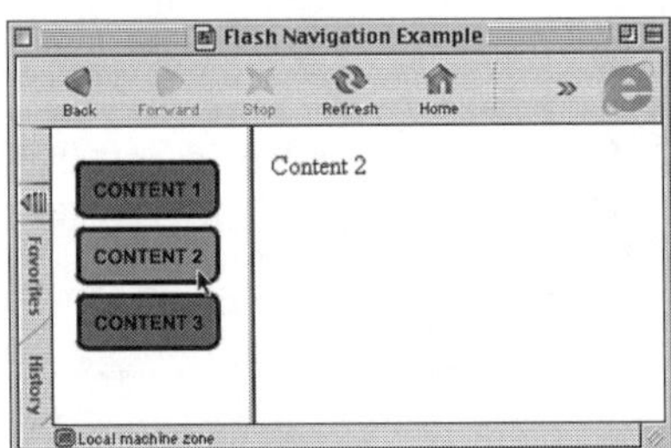

FIGURE 17.1
This Web page has two frames. The one on the left contains a Flash movie that controls the frame on the right.

You can find all these files in the folder 17navigation. Drag and drop the Navigation.html file on to your browser. The other .html files are support for that one. This example is not too exciting. As a matter of fact, you can do it pretty easily with plain HTML and no Flash movie at all. However, the brilliance of Flash shines through if you decide to animate the buttons; then it is less of a typical navigation bar.

ActionScript and JavaScript

If you are already familiar with JavaScript, you may be excited by the fact that ActionScript and JavaScript can communicate. However, this technology has one flaw: It doesn't work on all browsers.

The JavaScript communication is made possible by one of two technologies. The first is LiveConnect, a technology built into Netscape Navigator versions before version 6. The second technology is ActiveX, the interface between Internet Explorer and Flash.

However, Netscape Navigator 6.0 does not include LiveConnect. The technology has been abandoned. In addition, Internet Explorer on the Mac does not use ActiveX.

You are left with two bug exceptions to ActionScript/JavaScript communication: Internet Explorer on Mac and all Netscape 6 browsers. That's enough to make most Web development companies stay away from ActionScript to JavaScript communication altogether.

However, if you are operating in a situation where all your users are on Internet Explorer for Windows, you could potentially use this technology. Either way, it is probably worth taking the time to learn.

Sending Messages to JavaScript

Sending a message from ActionScript to JavaScript involves one line of ActionScript, but many changes to your HTML page.

If you choose the Flash with FSCommand option in the Publish settings, you will get an HTML page already modified to accept these messages. You just need to find the portion marked You Code Here and insert your own JavaScript code.

To better understand how this works, let's look at a slightly cleaned-up version of the HTML that Flash exports.

First, look at the OBJECT/EMBED tag. This has several new parts to it to support communication. There is an ID parameter in the OBJECT tag and a matching NAME parameter in the EMBED tag. These both name the Flash movie within the document so that JavaScript can address it. There is also an swLiveConnect parameter in the EMBED tag for older versions of Netscape that use LiveConnect to facilitate this kind of communication.

```
<OBJECT classid="clsid:D27CDB6E-AE6D-11cf-96B8-444553540000"
codebase="http://download.macromedia.com/pub/shockwave/cabs/
[ic:cc]flash/swflash.cab#version=5,0,0,0"
 ID=flashmovie WIDTH=120 HEIGHT=120>
<PARAM NAME=movie VALUE="17astojs.swf"> <PARAM NAME=quality VALUE=high>
➥<PARAM NAME=bgcolor VALUE=#FFFFFF>     <EMBED src="17astojs.swf"
```

```
➥quality=high bgcolor=#FFFFFF  WIDTH=120 HEIGHT=120
swLiveConnect=true NAME=flashmovie TYPE="application/x-shockwave-flash"
PLUGINSPAGE="http://www.macromedia.com/shockwave/download/
➥index.cgi?P1_Prod_Version=ShockwaveFlash"></EMBED>
</OBJECT>
```

Before the OBJECT/EMBED tag is a script. The first part is a JavaScript function named the same as your movie ID but with a `_DoFSCommand` appended to it. So if the movie is given the ID flashmovie, then it will be called `flashmovie_DoFSCommand`.

It is somewhat likely that you will want to send a message back to the Flash movie as a result of the function. Unfortunately, Internet Explorer and Netscape see the movie differently. Internet Explorer sees it as just `flashmovie`, assuming that is its ID, whereas Netscape sees it as `document.flashmovie`. A reference to the appropriate one is put in the variable *`flashMovieObj`*.

Finally, the function concludes by showing the contents of the two parameters passed to JavaScript.

```
<SCRIPT LANGUAGE=JavaScript>
function flashmovie_DoFSCommand(command, args) {
    if (navigator.appName.indexOf("Microsoft") != -1) {
        var flashmovieObj = flashmovie;
    } else {
        var flashmovieObj = document.flashmovie;
    }

    alert(command);
    alert(args);
}
```

But wait, there's more. It turns out that Internet Explorer doesn't facilitate communication between Flash and JavaScript at all. Instead, Flash can only communicate with VBScript, Microsoft's little-used JavaScript-like language. However, VBScript can communicate with JavaScript. So this next piece of code creates a VBScript function that just passes along the information to JavaScript.

```
if (navigator.appName && navigator.appName.indexOf("Microsoft") != -1 &&
    navigator.userAgent.indexOf("Windows") != -1 &&
    navigator.userAgent.indexOf("Windows 3.1") == -1) {
        document.write('<SCRIPT LANGUAGE=VBScript\> \n');
        document.write('on error resume next \n');
        document.write('Sub flashmovie_FSCommand(ByVal command, ByVal args)\n');
        document.write('call flashmovie_DoFSCommand(command, args)\n');
        document.write('end sub\n');
        document.write('</SCRIPT\> \n');
}
</SCRIPT>
```

So what about the ActionScript side of things? If the HTML is that complex, surely the ActionScript should be complex as well.

All you actually need is one line of code. The `fscommand` function passes two pieces of information along to the above JavaScript code. Here is an example:

```
fscommand ("alert", "This is alert 1.");
```

That's it. You can test this code with the HTML page 17astojs.html. The Flash movie example used is 17astojs.fla. Remember that this will not work in Internet Explorer for Mac, Netscape 6, or most older or lesser-known browsers.

You can do a lot by passing strings along to JavaScript. As a matter of fact, although the example is a little basic, it demonstrates one of the primary uses for ActionScript to JavaScript communication: the alert box. Flash can't generate a simple alert box on its own, but with help from JavaScript, you can pop up little messages to the user.

Getting Messages from JavaScript

Sending messages from the HTML page to your Flash movie is easier than the other way around. First, you need to make sure that you set an ID parameter for the OBJECT tag and a NAME parameter for the EMBED tag. Make them the same value. You will also need to set `swLiveConnect` to true in the EMBED tag.

Now you have a host of commands that you can send to the Flash movie. For instance, you can use `GotoFrame` to tell the movie to go to a specific frame number. Here is a button that tells the movie flashmovie to go to frame 2.

```
<FORM NAME="flashControlForm">
<INPUT NAME="gotoFrame1" TYPE=Button VALUE="Frame 1"
onClick="window.document.flashmovie.GotoFrame(1);">
</FORM>
```

If this code is supposed to make the movie go to frame 2, why is there a 1 in the `GotoFrame` command? This is another case where the numbering is zero-based. So frame 1 is 0, frame 2 is 1, and so on.

There are 24 more commands that you can use on a Flash movie. However, I don't want to spend too much time on this because, as I mentioned at the start of this section, JavaScript communication doesn't work on all browsers, so it is not considered by most developers to be of any use.

You can use `GetVariable` and `SetVariable` to look at and control variables on the main timeline. The `Zoom` command allows you to control the scale of the movie. The `isPlaying` and `percentLoaded` functions allow you to detect what the movie is doing at the time. The simple `Play` command moves the movie forward from its stopped state.

There is also a set of command that start with a capital T. These are called *targeted commands* because they target a movie clip. The first parameter in these commands is the target. This parameter uses an out-of-date format from Flash 3 and 4 to name movie clips. In this format, `"/"` is equivalent to `_root` and `/myMovieClip` is equivalent to `_root.myMovieClip`.

An example of a targeted command is `TgotoFrame`, which tells a movie clip to go to a frame number. It would look like this:

```
window.document.flashmovie.TGotoFrame("/myMovieClip", 1);
```

You can also use `TgotoLabel` to use a frame name rather than a number. The `TGetProperty` and `TSetProperty` commands seem simple enough, except that they can't refer to a property by its real name. Instead, they have to use a number to refer to each property. So `_x` is 0, `_y` is 1, `_visible` is 7, and so on.

To find out more about JavaScript communication, you'll have to go to the Macromedia Web site. The documentation has only a small amount of information and does not list the commands or the property numbers. Perhaps this is because of the doesn't-work-on-every-browser issue.

To get to the special section about this topic, go to `http://www.macromedia.com/support/flash/` and search on Flash Methods. You'll eventually find the document that contains a lot of information about this subject.

Task: Open a New Window

Perhaps the most common task that Flash developers demand from browser communication is the ability to open a new browser window. This is something that can be done with both the `getURL` command and JavaScript communication.

However, JavaScript has one distinct advantage: You can specify the size and properties of the new window. Here's how to do that:

1. Create a new Flash movie.
2. Place a button in the movie.
3. Attach this script to the button:
   ```
   on (release) {
     fscommand ("newwindow", "content.html");
   }
   ```
4. In the Publish settings, choose to export an HTML page as well as a Flash movie. In the HTML page, choose Flash with FSCommand as your template.

5. Publish the movie.
6. Open the HTML page in a text editor. Look for the portion of the JavaScript function where you can place your own commands. Insert this in that spot:

```
if (command == "newwindow") {
    window.open(args,"","width=320,height=240,location=no,toolbar=no,
➥menubar=no");
}
```

7. Create a simple HTML page named content.html.
8. If you open the HTML page in a browser capable of supporting JavaScript communication, you should be able to click on the button and get the window to appear. It should be 320×240 without a toolbar.
9. But what about browsers that don't support JavaScript communication? Well, we can use a `getURL` command to open a standard new window in them. However, the trick is knowing which command to execute in which situation.

   Back in the HTML page, add the following JavaScript function to the end of the JavaScript inserted by Flash's Publish command:

```
function initComm() {
    window.document.newWindowMovie.SetVariable("jsCommOK","OK");
}
```

   This function tries to set the variable *`jsCommOK`* in the Flash movie to the string `"OK"`. If the browser is capable of JavaScript communication, the command should be successful. If not, *`jsCommOK`* will remain undefined.

10. To run the `initComm` function at the right time, you need to edit the BODY tag of the HTML page:

```
<BODY bgcolor="#FFFFFF" onLoad="initComm();">
```

   This runs the function only after the HTML page is finished loading. If you run it any earlier, the Flash movie may not be there to get the message.

11. Now, go back to your button script. Change it to call either `fscommand` or `getURL` depending on the value of *`jsCommOK`*.

```
on (release) {
    if (jsCommOK == "OK") {
        fscommand ("newwindow", "content.html");
    } else {
        getURL ("content.html", "_blank");
    }
}
```

The folder 17newwindow contains all the files used to make up this example. In addition, the Flash movie has a dynamic text field linked to the variable *`jsCommOK`*. You should see this variable change values as the `initComm` function sends its message.

17

Task: JavaScript-Controlled Slideshow

Here's a task that can be performed easily with JavaScript, provided that the user has the right browser. In this task, we'll build a movie that doesn't have much of any ActionScript in it at all. The JavaScript on the HTML page, however, controls it completely.

1. Create a new Flash movie with three or more different frames in it. It doesn't matter what is on each frame, as long as you can easily tell the difference between frames.
2. Place a `stop()` command on the first frame so that the movie doesn't animate.
3. Publish the movie with a standard HTML page. There is no need to use the Flash with FSCommand template.
4. Using a text editor, open the HTML page.
5. Add an ID parameter to the OBJECT tag and a NAME parameter to the EMBED tag. Use "slideshow" as the value for both.
6. Also add an `swLiveConnect=true` to the EMBED tag.
7. Add two buttons to the HTML page. Use this code:

```
<FORM NAME="flashControlForm">
<INPUT NAME="next" TYPE=Button VALUE="Next" onClick="nextFrame();">
<INPUT NAME="prev" TYPE=Button VALUE="Previous" onClick="prevFrame();">
</FORM>
```

8. These two buttons call one of two functions. They both use `TcurrentFrame("/")` to get the number of the current frame and then `GotoFrame` to go to either the next or previous frame in the movie.

```
<SCRIPT LANGUAGE="JavaScript">
function nextFrame() {
  var frameNum = window.document.slideshow.TCurrentFrame("/");
  window.document.slideshow.GotoFrame(frameNum+1);
}
function prevFrame() {
  var frameNum = window.document.slideshow.TCurrentFrame("/");
  window.document.slideshow.GotoFrame(frameNum-1);
}
</SCRIPT>
```

Test your movie or use the files in the 17slideshow folder. The handy thing about this technique is that you can easily substitute any Flash movie and it instantly makes a slideshow presentation out of it. You'll either need to put a `stop()` at the start of the movie or add a `play=false` parameter in the tags so that the movie does not advance past the first frame when it starts.

Special Projector Commands

The `fscommand` command can also be used in projectors, which are standalone Flash movies. However, only a few special commands can be used.

The simplest command is `quit`. This takes no second parameter but simply exits the projector quickly. Here is a script for a projector quit button:

```
on (release) {
    fscommand("quit");
}
```

Two commands deal with scaling. The `fullscreen` command takes a `true` or `false` as a value and forces the projector to scale up to the full size of the user's screen. The `allowscale` command, if set to `true`, scales the movie to fit whatever size the projector window is currently.

The `showmenu` command turns on or off the menus that the user sees with the projector.

Finally, the `exec` command takes a given path and attempts to execute an application at that path. This could be another projector or something like Wordpad.

Summary

Using the `getURL` command, you can load a new Web page to replace the current one, or load a new Web page in another frame or window. You can use the special parameter `_blank` to load a new page in a new window.

ActionScript has the capability to communicate with JavaScript, provided that the browser supports this communication. You can use `fscommand` to send messages to the HTML page where a special JavaScript function intercepts it. From there, you have to write JavaScript code that uses the information sent.

You can also have JavaScript send information back to Flash. A whole set of commands can be sent to Flash, including ones that change frames and set variables.

The `fscommand` can also perform special tasks in projectors, such as quitting the projector, enlarging the projector to full screen size, or running another application.

Q&A

Q Can I use `getURL` to open HTML pages on the user's local hard drive?

A Yes, just like you could by using an <A HREF> tag in HTML. The `getURL` command just passes the information along to the browser. The browser does all the work. So anything a browser can do with a URL, the `getURL` command can do.

Q Can two Flash movies on one HTML page communicate with each other?

A If the browser supports JavaScript communication, you can write code to use JavaScript to pass messages between movies.

Q Is there any way at all to allow browsers that don't have JavaScript communication capability to open windows with custom options?

A Yes. You could use Flash to open a window with `getURL` and then have some JavaScript code on that page to have it resize itself and change its options.

Workshop

The quiz questions are designed to test your knowledge of the material covered in this hour. The answers to the questions follow.

Quiz

1. If you use the JavaScript command `GotoFrame(2)`, which frame of the Flash movie will be shown?
2. If you use `getURL` with the target `_top` in a movie that is in a frame, what will happen?
3. Will a user with Internet Explorer be able to use a Flash movie that communicates with JavaScript?
4. What three changes do you need to make to the OBJECT and EMBED tags to enable JavaScript communication?

Quiz Answers

1. Frame 3. Remember that `GotoFrame` uses zero-based numbering.
2. The entire contents of the window will be replaced, not just the current frame.
3. Only if the user is using a recent version of Internet Explorer in Windows. Mac versions do not support JavaScript communication.
4. You need to set an ID in the OBJECT tag and a NAME in the EMBED tag. You also need to set `swLiveConnect=true` in the EMBED tag.

HOUR 18

Sending Information to the Server

Until now, all the movies we have created have been standalone client-side productions. The experience takes place on the user's machine and does not result in anything beyond that. However, Flash can send information back to the server just like an HTML page form. So you can use Flash as a replacement for a form, or something more complex that gathers information and sends it back to your server.

In this hour, you will:

- Learn about the LoadVars object
- Create a simple server-side application
- Use Flash to send information to the server

The LoadVars Object

You are lucky to be learning Flash-server communication with Flash MX. In earlier versions of Flash, you had to create awkward movie clips to be able to send information to the server. But with Flash MX, you can use the LoadVars object.

The LoadVars object is a series of commands and a special type of variable object that allows you to send information to the server just like a post form in HTML. You can create a LoadVars object in the same way that you create a variable object, like the ones in Hour 12, "Objects and Arrays."

Loading Data

Here is an example. Instead of using `new Object()`, you simply use new `LoadVars()`. This creates an empty LoadVars object.

```
myVars = new LoadVars();
```

You can do one of two things with a LoadVars object. You can use it to get data from the server or send data to the server. Getting data from the server is done with the `load` command. All you need to do is specify the URL where the data needs to be loaded:

```
myVars.load("myURL.txt");
```

This works similarly to the `LoadVariables` command in Hour 10, "Creating and Controlling Text." However, the `LoadVariables` command just created or replaced variable values at the same level as the command. The LoadVars object populates itself with those variables as properties of the object.

For instance, suppose that you have a data file that looks like this:

```
name=George&ID=47
```

When you use load to get these variables into the *`myVars`* object, you end up with properties *`myVars.name`* and *`myVars.ID`* with the values "George" and "47".

Like the `LoadVariables` command, the `load` command in the `LoadVars` object only works if the data file is at the same subdomain as the Flash movie. The only exception is in projectors or the Flash test window. Otherwise, you just can't get data from a different server.

Sending Data

You can also send data with your `LoadVars` object. First, you need to put some data in the object. Then, you can use the `send` command to send it along to the server in the same format as an HTML form.

```
myVars = new LoadVars();
myVars.name = "George";
myVars.ID = 47;
myVars.send("serverprogram.cgi", "_self");
```

This code creates the variable *myVars* as a `LoadVars` object. It then adds two properties to it. Finally, it sends this information to the server, specifically to the CGI program named echo.cgi.

The `send` command works much like an HTML form. As a matter of fact, if you include the optional `_self` parameter, it will even replace the entire Web page with the results from the server, just like posting with an HTML form will replace the entire page with the results of the operation.

You can vary this a little by specifying another target frame or window with a second parameter to send. Then the results of the post are returned in another window, and the page with the Flash movie on it remains. You can use `_blank`, `_top`, or `_parent` as well as a specific window or frame name. If you omit the second parameter altogether, no response is sent.

18

However, there is another alternative. You can use the `sendAndLoad` command. This is a combination of both the `send` and the `load` commands. It sends the variables from one `LoadVars` object and loads the resulting variables into another. Here is an example:

```
mySendVars = new LoadVars();
myLoadVars = new LoadVars();
mySendVars.name = "George";
mySendVars.ID = 47;
mySendVars.sendAndLoad("serverprogram.cgi", myLoadVars);
```

When using the `sendAndLoad` command, no HTML page is replaced at all. The results of the server program need to be in the special format that `load` and `LoadVariables` use so that they can be read in and used to populate the second LoadVars object.

Load Status

Keep in mind that the `load`, `send`, and `sendAndLoad` commands do not happen immediately. The process starts when you issue the command, but then continues on independently of the rest of your code. So the next ActionScript line after a `load` command executes immediately, but the `load` command itself is just starting. The server is contacted, and the information is sent. This takes some time. How long depends on the responsiveness of the server and the speed of the network. It could be a fraction of a second or several whole seconds.

This means that you will not want to try to use the results of the `load` or `sendAndLoad` command right away. Instead, you'll need to detect when the process is complete. There are several ways to do this. The simplest way is to examine the loaded property of the LoadVars object. This will be true only when the process is complete.

You can have a looping movie clip that checks the loaded property, or perhaps just use it to deter the user from clicking a Next button until it is true.

If you want to check the status of the process, you can use the `getBytesLoaded` and `getBytesTotal` properties of the `LoadVars` object to see how far the process has gotten. However, this would only make sense if there is a large amount of data or a very slow network.

You can also define a function to be called when the process is complete. You do this in a similar way to creating a listener for other objects. Here is an example:

```
myLoadVars.onLoad = function(success) {
 if (success) {
  gotoAndStop("load done");
 } else {
  gotoAndStop("load problem");
 }
}
```

As you can see by this example, the `success` parameter gets either a true or false depending on whether the operation was a success.

But what exactly happens on the server side of things? The preceding examples include serverprogram.cgi as the name of the place where the LoadVars object gets sent, but what, exactly, happens on the server?

Server-Side Applications

It is not the purpose of this section, hour, or book to teach server-side programming. In fact, dozens, and perhaps hundreds, of books teach only that one subject. But I will try to give you the basics to further demonstrate the LoadVars object.

Server-side programs, also called CGI (Common Gateway Interface) programs, can be written in a variety of languages. The simplest is Perl, which is what we will use here. You can also write them using C, C++, PHP, JSP, ASP, and just about anything else that your server supports.

Perl is a simple language that is installed on most Web servers. It is the choice of beginning CGI programmers and of those who don't have full access to their server, such as people who use a separate Internet service provider for their Web hosting.

Here is a basic Perl program; it outputs the words "Hello World!" when called:

```
#!/usr/local/bin/perl
print "Content-type: text/html\n\n";
print "Hello World!";
```

The first line of the program simply defines it as a Perl program. It tells the Web server to use the program /usr/local/bin/perl to interpret and run the code. This is the typical location of Perl on a typical Web server.

The other lines of the program use the simple print command to output text. The first line defines the type of document, in this case a text/html document. Web browsers use this first line to figure out how to interpret the rest of the document. The last line just outputs the "Hello World!".

If you put this code into a file named helloworld.pl and upload this file to your Web server, you should be able to go to that location with a Web browser and get the words "Hello World!" back. For instance, if the file was uploaded to `http://www.mydomainname.com/test/helloworld.pl`, you can go to that URL with Internet Explorer or Netscape to run the program.

Try it. If this is your first time using CGI programs, you will probably not see "Hello World!" but instead something like this:

```
Forbidden
You don't have permission to access /test/helloworld.pl on this server.
```

Don't have permission! But it is *your* Web site!

Well, you have to set the permissions on this CGI program to allow it to run as a program. Otherwise, the security measures on your server forbid it from executing.

So how do you set the permissions of a file on your server? Well, this is where I stop. I can't tell you how to set the permissions on your server because there are many different types of servers, many different setups used by ISPs, and many different programs with different interfaces that allow you to set permissions. However, I will give you a list of things you can do to get your first CGI program up and running:

- Figure out what type of Web site you have. Is it a company Web site? Then you probably have a company system administrator who can help you.
- If you use a quality hosting provider, there are probably how-tos and help files that you can refer to on its Web site.

- Quality Web hosting companies will also have customer support that may be able to help you.
- If you are using a free or inexpensive Web hosting solution, you probably cannot run CGI programs at all.
- Seek out a friend who has created CGI programs before. Tell her that you need to get your first Perl program up and running. Someone who knows Web servers can figure out your hosting situation and show you how to set up a Perl program in no time.
- Partner with someone at your company who can write CGI programs. At most companies, Flash and CGI programming are considered different skills and are done by different people. So if you are asked by your company to set up a program that requires CGI programming, but you have never done it before, you may want to inquire about having someone else help you with the task.

For the rest of this hour, I'll assume that you were able to get CGI programs running on your server. Remember that you will have to upload the Flash movie to the same server where the CGI program is located. In most cases, you will want the movie and the CGI program to be in the same folder.

Here is an example of a simple CGI program that takes the input from an HTML form or a Flash movie and echoes them back to the user:

```
#!/usr/local/bin/perl
print "Content-type: text/html\n\n";
print "<HTML><BODY>\n";

read (STDIN,$QUERY,$ENV{CONTENT_LENGTH});

@data = split('&',$QUERY);
foreach $item (@data) {
 ($prop,$val) = split('=',$item,2);
 $val =~ s/\+/ /g;
 $val =~ s/%([\da-f]{1,2})/pack(C,hex($1))/eig;
 print "$prop: $val<BR>\n";
}

print "</BODY></HTML>\n";
```

Because this is a book about ActionScript, not Perl, I will quickly summarize what this code does. It takes the contents of an HTML form or a Flash `LoadVars` object and looks at each property/value pair, sending it back as a simple text page. It converts the text to normal text rather than the escape-character equivalent, which uses + rather than spaces and things such as `%20`. Both HTML forms and Flash convert the data to this format before submitting.

Here is the HTML that could be used to call this CGI program:

```
<HTML><HEAD>
<TITLE>Echo Test</TITLE>
</HEAD>
<BODY BGCOLOR="#FFFFFF">

<FORM ID="echoTest" NAME="echoTest" ACTION="echo.cgi" METHOD="POST">
NAME: <INPUT NAME="name" TYPE="text" SIZE="30"><BR>
ID: <INPUT NAME="ID" TYPE="text" SIZE="10"><BR>
<INPUT TYPE="submit" VALUE="ID">
</FORM>

</BODY>
</HTML>
```

You can find the CGI script on the CD-ROM in the folder 18send. It is called echo.cgi. The sample HTML is called echotest.html.

Upload these both to your server, set the permissions on echo.cgi to what your server requires for CGI programs, and open the HTML page in your browser. You should be able to type a name and ID in the HTML form, click Submit, and get back a list of the values you entered.

18

Now let's do the same thing in Flash. The movie 18echotest.fla contains two simple input text fields linked to the variables *`userName`* and *`userID`*. There is also a Submit button. The only script is on the Submit button. It creates a `LoadVars` object, sets two properties, and sends it.

```
on (release) {
 mySendVars = new LoadVars();
 mySendVars.name = userName;
 mySendVars.ID = userID;
 mySendVars.send("echo.cgi","_self");
}
```

The second parameter, `_self`, means that the entire HTML page with the Flash movie will be replaced by the result of the CGI program. This means that it will work just like a normal HTML form.

You can test this movie by uploading both the .swf and the .html files to your server, in the same location as the working CGI program. The result should be the same as if you used the HTML form.

Task: Recording Survey Results

Now let's make a Flash movie that is somewhat useful. We'll build a slightly more complex form that asks several questions. Then, we'll send all the data to the server, where a CGI program records it. It does this by appending the data to the end of a text file.

While building this movie, refer to Figure 18.1 to get an idea of what the final movie should look like.

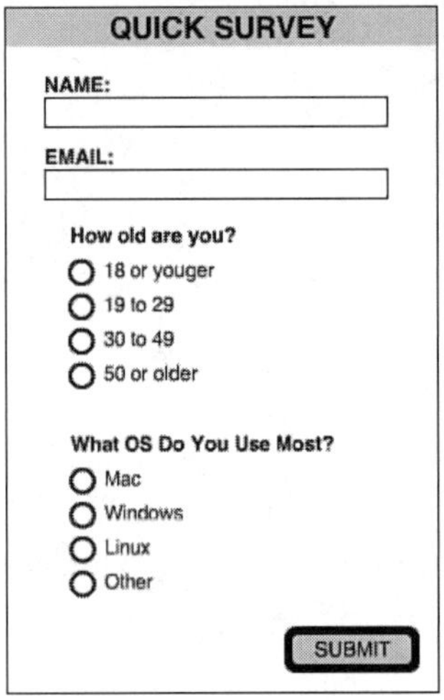

FIGURE 18.1
A simple survey form done with Flash elements.

1. Start a new Flash movie.
2. In this movie, place two input text fields, linked to the variables `userName` and `userEmail`.
3. Open the movie 15radiobuttons.fla that we used in Hour 15, "User Input Elements." Copy a single radio button from that movie's stage onto the new movie's stage. This should bring with it the movie clip and two buttons as Library elements.
4. Copy and paste to make a group of four radio buttons. Name each movie clip **ageGroup1**, **ageGroup2**, **ageGroup3**, and **ageGroup4**. Place text next to each one signifying a different age group. Select them all and choose Insert, Convert to Symbol. Make them all one movie clip named **ageGroup**.
5. Repeat step 5 to make another group of four radio buttons. Name them **OSmac**, **OSwindows**, **OSlinux**, and **OSother**. Place appropriate text next to them and group them together in a movie clip named **OS**. At this point, you may want to check the movie 18survey.fla in the folder 18survey to see how your movie matches my sample.

6. Add a Submit button to the bottom of the stage. Attach this script to it:

```
on (release) {
 sendVars = new LoadVars();
 sendVars.name = userName;
 sendVars.email = userEmail;
 sendVars.age = ageGroup.ageGroup1.getValue();
 sendVars.OS = OS.OSmac.getValue();
 trace(sendVars.toString());
}
```

   The `getValue` function is the one we made in Hour 15 that gets the name of the selected radio button. We can use any one of the button movie clips in the group to get the answer, but I used the first in each group.

7. Run the movie. Instead of submitting the data to the server, the movie uses the `trace` command, along with a `toString()` function to output the potential submission to the Output window. This allows you to test your movie before going forward and doing the CGI script. You should see a result like this:

```
OS=OSmac&age=ageGroup2&email=gary@xxx.com&name=Gary
```

8. The next step is to change the `trace` command to a `send` command. We'll use one that replaces the entire page.

```
sendVars.send("survey.cgi","_self");
```

9. The CGI program looks similar to the echo.cgi example from earlier this hour, but it writes the data to a text file instead. It then returns the text "Thank You!" as the Web page.

```
#!/usr/local/bin/perl
print "Content-type: text/html\n\n";

read (STDIN,$QUERY,$ENV{CONTENT_LENGTH});
open(FILE, ">>survey.txt");
print FILE "$QUERY\n";
close(FILE);
print "Thank you!";
```

Even if you have been able to get the echo.cgi program working on your server, you may not be able to get this one to work. This is because the program needs to have permission to create and append to a new file. You may need to adjust the permissions of the program or even the folder it sits in. You may have to create the survey.txt file yourself, as an empty text file, and then set its permissions. Some hosting providers may not allow CGI programs to create or write to files.

10. Test this movie and then examine the new contents of survey.txt on your server. You will see the data for your test there. A new line is added every time someone takes the survey. You can compute the results of the survey using a spreadsheet program, or even another CGI script specially written to compute the results with the existing data.

Summary

The `LoadVars` object allows you to send and receive information from a server. The `send` command works just like a <FORM> in HTML.

For the server to receive information, there must be a CGI script on the server written in Perl or some other language. Writing a CGI program takes a separate set of skills and is not usually done by the Flash programmer.

By combining a Flash movie with a LoadVars object and a CGI script on the server, you can record a user's input. This can be used for surveys' similar tasks.

Q&A

Q When should I use `LoadVariables` and when should I use the `LoadVars` object?

A Use `LoadVariables` in simple situations where you just need to get some quick external data into your movie. The `LoadVars` object should be used in more complex movies where you need to call out to the server many times and send data as well as receive. `LoadVars` is also more useful if you need to track the incoming data.

Q I've made a CGI program to send data to a movie, but that movie doesn't always get the data. Why?

A Make sure that you are using the right MIME type when returning the data. This corresponds to the Content-type: at the top of the Perl scripts in this hour. If you are generating a text or HTML page, then text/html is the right MIME type. However, if you are sending data directly to a Flash movie, use application/x-www-urlform-encoded.

Q In a program like the survey, how do I prevent the user from clicking the Submit button more than once?

A There are many ways. You could let the user click the button more than once, but just not send the data if it has already been done—set a variable to `true` the first time. Or, you could send the user immediately to another frame that says "please wait" when the user clicks the button.

Q How can I quickly determine whether my Web server supports Perl?

A The only way is to test it. Servers vary greatly in the software that runs them and the way they are configured. There is no surefire way to determine whether the server will run CGI programs unless you are an expert.

Q Do CGI programs see a difference between HTML post forms and Flash movies that use the LoadVars object?

A No. They look the same to CGI programs. This means that creating quick and simple HTML forms is a great way to test your CGI programs before trying to use them from a Flash movie.

Workshop

The quiz questions are designed to test your knowledge of the material covered in this hour. The answers to the questions follow.

Quiz

1. What is the difference between `loadVariables` and `load`?
2. How many ways are there to send data to the server with a `LoadVars` object?
3. Is there any way to send or load data from another server?
4. Name three ways to determine when a `sendAndLoad` command is finished.

Quiz Answers

1. The `loadVariables` command creates or replaces variables at the same level as the command. The `load` command creates properties in the `LoadVars` object.
2. There are two primary functions: `send` and `sendAndLoad`.
3. No. At least not while the movie is being run from a Web site. Data and CGI programs must be on the same server for security reasons.
4. You could define an `onLoad` function, you could test the `loaded` property of the `LoadVars` object, or you could test the `getBytesLoaded` and compare it to the `getBytesTotal` properties of the object.

Hour 19

Using XML with Flash

- XML Basics
- The XML Object
- Task: XML-Powered Display
- Recursive XML Parsing
- Q&A

Flash has a set of commands for handling XML (eXtensible Markup Language). XML is being used more frequently for databases and Internet data transfer.

In this hour, you will:

- Find out about XML
- Learn about Flash's XML object
- Read in an external XML file and apply it to a movie

XML Basics

An XML document is a text document that stores data. XML is similar to HTML because of the use of tags. However, XML differs from HTML in that HTML uses specific tags and is used for a specific purpose.

XML, on the other hand, can use a completely custom tag set and can be used for any purpose where you need data. For instance, here is a simple XML document:

```
<user>
    <name>Gary</name>
    <ID>47</ID>
</user>
```

This document defines a user. A user has two pieces of information stored: name and ID.

NEW TERM In the preceding example, user, name, and ID are all XML *elements*. Each element is also known as a *node*. In addition, the data stored in elements are also nodes, known as *text nodes*.

Figure 19.1 illustrates what nodes are. In it, you see a visual representation of the preceding XML example. You can see the five nodes: user, name, ID, the text node with "Gary," and the text node with "47."

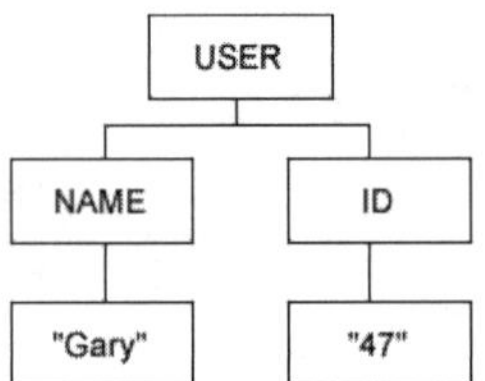

FIGURE 19.1
This diagram illustrates a simple XML file with three elements and two text nodes.

So why are XML documents so popular? The key is that they are both machine-readable and human-readable. Most other forms of databases are good for one or the other but not optimized for both.

XML documents can be created by people with simple text editors. Creation can also be facilitated by XML editing programs. On the other hand, programmers can easily write programs that access XML data.

Flash makes it easy to access the data in XML documents. The XML object can automatically parse an XML text document and then provide many functions and properties to access the information inside it.

It is unlikely, as a Flash programmer, that you will find a need to create an XML database for your movies. However, it is likely that you will be asked to write a Flash movie that accesses an existing XML database.

This data may take the form of a ready-made text file such as the examples later in this hour. Or, you could be calling out to CGI programs that return XML documents when queried.

The XML Object

Flash's XML object is a collection of functions and properties that allow you to easily get data from XML documents. The first step in using the XML object is to create a variable that holds XML. Here is an example:

```
myXML = new XML();
```

Parsing Text into XML

This XML document is empty. However, you can quickly populate it by using the `parseXML` command. This takes a text string and deconstructs it to get the XML data inside.

```
myXML = new XML();
myXML.parseXML("<user><name>Gary</name><ID>47</ID></user>");
```

Another way to do this same thing is to feed the string into the `new XML()` function:

```
myXML = new XML("<user><name>Gary</name><ID>47</ID></user>");
```


Now just because you say that a string represents XML doesn't make it true. Suppose that there is a mistake in your XML code. In that case, ActionScript won't be able to parse the string. You can find out whether there was a problem by monitoring the `status` property of the object. Here is an example:

```
myXML = new XML("<user><name>Gary</name><ID>47</user>");
trace(myXML.status);
```

The result is -9. This is because the closing </ID> tag is missing. The code -9 translates to a start tag without an end tag. A -10 is an end tag without a start tag. But if you get a 0, that means that the string was parsed without any problems.

Getting Data from XML

So how do you access the information inside the XML object now that you have it? There are many functions for doing this. For instance, you can use `firstChild` to get the first child node of the object:

```
myXML = new XML("<user><name>Gary</name><ID>47</ID></user>");
trace(myXML.firstChild);
```

The result is "<user><name>Gary</name><ID>47</ID></user>". This is the first child of the XML object. Now let's dig deeper:

```
myXML = new XML("<user><name>Gary</name><ID>47</ID></user>");
trace(myXML.firstChild.firstChild);
```

Now the result is <name>Gary</name>. The *name* element is the first child of the *user* element.

Another way to do this, instead of using firstChild, is to use childNodes, an array of nodes. Here is the same example, but with childNodes:

```
myXML = new XML("<user><name>Gary</name><ID>47</ID></user>");
trace(myXML.childNodes[0].childNodes[0]);
```

Is that it? No, you can still go further. Refer back to Figure 19.1. There is a node under the user node that holds the text.

```
myXML = new XML("<user><name>Gary</name><ID>47</ID></user>");
trace(myXML.childNodes[0].childNodes[0].childNodes[0]);
```

The result is now Gary. This is the text node of the name node of the user node. So that's the bottom? No. This is the last node, but it is still a node, not a text string like we would probably need if we were looking for the data in the XML document. To access the string in a text node, you need to use the nodeValue property. Here is the way to get the username from the XML document:

```
myXML = new XML("<user><name>Gary</name><ID>47</ID></user>");
trace(myXML.childNodes[0].childNodes[0].childNodes[0].nodeValue);
```

But what if we wanted the user ID? That would be the second node of the user node. Here is the code:

```
myXML = new XML("<user><name>Gary</name><ID>47</ID></user>");
trace(myXML.childNodes[0].childNodes[1].childNodes[0].nodeValue);
```

Creating XML from Scratch

What if you didn't have a text string but wanted to create the XML code from scratch? You can use createElement to make a new element and createTextNode to create a new text node. However, neither of these commands actually adds the node to the XML object; they just prepare a new node. You have to use appendChild to add a new node.

For instance, to re-create the XML object from the previous example, you would do this:

```
myXML = new XML();
newElement = myXML.createElement("user");
myXML.appendChild(newElement);
```

```
newElement = myXML.createElement("name");
myXML.childNodes[0].appendChild(newElement);
newText = myXML.createTextNode("Gary");
myXML.childNodes[0].childNodes[0].appendChild(newText);
newElement = myXML.createElement("ID");
myXML.childNodes[0].appendChild(newElement);
newText = myXML.createTextNode("47");
myXML.childNodes[0].childNodes[1].appendChild(newText);
```

If you want to change the value of a text node, you need to set the `nodeValue` property:

```
myXML.childNodes[0].childNodes[1].childNodes[0].nodeValue = 53;
```

Attributes

XML elements can also have attributes. An *attribute* is a property and value pair that further defines an element. For instance, in the following XML, the attribute *`type`* helps to define the element *`name`*:

```
<user>
    <name type="alias">Gary</name>
    <ID>47</ID>
</user>
```

If you wanted to read this into an XML object, you would have to use a single quote or a backslash followed by a quote, in place of the quotes around `"alias"`. Otherwise, the ActionScript line would have a syntax error.

```
myXML = new XML("<user><name type='alias'>Gary</name><ID>47</user>");
```

To access this attribute, you need to refer to the `attributes` property of the node and then the specific attribute name:


```
trace(myXML.childNodes[0].childNodes[0].attributes.alias);
```

Another way to do this uses brackets:

```
trace(myXML.childNodes[0].childNodes[0].attributes["alias"]);
```

You can set, change, or even add an attribute to a node like this:

```
myXML.childNodes[0].childNodes[0].attributes["alias"] = "real";
```

If the attribute *`alias`* wasn't already there, it would be created.

Unfortunately, the `attributes` property is not an array. So you can't get its `length` or examine the property name and value of each element by number. You can, however, use a `for in` loop to discover each attribute.

```
myXML = new XML("<user><name type='alias' validity='verified'>Gary</name>➥
<ID>47</user>");
```

```
for(attr in myXML.childNodes[0].childNodes[0].attributes) {
    trace(attr+": "+myXML.childNodes[0].childNodes[0].attributes[attr]);
}
```

More XML ActionScript

You should know several other things about the XML object. Most important, remember that any part of an XML object is another XML object. For instance, you can take the first node of an XML object and refer to it with another variable. Here is an illustration:

```
myXML = new XML("<user><name>Gary</name><ID>47</user>");
thisUser = myXML.childNodes[0];
thisUserName = thisUser.childNodes[0];
thisUserNameText = thisUserName.childNodes[0].nodeValue;
thisUserID = thisUser.childNodes[1];
thisUserIDText = thisUserID.childNodes[0].nodeValue;
```

You can get the number of nodes inside a node by using the `length` property of the `childNodes` property of that node. So to find that the *`user`* node has two nodes inside it, you could do this:

```
myXML = new XML("<user><name>Gary</name><ID>47</user>");
trace(myXML.childNodes[0].childNodes.length);
```

In addition to being able to find out the `nodeValue` of a text node, you can find out the name of a regular element node with `nodeNode`. So you could determine that the first node under *`user`* is *`name`* with this:

```
myXML = new XML("<user><name>Gary</name><ID>47</user>");
trace(myXML.childNodes[0].childNodes[0].nodeName);
```

You can determine whether a node is an element or a text node by using the `nodeType` property. A value of 1 means that it is a regular element with possibly more nodes under it, or a value of 3 tells you that it is a text node.

Loading External XML

You can get XML files from an external source. The XML object has the same basic commands and properties as the LoadVars object in Hour 18, "Sending Information to the Server."

First, you would create the XML object. Then you would use the `load` command to initiate a server call. The results would happen some time later, which you can check for using the `loaded` property of the object or defining an `onLoad` function.

For instance, this code starts to load the XML document xmldata.txt from the same folder as the Flash movie. When it is finished, it calls the function `dealWithXML`:

```
data = new XML();
data.ignoreWhite = true;
```

```
data.load("xmldata.txt");

data.onLoad = function(success) {
    if (success) {
        if (data.status == 0) {
            // take data from this user
            dealWithXML(thisUser);

        } else {
            // could not parse the XML data
            trace("Parse Error: "+data.status);
        }

    } else {
        // could not get the XML
        trace("Load Error");
    }
}
```

A few more things in the preceding function need explaining. The `ignoreWhite` property of the XML object tells it to ignore whitespace: tabs, returns, line feeds and other nonvisible characters. This means that the XML file can have multiple lines and use tabs to make it easier to read. Flash ignores these characters when it parses the XML data. This is necessary when using human-created XML files, or even files generated by programs but meant to be examined by humans.

The `onLoad` function takes a single parameter that will be true if the load was a success. If not, there was an error, and the preceding function handles that case. In addition, I use the `status` property to make sure that Flash can parse the XML file.

19

Now that you know how to get an external XML file and manipulate it in a number of ways, let's create a simple XML display.

Task: XML-Powered Display

Let's read an external HTML file and use it to populate a set of text fields. The XML data will look like this:

```
<list>
    <user>
        <name>
            <last>Doe</last>
            <first>John</first>
        </name>

        <ssnumber>000-00-0000</ssnumber>

        <address>
```

```
            <street>123 Street Road.</street>
            <city>Metropolis</city>
            <state>New York</state>
            <zip>12345</zip>
        </address>

        <phone>
            <work>212-555-1212</work>
            <home>212-555-0000</home>
        </phone>

        <email>test@test.com</email>

        <dateofbirth>10/29/1969</dateofbirth>

        <emergencycontact relation="Wife">Jane Doe</emergencycontact>
    </user>
</list>
```

You can find this document on the CD-ROM in the 19xmldisplay folder. It is named xmldata.txt.

Notice that its first node is <list>, suggesting that more than one user might be in the final document. In this example, however, there is just one user. Then there are nodes for the user's name, social security number, address, phone, e-mail, date of birth, and emergency contact information. Most of these nodes are divided still further. For instance, there is a node for the last name and a node for the first name.

Now let's make a movie that reads in this data and displays it.

1. Start with a new Flash movie.
2. You'll need to create a whole series of dynamic text fields. You can see them all in Figure 19.2. There is one static text field for each dynamic one that acts as a label.

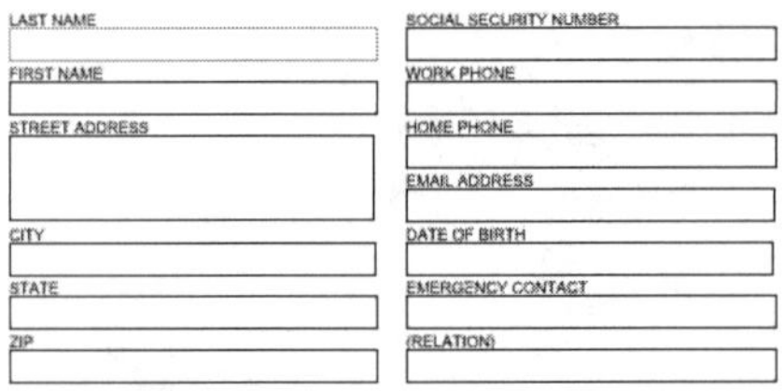

FIGURE 19.2
This application displays the information found in an XML file.

3. Each of the dynamic text fields needs to be set to link to a specific variable. All these names have two words. Here is a complete list: last name, first name, address street, address city, address state, address zip, user ssnumber, phone work, phone

home, user email, user dateofbirth, user emergencycontact, and emergencycontact relation. You'll find out why these need these specific names in the next task.

4. Now we need to read in the XML data. This sequence of commands is almost identical to the example earlier in this hour. It needs to be placed in the first and only frame of the movie.

```
// get XML data from file
data = new XML();
data.ignoreWhite = true;
data.load("xmldata.txt");

data.onLoad = function(success) {
    if (success) {
        if (data.status == 0) {
            // get first user
            thisUser = data.childNodes[0].childNodes[0];
            // take data from this user
            parseData(thisUser);

        } else {
            // could not parse the XML data
            trace("Parse Error: "+data.status);
        }

    } else {
        // could not get the XML
        trace("Load Error");
    }
}
```

The main addition to this code is that the variable *thisUser* is defined as the `user` node in the XML data. Then, this node is passed into the function `parseData`.

19

5. The `parseData` function examines every text node in the document plus the one attribute. It assigns these values to the variables linked to the dynamic text fields.

```
// get all data from user node
function parseData(user) {
    this["name last"] = ➥
user.childNodes[0].childNodes[0].childNodes[0].nodeValue;
    this["name first"] = ➥
user.childNodes[0].childNodes[1].childNodes[0].nodeValue;
    this["user ssnumber"] = user.childNodes[1].childNodes[0].nodeValue;
    this["address street"] = ➥
user.childNodes[2].childNodes[0].childNodes[0].nodeValue;
    this["address city"] = ➥
user.childNodes[2].childNodes[1].childNodes[0].nodeValue;
    this["address state"] = ➥
user.childNodes[2].childNodes[2].childNodes[0].nodeValue;
    this["address zip"] = ➥
```

```
user.childNodes[2].childNodes[3].childNodes[0].nodeValue;
    this["phone work"] = ➥
user.childNodes[3].childNodes[0].childNodes[0].nodeValue;
    this["phone home"] = ➥
user.childNodes[3].childNodes[1].childNodes[0].nodeValue;
    this["user email"] = user.childNodes[4].childNodes[0].nodeValue;
    this["user dateofbirth"] = user.childNodes[5].childNodes[0].nodeValue;
    this["user emergencycontact"] = ➥
user.childNodes[6].childNodes[0].nodeValue;
    this["emergencycontact relation"] = ➥
user.childNodes[6].attributes["relation"];
}
```

6. Keeping track of all those node numbers can be a pain and difficult to debug. Instead, you can break up the `user` node further and refer to the pieces. Here is an improved `parseData` function:

```
function parseDataAlt(user) {
    userName = user.childNodes[0];
    this["name last"] = userName.childNodes[0].childNodes[0].nodeValue;
    this["name first"] = userName.childNodes[1].childNodes[0].nodeValue;

    this["user ssnumber"] = user.childNodes[1].childNodes[0].nodeValue;

    userAddress = user.childNodes[2];
    this["address street"] = ➥
userAddress.childNodes[0].childNodes[0].nodeValue;
    this["address city"] = ➥
userAddress.childNodes[1].childNodes[0].nodeValue;
    this["address state"] = ➥
userAddress.childNodes[2].childNodes[0].nodeValue;
    this["address zip"] = ➥
userAddress.childNodes[3].childNodes[0].nodeValue;

    userPhone = user.childNodes[3];
    this["phone work"] = userPhone.childNodes[0].childNodes[0].nodeValue;
    this["phone home"] = userPhone.childNodes[1].childNodes[0].nodeValue;

    this["user email"] = user.childNodes[4].childNodes[0].nodeValue;

    this["user dateofbirth"] = user.childNodes[5].childNodes[0].nodeValue;

    userContact = user.childNodes[6];
    this["user emergencycontact"] = userContact.childNodes[0].nodeValue;
    this["emergencycontact relation"] = userContact.attributes["relation"];
}
```

Although this is easier to read, it still relies on all the information being specifically numbered nodes. In the next section, we'll look at a better way to do this.

Run this example movie, found on the CD-ROM as 19xmldisplay.fla in the 19xmldisplay folder. Examine both the xmldata.txt file and the code in the Flash movie. Try changing the XML data values to see the change reflected the next time you run the movie.

Recursive XML Parsing

The problem with the preceding task is that it depends on specific pieces of information being at specific node locations. What's the point of calling a node `email` if you are not even going to refer to it by name? Besides, what if the creator of the XML file accidentally moves the `ssnumber` tag to the end of the `user`? Then everything is out of whack, and your code won't find the right values at the right node numbers.

Fortunately, there is a way to parse an XML file one node at a time, check what is there, and populate fields based on the name of the node.

XML is recursive. This means that an XML document is an XML document. A node in that XML document is also an XML document. A node in *that* XML document is also an XML document and so on.

You can write code that parses an XML document using a recursive function. This function is told to examine the current XML document and determine whether it is an element or a text node. If it is a text node, it is simply data that needs to be placed somewhere. If it is an element, it is a smaller XML document that needs to be parsed.

To explain further, let's look at the code:


```
function parseData(dataPart,parent,grandparent) {
    if (dataPart.nodeType == 3) { // get value of text node
        this [grandparent+" "+parent] = dataPart.nodeValue;

    } else if (dataPart.nodeType == 1) {

        // loop through attributes
        for(var attr in dataPart.attributes) {
            this[dataPart.nodeName+" "+attr] = dataPart.attributes[attr];
        }

        // loop through child nodes
        for(var i=0;i<dataPart.childNodes.length;i++) {
            parseData(dataPart.childNodes[i],dataPart.nodeName,parent);
        }
    }
}
```

This function looks at the XML object passed in, which is in the parameter `dataPart`. If it is type 3, it is a text node. In that case, it places the text into a text field that has the name as its grandparent and parent. For instance, the text node in the `last` node has the parent `last` and the grandparent `name`. So the name of the text field should be `name last`. That is where the text would go.

If the XML object is not just a text node, two loops occur. The first looks for any attributes of the node. It puts the contents of the attribute in a text field named after the parent and the attribute name. So the `emergencycontact` node has the attribute `relation`. It's content will be put in the `emergencycontact relation` text field.

The second loop looks at all the child nodes in the node. For each of these, it calls `parseData` with the new node. It sends in the parent's name as the grandparent and the current node name as the parent. This is the recursive bit. The function is calling itself.

By doing recursion, the program is breaking the XML object into smaller and smaller pieces until it has piece so small that they are just text nodes. It uses the name of the text node's parent and grandparent to determine what text field to place the text node value into.

This little function does the same job as the `parseData` function in the previous task. However, it never refers to any node by number. So the XML document can be in any order and even contain additional, unused information. If information is missing, the text fields will simply be left blank.

Check out the movie 19xmlrecursivedisplay.fla to see this one in action. Note that the first time `parseData` is called in the `onLoad` function, it is sent `list` and `xmldoc` as its parent and grandparent. These really aren't important because the text nodes are much farther down.

Summary

XML is a popular way for encapsulating data. It looks like HTML but is completely customizable and can be used for any type of data. It is readable both by people and computers.

The XML object in ActionScript allows you to import, manipulate, and create XML. You can convert a text document or a simple string into an XML object provided that it is formatted correctly.

Using dot syntax and XML object properties, you can access any of the nodes of an XML document. You can deconstruct XML and display the data in text fields or use it in your applications.

Q&A

Q Can I use Flash to create and send XML documents?

A Sure. You can populate an XML object and then use `send` to send it to a server just like you would with the LoadVars object.

Q How do I know whether to use XML documents or lists of variables like what LoadVars expects?

A Use XML in cases where the data is already in XML format. You can also use it if you are building the system and feel like XML is needed. However, for small pieces of data, you should be able to stick with plain text files.

Q Can I remove nodes from an XML object?

A Yes. There is a `removeNode` command that will delete one. Read the XML section of the documentation for a complete list of commands and properties.

Q Isn't recursion supposed to be some difficult concept that only expert programmers understand?

A Although it is true that some people have trouble understanding the idea of a recursive function, many non-programmers can see how it works. However, don't be frustrated if you don't get it. Many freshmen computer science students switch majors shortly after trying to learn recursion.

Workshop

19

The quiz questions are designed to test your knowledge of the material covered in this hour. The answers to the questions follow.

Quiz

1. How many nodes are shown in Figure 19.1?
2. Name the nodes in the XML document `<test>Hello World!</test>`.
3. What two steps need to be done to insert a new node into an XML document?
4. How would you get to the text "Hello World" in the document `<test>Hello World!</test>`?

Quiz Answers

1. Five. There are three elements and two text nodes for a total of five nodes.
2. There is the `test` node and the text node under it containing "Hello World!".

3. You need to first use `createElement` or `createTextNode` to make the node and then use `appendChild` or, alternatively, `insertBefore`, to put the node in the XML object.
4. The text is the `nodeValue` of the first child of the first child. So you could do this: `myXML.childNodes[0].childNodes[0].nodeValue`.

HOUR 20

Printing

Although not as complex as browser or server communication, printing is another way that Flash communicates with the outside world. Flash's printing capabilities are useful because they allow you to build documents that the user can print from inside your interface. This is often a better design option than relying on the browser's print function.

In this hour, you will:

- Learn how to set up your movie for printing
- Find out how to use the print commands
- Create a printable form

Setting Up Your Movie for Printing

You need to do a few things to your movie before you can use any ActionScript print commands. Unfortunately, the print commands are not versatile. If used without any preparation, they will print the entire contents of the movie, frame by frame.

This is usually not what you want. You may want only the current frame printed, perhaps a frame inside a specific movie clip, or maybe a small series of frames. But rarely will you want every single frame printed.

Labeling Frames for Printing

You specify that a frame should be printed by labeling it with a **#p**. If you don't place a **#p** label on any frame, the print commands will print all frames in your movie. On the other hand, if you place more than one **#p** frame in your movie, just those frames will be printed.

Figure 20.1 shows a timeline with two frames labeled for printing. Notice that those same frames are also labeled in another layer. You can place more than one label on a frame this way. This comes in handy because you probably don't want to use **#p** as a real label, and you may want to have more than one frame with a **#p** label.

FIGURE 20.1
Frames 2 and 4 are labeled for printing.

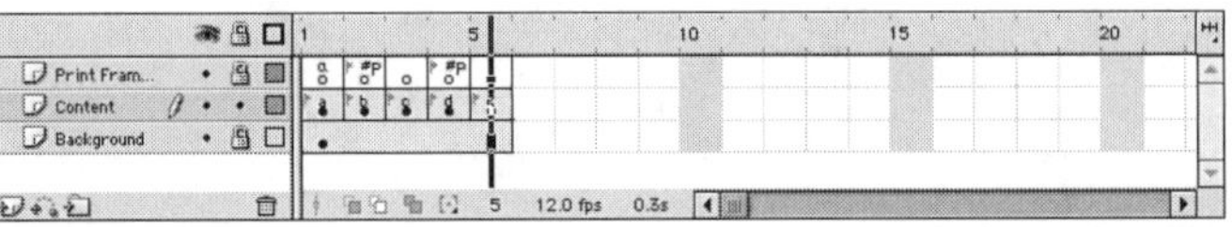

When you label more than one frame with a **#p**, you will get a warning when you test the movie: "WARNING: Duplicate label...". It is unfortunate that this happens, but it will not affect your movie unless you try to use the **#p** labels in `gotoAndStop` commands and such.

A Printing Strategy

You really need to think ahead to build printing into your movie. Because you can't just print the current frame, you will need to build special printable frames.

Note that everything visible on the frame gets printed. This includes a Print button, if you have one, plus any navigation buttons. So you probably want to have a Print button on one frame, and then have a frame that is identical to that one but without the Print button or other unwanted elements. This frame has the **#p** label on it.

You can organize this using the main timeline layers. For instance, you could have Print and navigation buttons on separate layers from the page's content. These layers, which you do not want printed, will not extend to the print frame.

Figures 20.2 and 20.3 illustrate this kind of system. Figure 20.2 is the frame that the user sees on the Web page. It features the content, a navigation button, and a Print button.

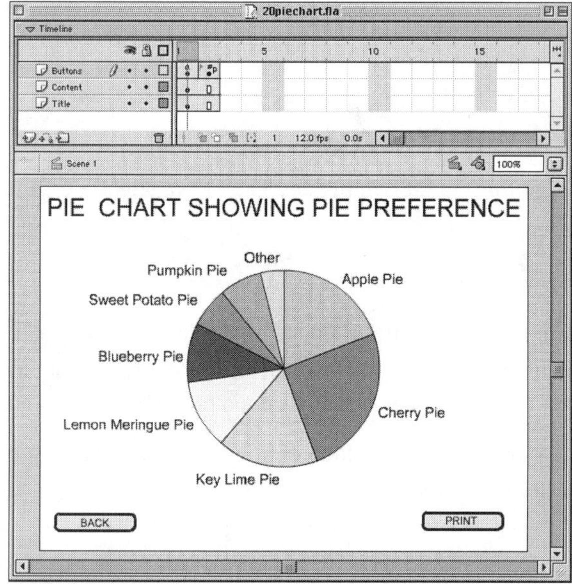

FIGURE 20.2
This is the frame the user sees onscreen, which includes elements that shouldn't be printed.

On the other hand, Figure 20.3 shows a frame that the user never sees—at least not on the screen. It is labeled with a **#p**, which you can see in the timeline. The Buttons layer does not use the same key frame as the previous frame. Instead it uses a new key frame that excludes the button but includes additional information meant for the printout only.

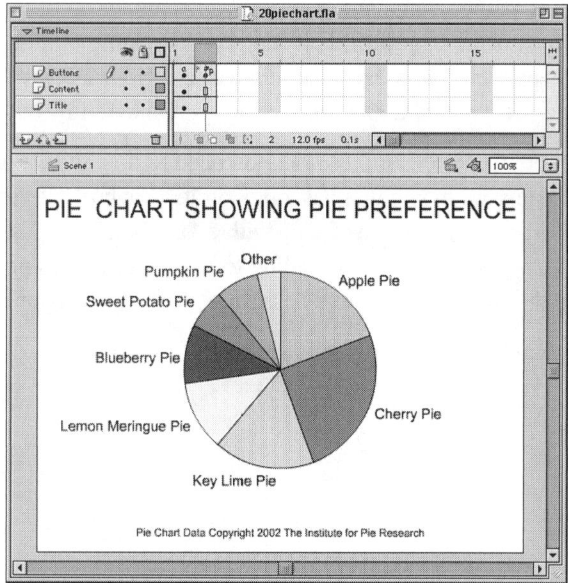

FIGURE 20.3
This frame is meant to be printed.

Now that you know how to prepare your movie, let's look at the ActionScript needed to print.

The Print Commands

There are two primary print commands. They have slightly different uses but work basically the same.

Print

The first is simply `print`. This command takes two parameters. The first is the target to be printed. Usually this is the main timeline, or `_root`. You can also use `this`. However, if you do want to print frames inside a movie clip, you can use a reference to that clip.

The second parameter is one of three options: `bframe`, `bmovie`, or `bmax`. These relate to how Flash scales the frames printed.

Flash scales the printable material up to the size where it fills the page as much as possible without distorting it. So if a frame is 550×400, it will most likely make the 550 pixels of the frame fit across the page. The vertical dimension will remain proportional.

If you use the `bframe` option, each frame printed scales to its own size to fill the page. If one frame fills 550×400 and a second frame has content that only fills 275×200, the second frame scales to twice the size of the first, so that they both fill their pages as much as possible.

If you use `bmax` as the second parameter, Flash examines all of the frame to be printed to determine which is the largest. It then chooses the scaling of all pages based on that one page. This keeps each frame the same relative size. So if a 550×400 screen is the largest, it fills the page. But a 275×200 screen in the same movie fills only half the page.

The third option is `bmovie`. In this case, you need to do a little more work. You need to create a frame in your movie that has a box on it. This box determines the maximum size to be printed. You must label this frame with a **#b** label. Then Flash uses the size of the box on this frame to determine the scaling to use on all frames printed. If there is something outside this area on a frame to be printed, it should not appear on the printout.

Here is an example of the `print` command:

```
on (release) {
    print(this,"bframe");
}
```

As you can see, the boundary option is actually passed in as a string. You must put quotes around it.

You can see an example of the `print` command in action in the movie 20piechart.fla.

PrintAsBitmap

The companion command to `print` is `printAsBitmap`. This command works just like `print`, with the same two parameters.

The difference between `print` and `printAsBitmap` is that `print` actually sends vector graphics and fonts to the printer. The printer then re-creates the vectors and text when building the page.

On the other hand, `printAsBitmap` converts the entire screen to a large bitmap image and sends that to the printer.

The main advantage of `printAsBitmap` is that alpha transparencies can be printed; so if you have semitransparent graphics, you will need to use this. It also works with a wider variety of print devices.

The `print` command has the advantage of producing nice, smooth curves and text on higher-end printers. It may also be faster if printing over a network.

A good general rule to follow is to use `printAsBitmap` at times when you want to be assured that printing works and that the results mirror what is seen onscreen. Use `print` when accuracy is not critical or when you are making the movie for a controlled environment like a corporate intranet.

> If you are streaming your movie over the Internet, note that printing should work only after all the frames you want printed have loaded. You may just want to check to make sure that the whole movie has been loaded before allowing the user to print. See Hour 23, "Managing Movie Streaming," to learn about streaming and how to detect whether a movie is fully loaded.

Task: Printable Form

One thing I hate to see on the Web is a printable form that you need to print out, fill out, and then mail in. It is the filling out that I object to. I'm using a computer, but then I suddenly have to find a pen and a clear spot on my desk to write?

So why not allow the user to fill out the form right on the screen? Then you can print out the form, complete with the text the user entered.

Doing this is simple with Flash and has some definite advantages over placing an HTML form on a page and asking the user to print out the entire Web page. You can completely control what gets printed, so that miscellaneous elements on the page get ignored, and new elements, such as a mailing address for the form, can be added.

1. Create a new Flash movie.
2. Add a lot of input text fields on a layer named content. You can see which fields to add in Figure 20.4. This layer should be named **Content**.

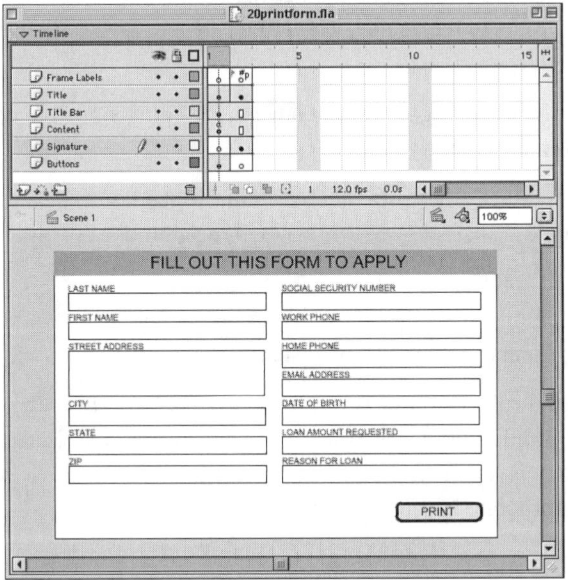

FIGURE 20.4
This form contains various fields to be filled out, plus a Print button.

3. Add a title to the top, complete with a title bar under it. Place these on two separate frames named **Title** and **Title Bar**.
4. Create a Print button and place that on its own frame named **Buttons**.
5. Add this script to the button:

```
on (release) {
    print(this,"bmax");
}
```

6. Now add a second frame to the movie. Stretch the Title Bar and Content layers onto this second frame. However, create new blank key frames for the Buttons and Title layers. They will have different content on frame 2.

7. In the second frame of the Title layer, put a different title. For instance, if the first frame is titled Fill Out This Application, the second frame can be titled just Application. After all, if the printed application is already filled out, the original title doesn't make sense anymore. You can see this new title in Figure 20.5.

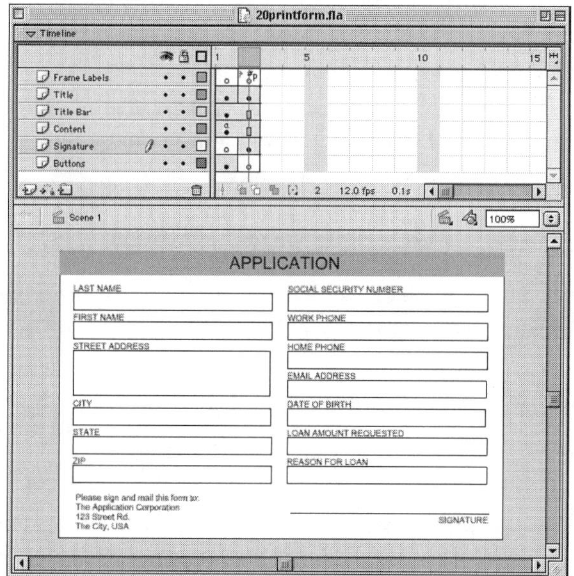

FIGURE 20.5
This frame has a different title, and is missing the Print button, but has a signature line and mailing instructions.

8. Add a new layer named **Signature**. Put a key frame on the second frame of this layer. Add a signature line and mailing instructions to this key frame, as shown in Figure 20.5. These should not be visible on the first frame, only the second.
9. Add a **Frame Labels** layer. Place two key frames on it. The second key frame, in the second frame of the movie, needs a **#p** label on it. Use the first key frame to place a `stop()` script so that the movie stops on frame 1.

   Test your completed movie. You should be able to fill out the form and then click the Print button. The second frame prints, complete with a new title, signature line, and mailing instructions.

The sample movie 20printform.fla contains my version of this example.

Summary

To print frames of a movie, you first need to label those frames with a **#p** label. You can label one or more frames for printing.

Everything on the **#p** frames will be printed, so you will probably want to make up custom frames for printing, ones that don't have screen elements like navigation buttons.

You can use the `print` command to print the frames using vector shapes sent directly to the printer. However, if you need to print semitransparent graphics or be assured that the printing works the same for all users, use `printAsBitmap`.

Q&A

Q How can I make a Flash movie where a Print button prints the current frame?

A Place most or all of the frame's contents into its own single-frame movie clip. Label that frame in the movie clip with a **#p**. Use the `print` or `printAsBitmap` command with the target set to that movie clip. Do this for each frame.

Q How can I bring up the Page Setup dialog for the user so that she can change her settings before printing?

A When you use `print`, both the Page Setup and Print dialogs are displayed, one after the other. This may depend a little on your system configuration and print drivers.

Q How can I test the `print` command without wasting paper?

A Many print drivers come with a print preview option. This means that you can select Preview instead of Print in either the Page Setup or Print dialog. This is a great way to test printing. Many recent color ink jet printers come with such print drivers, but basic business printers usually do not.

Workshop

The quiz questions are designed to test your knowledge of the material covered in this hour. The answers to the questions follow.

Quiz

1. What must be done to a frame to indicate that it should be printed?
2. If you have semitransparent graphics on the screen, which print command should you use?
3. Is there any difference between using the `bframe` and `bmax` boundary options if you are printing just one frame?
4. Do you have to show a frame on the screen to be able to print it?

Quiz Answers

1. Put a **#p** label on a frame that you want printed.
2. Use `printAsBitmap` because `print` will not handle semitransparent graphics.
3. None. The `bmax` option would use the bounding box of the largest frame, but because there is only one frame, it doesn't matter.
4. No. You can print frames labeled with a **#p** that have never been shown. However, if your movie is in the process of streaming, printing will not work until all frames labeled for printing have been loaded.

PART VI
Advanced Topics

Hour

HOUR 21

Using Components

Components are prebuilt interface objects such as check boxes, radio buttons, and pop-up menus. A set of these comes with Flash MX that includes some of the most common user interface elements. In Flash 5, these were known as Smart Clips.

In this hour, you will:

- Review all the built-in components
- Find out how to use ActionScript related to components
- Create a user input form with components
- See how to make style changes to the components

ActionScript for Flash's Built-In Components

There are seven different built-in components. Figure 21.1 shows the Components panel, which includes the names and icons for each of these.

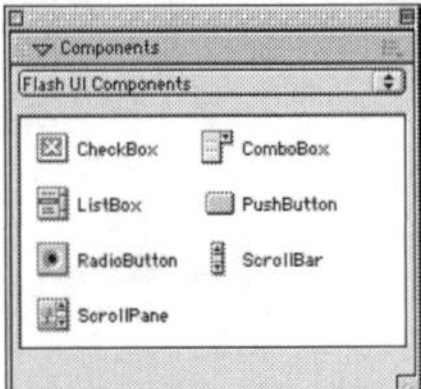

FIGURE 21.1
The Components panel is where you select components to add to your movie.

To add a component to your movie, you can either double-click on a component in the panel, or click and drag a component to the stage.

PushButton

Click and drag the PushButton component to the stage. This creates a new instance of the PushButton component on the stage. It also adds a ton of Library elements to your movie. Fortunately, these Library elements are stored in neat folders, so they won't get in your way too much.

Figure 21.2 shows the PushButton component on the stage. It is a simple box with the words "PushButton" in the middle.

FIGURE 21.2
The PushButton is the simplest of the components.

If you happen to have the Live Preview feature of Flash turned off, the PushButton will look far worse on your screen and very different from what you get when you run the movie. You can turn on Live Preview by choosing Control, Enable Live Preview.

After the PushButton is on the stage, you can select it and open the Properties panel to change its name. Figure 21.3 shows the Properties panel for this component.

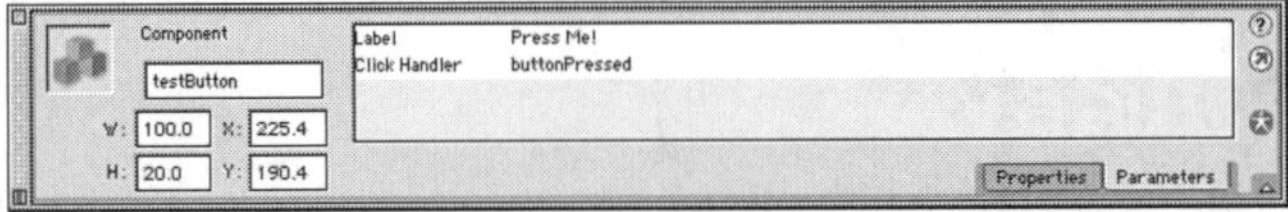

FIGURE 21.3
The Properties panel for components features Properties and Parameters tabs. You can switch between these two modes to see different information about the component.

Two parameters can be set for the PushButton component. The first is the Label; change that to **Press Me!** The second is the Click Handler. This is the name of the function that will be called when the button is clicked. This function must be in the same timeline as the button; so if the button is at the root level, the function should be in the main timeline. Set the Click Handler to **buttonPressed**.

Also, name the component instance **testButton** as shown in Figure 21.3.

Now all you have to do is to create the `buttonPressed` function. Here is a simple example. It just sends some text to the Output window:

```
function buttonPressed(buttonInstance) {
    if (buttonInstance == testButton) {
        trace("Test Button Pushed.");
    } else {
        trace(buttonInstance._name);
    }
}
```

A button handler function is passed one parameter: a reference to the button that called it. So you can test this instance to see whether it is `testButton`. This sample function prints out a special message if it is that button, and the button instance name if it is not.

You can see this example in the movie 21pushbutton.fla.

CheckBoxes

The CheckBox component is similar to the one we created in Hour 15, "User Input Elements." You can see three of them in Figure 21.4.

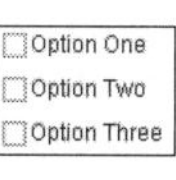

FIGURE 21.4
CheckBox components allow the user to select nonexclusive options.

To make a CheckBox component, double-click it in the Components panel, or click and drag it to the stage. To make a second one, go to the Library and open the Flash UI Components folder that was created when you added the first component. Drag the CheckBox component from there onto the stage.

In the example movie 21checkboxes.fla, I have created three CheckBoxes. If you select any one of these and bring up the Properties panel, you will see that it includes a few more parameters than the PushButton Properties panel, shown in Figure 21.3.

In addition to Label and Change Handler parameters, you now also have Initial Value and Label Placement parameters. The Initial Value parameter is either true or false, depending on whether you want the CheckBox to start off checked. The Label Placement parameter allows you to select right or left. Right is the default placement, which is shown in Figure 21.4. If you switch to left, the text will be to the left of the box instead.

In the example movie, I have named the three CheckBox instances option1, option2, and option3. I also labeled them Option One, Option Two, and Option Three. The Change Handler for each is set to changeOptions.

I placed the `changeOptions` function in the main timeline. This will be triggered any time one of the CheckBoxes is clicked. It will send the name of the CheckBox and its new state to the Output window.

```
function changeOptions(checkBoxInstance) {
    trace(checkBoxInstance._name+": "+checkBoxInstance.getValue());
}
```

In 21checkboxes.fla, I also added a PushButton component. This button is named doneButton and calls the `buttonPressed` function. This function loops through all the CheckBoxes and sends its state to the Output window.

```
function buttonPressed(buttonInstance) {
    if (buttonInstance == doneButton) {
        trace("Option One: "+option1.getValue());
        trace("Option Two: "+option2.getValue());
        trace("Option Three: "+option3.getValue());
    }
}
```

Instead of sending the results to the Output window, you will probably want to use them in some other fashion. For instance, you might want to placed them in a LoadVars object so that they can be sent to a server.

RadioButtons

RadioButtons are similar to CheckBoxes, except that they are arranged in groups. Only one RadioButton in a group can be on at one time. You can see what RadioButtons look like in Figure 21.5.

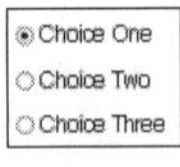

FIGURE 21.5
RadioButton components allow the user to select exclusive options.

The example movie 21radiobuttons.fla has three RadioButtons. If you select one of the buttons and bring up the Properties panel for that button, you will see that it has more parameters than the CheckBox or PushButton components.

In addition to the parameters seen in the CheckBox component, there are Group Name and Data parameters. The Group Name parameter specifies which group the RadioButton belongs to. In the example movie, all three RadioButtons have this set to firstGroup. If there was a second group of buttons with a different name, these two groups would be treated separately when it comes to deciding which RadioButton is on.

The Data parameter is an optional one that can be used by you in your scripts. You can access it with the `getData()` function. You can store instructions that your script can pick up on when the choice is made. Or, you could avoid the Data parameter and refer to the name of the RadioButton.

In the example movie, the three RadioButtons are named choice1, choice2, and choice3. The labels for these buttons are Choice One, Choice Two, and Choice Three.

Determining which choice the user has made is done when the PushButton in the movie is clicked. The PushButton then runs this script to determine which choice has been made. The script loops through the three buttons looking for a button that returns a true from the `getState()` function. This is the RadioButton that is turned on.

```
function buttonPressed(buttonInstance) {
    if (buttonInstance == doneButton) {
        var choice = "none";
        for(i=1;i<=3;i++) {
            if (this["choice"+i].getState()) {
                choice = this["choice"+i]._name;
            }
        }
        trace("Choice: "+choice);
    }
}
```

ListBox

A ListBox is a simple way to allow the user to select one or more options. A ListBox can take the place of either a set of CheckBoxes or a set of RadioButtons. It is particularly useful when you have many choices but limited screen space.

Figure 21.6 shows a ListBox with three choices. It looks a lot like a scrolling text field—in fact, it is. Each line represents a different choice for the user. If there were more choices than could fit in the space, the user could scroll up and down the list to see them all.

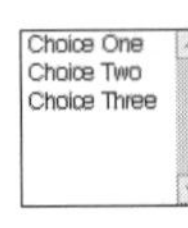

FIGURE 21.6
The ListBox component allows the user to select one or more choices.

When you create a new ListBox instance, you must set its Select Multiple parameter. If true, the user can use the Shift, Command, or Ctrl keys to select more than one line. If false, only one line may be selected at a time.

In addition, you must set the Labels parameter. However, this is not a single value but an array of values. Flash has a special interface for entering these values. When you click on the Labels parameter in the Properties panel, you get a dialog that looks like Figure 21.7.

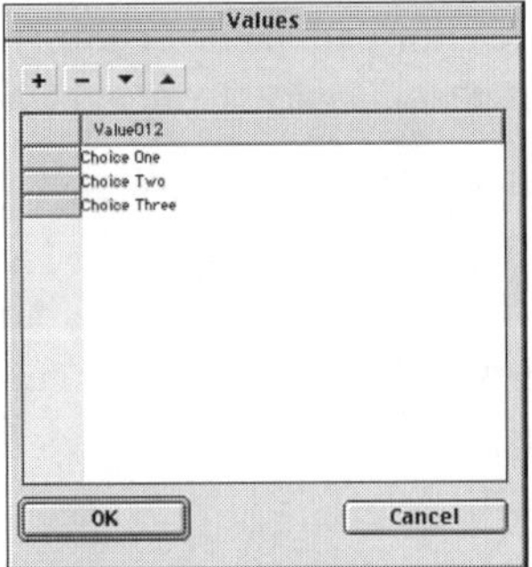

FIGURE 21.7
The Values dialog lets you enter an array of items for different component parameters.

You also have a Data parameter that can take an array of data. This Data parameter, like the one used with radio buttons, allows your code to get additional information about the choice(s) that the user made. However, it is not required.

In the example movie 21listbox.fla, I have placed a ListBox component with three choices on the screen. It is set to accept multiple selections. When the user clicks on a line, the `listBoxChange` function is called. This is specified by its Change Handler parameter. This function tells you which line was just selected:

```
function listBoxChange(listBoxInstance) {
    trace(listBoxInstance.getValue());
}
```

There is also a PushButton component in the example movie. When it is clicked, it runs this function. It uses the `getSelectedItems()` function to get an array of the choices selected in the list box. Each item in the array is an object with a `label` and `data` property. Because we didn't use the `data` properties of the list box, we'll get the labels instead.

```
function buttonPressed(buttonInstance) {
    if (buttonInstance == doneButton) {
        items = myListBox.getSelectedItems();
        for(var i=0;i<items.length;i++) {
            trace(items[i].label);
        }
    }
}
```

You can also add or remove lines from the list box using ActionScript. For instance, `addItem` adds an additional choice to the list box.

```
myListBox.addItem("Choice Four");
```

You can use `addItemAt`, `removeItemAt`, and `replaceItemAt` to make even more changes to the list box with ActionScript.

ComboBox

A combo box is something that Windows users will be familiar with, but no such thing exists in standard Macintosh interfaces. It is a pull-down menu where the user can also type in a value manually.

Fortunately, you can also turn off the option to edit the value. This turns the combo box into a normal pull-down menu. The parameter for doing this is the first one in the Properties dialog for a combo box, named Editable. In addition to that parameter, you can also provide arrays for the Labels and Data.

Another parameter for a combo box is the Row Count. Combo boxes can act a little like list boxes. When the user clicks them, they expand into a list of choices. If the number of choices exceeds the Row Count, a scrolling bar appears to the right to allow the user to scroll through the choices.

Figure 21.8 shows all three variations of a combo box. The box on the left is what a combo box looks like when it is inactive. The second box shows what happens when the user clicks the combo box. The third box shows what happens when there are more choices than rows.

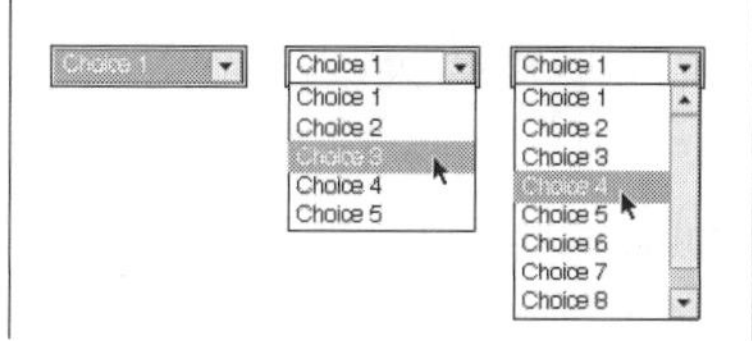

FIGURE 21.8
Three different looks for the combo box.

21

When a user selects a new choice in the combo box, the Click Handler is called. Here is one that simply tells you the label that was selected:

```
function comboBoxChange(comboBoxInstance) {
    trace(comboBoxInstance.getValue());
}
```

You can also use `getSelectedIndex()` to get the zero-based number of the selected choice.

The example movie 21combobox.fla shows an example of a ComboBox component.

ScrollPane

The next two components are different from the previous five. They are not used to allow the user to make choices, but are instead used to display large amounts of information in small spaces.

The ScrollPane component consists of a vertical and horizontal scrollbar and a rectangular viewing area. Its main parameter is Scroll Content. This is the Linkage name for a movie clip. When you run the movie, the movie clip is copied from the Library and placed in the view area of the scroll pane. The scrollbars then allow the user to view different parts of the movie clip.

Figure 21.9 shows the ScrollPane with a movie clip inside. You can see this example in the movie 21scrollpane.fla.

FIGURE 21.9
The ScrollPane allows the user to view a large movie clip in a small space.

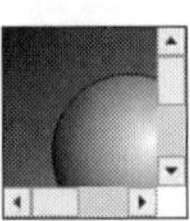

If you set the Drag Content parameter to true, the user can also click in the display area and drag the image around. The scrollbars follow the dragging.

Although the ScrollPane does not require any ActionScript at all to work, there are plenty of functions that you can use to determine which part of the movie clip is being viewed or to change the width and height of the pane.

You can also use the Properties panel to change the width and height of the scroll pane. When you do this, the scroll pane looks distorted in Flash, but it looks fine when you run the movie.

One useful ActionScript command is the `loadScrollContent` command. This command takes a URL and gets an external movie clip to display in the pane.

```
myScrollPane.loadScrollContent("myMovieClipFile.swf");
```

The scroll pane can be useful as an image browser.

ScrollBar

The last component is the ScrollBar. This adds scrolling bars to text fields. You can use this component without any ActionScript at all. Just drag and drop a ScrollBar component to a text field, and it adds itself there.

The ScrollBar component does have a small list of ActionScript-accessible properties. For instance, you can use `getScrollPosition()` to get the current scroll position and `setScrollPosition()` to change it.

Task: Form with Components

Now let's combine five different components to make a data entry form. Figure 21.10 shows such a form. It uses the CheckBox, RadioButton, ComboBox, ListBox, and PushButton components.

FIGURE 21.10
This form uses only Flash components.

1. Create a new Flash movie.
2. Make three CheckBox components. Name them **checkbox1**, **checkbox2**, and **checkbox3**. Label them as you see in Figure 21.10.
3. Make three RadioButton components. Name them **radiobutton1**, **radiobutton2**, and **radiobutton3**. Label them as you see in Figure 21.10.
4. Create a ComboBox component. Name it **combobox**. Add several labels to it so that the user has some choices to make.
5. Create a ListBox component. Name it **listbox**. Add as many labels to it as you can. Don't worry about the order in which they appear because we'll sort them later. Set the ListBox Multiple Selections parameter to false. Use the Properties panel to make the list box 200 pixels wide by 200 pixels high.

6. Add a PushButton component. Set its label to **Done** and its Click Handler to **buttonPressed**.
7. Add the following line to the frame script. This sorts the items in the ListBox component.

   ```
   listbox.sortItemsBy("label","Asc");
   ```

   The `sortItemsBy` command works with the ComboBox component as well. You can use "label" or "data" as the first parameter. This determines whether the labels or the data fields will be used for sorting. The second parameter can be "Asc" for sorting by ascending order or "Desc" for sorting by descending order.
8. The PushButton component calls `buttonPressed`. Let's build this function piece by piece to process each of the sections of the form.

   The function starts off by creating a new array. It then checks each check box to see whether its `getValue()` function is true. If it is, the label from that check box is added to that array. When this loop is finished, the array `own` contains any user selections made with the check boxes.

   ```
   function buttonPressed(buttonInstance) {
       if (buttonInstance == doneButton) {

           // compile array of CheckBoxes selected
           own = new Array();
           for(var i=1;i<=3;i++) {
               if (this["checkbox"+i].getValue()) {
                   own.push(this["checkbox"+i].getLabel());
               }
           }
           trace("Computers Owned: "+own);
   ```

9. The next piece of code checks all the RadioButton components and remembers which one is turned on:

   ```
           // determine which RadioButton selected
           favorite = "none";
           for(var i=1;i<=3;i++) {
               if (this["radiobutton"+i].getState()) {
                   favorite = this["radiobutton"+i].getLabel();
               }
           }
           trace("Favorite: "+favorite);
   ```

10. The simplest component to check is the combo box. This piece of code simply returns its value:

   ```
           // get value of ComboBoxComboBox
           nextPurchase = comboBox.getValue();
           trace("Next Purchase: "+nextPurchase);
   ```

11. To check the multiple selections of the list box, you will need to loop through the array returned by `getSelectedItems()`. You then need to examine the `label` property of each item.

    The following code does this and builds an array of labels selected:

```
            // compile list of ListBox selections
            uses = new Array();
            items = listbox.getSelectedItems();
            for(var i=0;i<items.length;i++) {
                uses.push(items[i].label);
            }
            trace("Uses: "+uses);
        }
    }
```

If you were building this for actual use, you would probably do something more constructive than using `trace` commands. For instance, you could make a LoadVars object that then gets submitted to the server.

Changing the Style of a Component

Flash's components have a nice look to them. But if all Flash developers start using them, soon all our Flash movies will look alike.

Fortunately, you can customize the components in many different ways. You can even create custom skins for them. Let's take a look at three ways to customize components using ActionScript.

Global Customization

Using the `globalStyleFormat` object, you can customize the look of all your components at once. Here is an example that changes the text color of all text in all components to blue:

```
globalStyleFormat.textColor = 0x0000FF;
globalStyleFormat.applyChanges();
```

The `applyChanges` command causes the change to occur. Until then, you can set more properties. Here is a more detailed change:

```
globalStyleFormat.textColor = 0x0000FF;
globalStyleFormat.textFont = "Arial";
globalStyleFormat.textSize = 18;
globalStyleFormat.textBold = true;
globalStyleFormat.applyChanges();
```

You can change much more than just the font. The number of style items is too long to list here. You can change the color and style of checks in CheckBoxes, circles in RadioButtons, arrows in ScrollBars, background colors, highlight colors, selection colors, and so on. Check any of the various Flash help systems to see a complete list.

Grouped Customization

Although the `globalStyleFormat` object is used by all the components on the stage, you can create your own style objects that can be used by one or more components that you specify.

You do this by creating an `FStyleFormat` object. When you do this, your new object has the same set of properties as the `globalStyleFormat` object.

For instance, you can create a style object and set its color to magenta like this:

```
myStyle = new FStyleFormat();
myStyle.textColor = 0xFF00FF;
```

Any style elements that are not explicitly set are just not included in the style object. So when you apply this style to a component, that aspect of its style will not change.

To apply the style to a component, use the `addListener` command:

```
myStyle.addListener(radiobutton1);
```

If this seems like an odd use for `addListener`, you are right. But think of it like this: You are telling the component to listen to the style object.

Single Component Customization

You can also set any one of the style attributes for a component directly. However, you can't do it using nice and neat dot syntax like you would expect. Instead, you need to use the `setStyleProperty` command. This takes the style property as a string in the first parameter and the value you want to set it to as the second parameter.

```
checkbox1.setStyleProperty("textColor",0xFF0000);
```

So using these three methods of setting component styles, you can customize your components to your heart's content.

Summary

Components are complex movie clips built in to Flash. They re-create some common user interface elements such as check boxes, radio buttons, pushbuttons, pull-down menus, and scrollbars.

When you add a component to your movie, you need to set various parameters of the component. Most components have an ActionScript callback function that is triggered when the component is used. You can also access the state of a component at any time.

You can change the style of components using ActionScript. You can either change all the components, a group of components, or just one component. Use this capability to customize your components so that they don't look like everyone else's.

Q&A

Q When should I use components instead of my own interface movie clips?

A Use components when time is short or you are not sure that your ActionScript abilities will allow you to get the results you want. However, components will never be as easy to customize as your own movie clips. In addition, components tend to slow down your movies. If reaction time is important, you will want to make your own components that are optimized to perform exactly as you need.

Q Can I use the ScrollBar component on something besides text fields?

A Yes. In fact, the ListBox and ComboBox components use it. If you are an expert ActionScript programmer, you can read the documentation to find out how to access the properties of the ScrollBar so that you can use it in other ways.

Q Can I use the scroll pane to show an image rather than a movie clip?

A Yes and no. The scroll pane shows only movie clips. But that doesn't stop you from making a movie clip that contains an image. In fact, that is how you should work things if you want to build an image browser. Some programs, such as Macromedia Fireworks, allow you to save images as Flash files. These can then be read in using `loadScrollContent`.

Q So how can I customize components even more?

A You don't even need ActionScript for this. But you do need to check out the documentation about how to alter and create component skins.

Workshop

The quiz questions are designed to test your knowledge of the material covered in this hour. The answers to the questions follow.

Quiz

1. Which components can be used to allow the user to make an exclusive choice?
2. Which components can be used to allow the user to make a nonexclusive choice?

3. How do you link a scrollbar to a text field?
4. Which component allows the user to type in a text response?

Quiz Answers

1. Radio buttons, combo boxes, and list boxes. Technically, push buttons also allow you to make a single choice, but they also usually perform some other task.
2. Check boxes and list boxes. List boxes can be set to allow only one item to be selected at a time, or they can be set to allow multiple items to be selected at one time.
3. Drag it onto the text field.
4. You can set the Editable parameter of a combo box to true, which allows the user to type in a response as well as select one from the pull-down menu.

HOUR 22

Controlling Sound with ActionScript

There are two ways to add sound to Flash movies. The first is to lay it into the timeline. This doesn't require ActionScript. Another way is to use ActionScript to trigger sounds stored in the Library.

In this hour, you will:

- Find out how to access sounds with ActionScript
- Learn how to control sound balance
- Use sound properties to monitor a sound
- Build an ActionScript beat box

Playing a Sound

Unfortunately, there is no simple way to play a sound. You will have to import the sound, write several lines of code, and then write several more lines of code to play the sound in anything but the standard way.

Linking and Playing Sounds

The first thing you need to do before playing a sound with ActionScript is to link it. Import the sound into the Library, select Linkage from the Library panel's menu, and set the sound to export with the movie. You can also assign a different linkage name to the sound, but Flash starts you off with the same name as the Library element, which is the same name as the file.

If you are working with a movie that has a lot of sound, it is a good idea to set the default sound compression to Raw in the Publish Settings. When you test your movie, Flash will not take the time to compress the sound. This way, you can test your movie as quickly as possible. Then, change the default sound compression setting to what you really want before publishing a copy for the Web.

For instance, if you import the file mysound.wav, it will appear in the Library as `mysound.wav`. When you set its Linkage properties so that it exports with the file, it will be assigned the linkage name `mysound.wav`, but you can change that to anything you want. It is this linkage name that you will use to refer to the sound in your code.

To play a sound, you have to perform at least three steps. The first step is to create a new sound object:

```
mySound = new Sound();
```

Then, you need to attach the sound in the Library to this sound object:

```
mySound.attachSound("mysound.wav");
```

Finally, you have to tell the sound object to play the sound:

```
mySound.start();
```

Here is a simple button handler that plays a sound from the Library:

```
on (release) {
    mySound = new Sound();
    mySound.attachSound("poof.wav");
    mySound.start();
}
```

You can find this simple example in the movie 22playsound.fla. You can find a slightly more sophisticated approach in the movie 22playsoundfunction.fla. In this movie, a function called `playSound` is placed in the main timeline. This function includes all the code you need to play a simple sound.

```
function playSound(soundName,balance) {
    var mySound = new Sound();
    mySound.attachSound(soundName);
    mySound.start();
}
```

By using this function, you can simplify your ActionScript so that you can play a sound with only one line. Here is a button script that uses this function:

```
on (release) {
    playSound("poof.wav");
}
```

The `start` Command

The `start` command in the previous example can be used in a few different ways. You can add up to two additional parameters to it to alter the way the sound plays.

The first parameter you can add is an offset. This starts the sound somewhere in the middle, rather than at the beginning. For instance, this line starts the sound off 1000 milliseconds, or 1 second, into the sound:

```
mySound.start(1000);
```

The second parameter the `start` command can take is the number of loops. For instance, if you want to start the sound off at 1 second and loop it three times, you would do this:

```
mySound.start(1000,3);
```

If you want to start the sound at the beginning and loop it three times, just use 0 as the offset:

```
mySound.start(0,3);
```

The companion command to `start` is `stop`. If you are playing a long sound, you can issue a `stop` command at any time to halt the sound in its tracks. You must supply the sound name again as a parameter. Otherwise, the `stop` command stops all sounds playing.

```
mySound.stop("poof.wav");
```

Adjusting Volume

You can alter a sound both before and during playback with a variety of commands. All these commands somehow alter the volume of the sound, in both speakers together or separately.

The `setVolume` command is the simplest of these adjustments. By setting the volume to a number from 0 to 100, you can raise, lower, or silence a sound:

```
mySound.setVolume(50);
```

The example movie 22playsoundvolume.fla features a Play button and four different volume buttons. The top one sets the volume to 0, the next one to 10, the next to 50, and the bottom button to 100. The Play button plays a sound 100 times so that you can have the chance to adjust the volume while it plays.

You can click a button during playback to adjust the volume. Note that adjusting the volume of a specific sound does not affect the volumes of other sounds being played at the same time. This means that you can have separate controls for different sounds—such as background music and instance sounds.

Sound Properties

Sound objects have two properties that you should know about. The first is `duration`. This is the how long the sound is, in milliseconds.

The sibling property to this is `position`. This is the location of the current bit of sound being played, in milliseconds.

For instance, if a sound has a `duration` of 3000, it is 3 seconds long. If the `position` of the sound is 1500, the sound is right in the middle of being played.

The example movie 22tracksound.fla demonstrates using `position` and `duration` to show the playback of a sound visually.

After starting a sound, a movie clip script positions a movie clip named mark at a position along the width of a movie clip named bar.

```
onClipEvent(enterFrame) {
    // how far along is the sound (0.0 to 1.0)
    percentPlayed = thisSound.position/thisSound.duration;

    // how wide is the bar
    barWidth = _root.bar._width;

    // set the mark
    _root.mark._x = _root.bar._x + barWidth*percentPlayed;
}
```

When a Sound Ends

You can use the `duration` and `position` of a sound to determine when a sound ends. They will be equal to each other. However, if a sound loops, the `duration` and `position` of a sound will be equal to each other for a moment at the end of each playback of the sound.

A better way to determine the end of a sound is to use the `onSoundComplete` listener.

This is a function triggered when the sound is finished playing.

```
mySound = new Sound();
mySound.attachSound("mySound.aif");
mySound.onSoundComplete = function () {
    trace("sound done!");
}
mySound.start();
```

Setting the Balance

You can also direct the sound more to one speaker than the other with the `setPan` command. This is similar to the balance control on a stereo.

You can set the pan of a sound to a value from -100 to 100. If you set it to -100, all sound comes from the left speaker. Setting it to 100 means that all sound comes from the right speaker.

```
mySound.pan(-100);
```

The movie 22monopan.fla has a single-channel (mono) sound in it. When you click the button on the left, the sound plays completely from the left speaker. When you click the button on the right, the sound plays completely from the right speaker.

This is done by setting to the pan to -100 or 100 before playing the sound.

Task: Panning Sound

You can also adjust the pan of a sound while the sound is playing. You can use this to make sounds appear to come from one side and travel to the other.

1. Create a new movie.
2. Import the sound 22airplane.wav from the CD-ROM.
3. Set the sound's Linkage properties so that it exports with the movie and its linkage name is **22airplane.wav**.
4. Create a simple shape and convert it to a movie clip. Name it **actions**.
5. The `load` handler attached to this movie clip starts the sound playing. It sets the pan to -100 so that the sound comes only from one side.

```
onClipEvent(load) {
    // load sound
    thisSound = new Sound();
    thisSound.attachSound("22airplane.wav");

    // set initial pan
    thisSound.setPan(-100);
```

```
    // play three times
    thisSound.start();
}
```

6. The `enterFrame` handler looks at the `position` and `duration` properties of the sound object. These are both measured in milliseconds. By dividing these by each other and multiplying by 200, you get a value from 0 to 200. Subtract 100 to get a value from -100 to 100. Then, set the pan to this value:

   ```
   onClipEvent(enterFrame) {
       // get value from -100 to 100 based on position
       pan = 200*thisSound.position/thisSound.duration - 100;

       // set pan
       thisSound.setPan(pan);
   }
   ```

   The result is that the sound starts on one side, coming completely out of one speaker. Then the sound travels to the other side as `setPan` is used to set the pan to values between -100 and 100. The sound should end with a pan of 100.

Try the movie 22airplane.fla to see this in action.

Sound Transforms

Although `setVolume` and `setBalance` seem to provide a lot of control over a sound, you can go even further. By creating sound transform objects, you can precisely control stereo sounds—which sound channel comes out of which speaker.

In a typical sound played in a typical way, the left channel's sound comes out of the left speaker, and the right channel's sound comes out of the right speaker.

However, you can change this by creating a sound transform object and applying it to the sound object with a `setTransform` command.

A sound transform object is actually just a plain variable object. But it needs to have four specific properties. Here is an example:

```
mySoundTransform = {ll: 75, rr: 25, rl: 25, lr: 75};
```

The four properties have two characters in each of their names. The first character represents the speaker. The second character represents the channel. So `ll` is the property that determines how much of the left channel comes out of the left speaker. `rl` is how much of the left channel comes out of the right speaker.

You obviously need a stereo sound to use a sound transform normally. However, if you use Flash's default compression settings, your stereo sound will be compressed into a mono sound when you test or publish the movie.

Using sound transforms, you can switch which channel comes out of which speaker. All you need to do is put 100 percent of the left channel out of the right speaker and 100 percent of the right channel out of the left speaker. Here is a button that does this:

```
on (release) {
    var mySound = new Sound();
    mySound.attachSound(soundName);
    var mySoundTransform = new Object();
    mySoundTransform = {ll: 0, rr: 0, lr: 100, rl: 100};
    mySound.setTransform(mySoundTransform);
    mySound.start();
}
```

The example movie 22steropan.fla includes several demonstration buttons. It also includes a sound where the left and right channels play completely separate sounds. The left channel features a robin singing away, whereas the right features a cardinal.

If you are using a sound transform with a mono sound, note that the entire sound is stored in the left channel. So only `ll` and `rl` properties will have any effect.

You can use one of the top three buttons to play the sound normally, but with the pan set to either the left, middle, or right. The left and right buttons allow you to hear only one channel at a time.

Then there are two buttons below that use sound transforms to play only one channel at a time, but in the opposite speakers.

Task: Beat Box

Figure 22.1 shows a simple beat box application. To focus on the sound portion of the ActionScript, I have used the CheckBox and PushButton components.

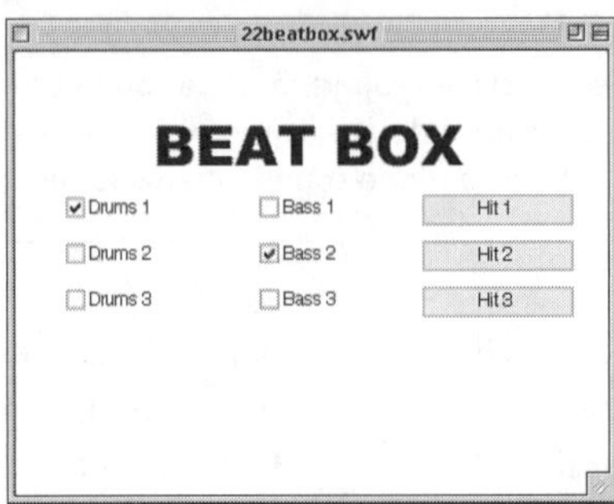

FIGURE 22.1
A simple beat box application that allows the user to play with music.

1. Open the movie 22beatboxnoscripts.fla.
2. There are three columns of buttons. The first column is for the drum sounds. Select the first drum button and see that its Click Handler is set to `buttonSound`. In fact, each CheckBox and PushButton component has the Click Handler `buttonSound`.
3. Where they differ, however, is their names. The drum check boxes are named **drumSwitch1**, **drumSwitch2**, and **drumSwitch3**. The three bass buttons are named **bassSwitch1**, **bassSwitch2**, and **bassSwitch3**. The three push buttons are named **hitSwitch1**, **hitSwitch2**, and **hitSwitch3**.
4. This entire movie works with only two functions. The first is an advanced version of the `playSound` function from earlier in the hour.

   It uses four parameters. The first is a true or false value that determines whether the sound is supposed to start or stop. The second is the name of the variable to use as the sound object. The third is the name of the sound from the Library. The last parameter is whether the sound is supposed to loop.

```
function playSound(startOrStop,varName,soundName,loop) {
    if (startOrStop) {
        this[varName] = new Sound();
        this[varName].attachSound(soundName);
        if (loop) {
            this[varName].start(0,9999);
        } else {
            this[varName].start(0,1);
        }
    } else {
        this[varName].stop(soundName);
    }
}
```

5. Each of the nine components in the movie calls `soundButton`. This calls `playSound` in one of nine different ways, depending on the component clicked. It uses `getValue()` in many cases to determine whether the check box has been clicked on or off.

```
function soundButton(button) {
    if (button == bassSwitch1) {
        playSound(button.getValue(),"bassSound1","bassLoop1",true);
    } else if (button == bassSwitch2) {
        playSound(button.getValue(),"bassSound2","bassLoop2",true);
    } else if (button == bassSwitch3) {
        playSound(button.getValue(),"bassSound3","bassLoop3",true);
    } else if (button == hitSwitch1) {
        playSound(true,"hitSound1","hit1",false);
    } else if (button == hitSwitch2) {
        playSound(true,"hitSound2","hit2",false);
    } else if (button == hitSwitch3) {
        playSound(true,"hitSound3","hit3",false);
    } else if (button == drumSwitch1) {
        playSound(button.getValue(),"drumSound1","drumLoop1",true);
    } else if (button == drumSwitch2) {
        playSound(button.getValue(),"drumSound2","drumLoop2",true);
    } else if (button == drumSwitch3) {
        playSound(button.getValue(),"drumSound3","drumLoop3",true);
    }
}
```

Try the sample movie. You can see the finished product as 22beatbox.fla.

Summary

You can use ActionScript to trigger sounds after their Linkage properties have been set so that they will export with the movie. You need to refer to the sound by its name specified in its Linkage properties.

To play a sound, you must first create a sound object. Then you must use `attachSound` to associate the sound with the sound object. Then you need to use the `start` command.

You can adjust the volume of a sound with the `setVolume` command. You can adjust the stereo balance of a sound with the `setPan` command.

You can create more complex variations of your sound by creating a sound transform object. This allows you to modify how much sound from each stereo channel goes to each speaker.

You can track the progress of a sound using the `position` property of the sound object. The total length of a sound can be determined with the `duration` property. This can be used to determine when a sound is finished playing, or you can use an `onSoundComplete` function.

Q&A

Q Can you play more than one sound at the same time?

A Yes. However, you will have to use different sound object variables for each sound.

Q Does it matter to ActionScript what sort of sound compression you use for sounds?

A Only if you compress the sound with the Convert Stereo to Mono option turned on, and then expect there to be two separate channels to be used by a sound transform. Otherwise, all other ActionScript works the same.

Workshop

The quiz questions are designed to test your knowledge of the material covered in this hour. The answers to the questions follow.

Quiz

1. What do you need to do to a sound in the Library to allow ActionScript to be able to access it?
2. How do you get a sound to loop infinitely?
3. What are two ways to determine whether a sound is finished?
4. What sound transform would silence the left channel, but play the right channel at half volume in both speakers?

Quiz Answers

1. You need to set its Linkage properties to export with the movie and give it a linkage name.
2. You can't. Instead, set it to loop a large number of times, like 9999.
3. If the sound is not looping, `position` equals `duration`. However, if the sound loops, the only way to tell is to make an `onSoundComplete` function.
4. You would use the transform {ll: 0, lr: 50, rr: 50, rl: 0}.

HOUR 23

Managing Movie Streaming

Flash movies come in all sizes. There are little ones that load in a few seconds, medium-sized ones that keep the user waiting for a few more seconds, and huge ones that seem to take forever to load. If you are building one of these large movies, you can use some ActionScript to help keep the user informed, or perhaps entertained, while he waits.

In this hour, you will:

- Find out how to monitor the movie as it loads
- Build a simple loading screen
- Build a complex loading screen
- Learn how to load a new movie in Flash
- Load in new movie clips, images, and sounds as external media

Monitoring Loading

All Flash movies stream. This means that the first frame of a Flash movie starts playing as soon as it is ready, no matter how far off the last frame is from loading.

You may not want this to happen. If your entire movie is a quick animation, you may not want to start until the entire movie has been downloaded from the Web and is waiting in the user's browser cache to be played.

There are several ways to force the movie to wait for loading to complete. The most common way is to have a *loader frame*. This is the first frame of the movie. It watches certain properties of the movie to determine when the movie is finished loading.

To find out how many frames of a movie have been loaded, you can use the `_framesLoaded` property of the movie. You can compare this to the `_totalFrames` property to see how far along the loading is.

You can use this in some simple cases. For instance, you can place a `stop()` on the first frame of your movie. There can be a button that allows the user to continue. When the user clicks the button, you can use a script like this to determine what to do next:

```
on (release) {
    if (_root._framesLoaded == _root._framesTotal) {
        play();
    } else {
        textDisplay = "Wait a few seconds and press again.";
    }
}
```

If the entire movie is not ready, the text field linked to the variable *`textDisplay`* informs the user of the delay.

You could also use this technique on parts of a long movie. For instance, this button can be on frame 50 and let the user continue only if the next 50 frames are ready. A script attached to a small movie clip can monitor the status and move the movie forward automatically when the time is right.

```
onClipEvent(load) {
    _root.textDisplay = "Waiting for the next sequence to load.";
    _root.stop();
}

onClipEvent(enterFrame) {
    if (_root._framesLoaded >= 100) {
        _root.play();
    }
}
```

This is the heart of a basic loader script. However, there are more accurate ways to monitor loading than by frames. You can use the `getBytesLoaded` and `getBytesTotal` functions to find out the actual size of the file and how much has been loaded.

Here is a script that sits on a movie clip in the first frame of a movie. The first frame should also have a `stop()` command on it.

```
onClipEvent(enterFrame) {
    if (_root.getBytesLoaded() == _root.getBytesTotal()) {
        _root.play();
    }
}
```


Because this script runs once per frame, it is constantly checking the two functions against each other. The statement becomes true the moment the movie is completely loaded. Then the `play` command moves the movie forward.

Task: Simple Loader

Here is how to build a simple loader frame that waits for the entire movie to load before continuing past frame 1:

1. Start with a blank movie.
2. Place a blank key frame at frame 1.

Start a new key frame at frame 2. Play some content starting at frame 2 and continuing on. It should be at least 100K worth of content. A good way to get fast content is to import a video.

4. Back at frame 1, we want to have the movie wait until the entire movie has been loaded before continuing to frame 2. Start by placing a `stop()` command on the frame.
5. Create a simple shape, convert it to a movie clip, and move it off the screen. Assign this script to it:

```
onClipEvent(enterFrame) {
    bytesLoaded = _root.getBytesLoaded();
    bytesTotal = _root.getBytesTotal()
    percentLoaded = Math.round(100*bytesLoaded/bytesTotal);
    _root.displayText = "Loading: "+percentLoaded+"%";
    if (bytesLoaded == bytesTotal) {
        _root.play();
    }
}
```

The script looks at `getBytesLoaded` to see whether the movie has finished loading; it uses this to also calculate the percent of the movie loaded. It places this number into the variable *`displayText`* at the root level.

6. Create a dynamic text field and link it to the variable *`displayText`*.
7. It will be difficult to test this movie on your hard drive because it will load too quickly. Instead, Publish it, complete with a Web page. Upload it to a test directory on your Web site.
8. Go to the Web page with your browser. You should see its loading progress reported in the text field. When it reaches 100 percent, the movie should automatically continue.

You can compare your movie with 23simpleloader.fla.

Task: Complex Loader

Although the simple loader may be all that you need, most large movies have something more elegant on the front end. Usually, there is a progress bar, as shown in Figure 23.1.

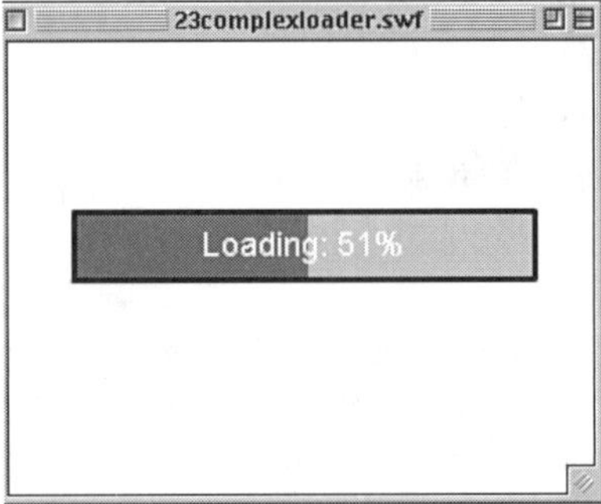

FIGURE 23.1
A progress bar, halfway through a load.

1. Start a new movie.
2. Draw a wide rectangle, complete with a border.
3. Select the entire rectangle and turn it into a movie clip by choosing Insert, Convert to Movie Clip.
4. Double-click on this new movie clip to edit it.
5. Separate the rectangle's fill and border into two separate layers.
6. Copy the rectangle fill and create a new layer to paste it into. This layer should have the border layer in front of it and the original rectangle behind it.

7. Select the new rectangle and fill it a darker color. It should sit right on top of the lighter original rectangle.
8. Now turn the darker rectangle into a movie clip by choosing Insert, Convert to Movie Clip. Give it any Library name you want, but give it the instance name **bar** in the Properties panel.
9. Double-click on the dark rectangle movie clip to edit it. You'll need to reposition the rectangle so that the upper-left corner of the rectangle is at the movie clip's registration point (see Figure 23.2).

FIGURE 23.2
The rectangle's upper-left corner is at the registration point.

10. Back in the main movie clip, create a fourth layer. Put a dynamic text field there. Link it to the variable *displayText*. Make it a nice big font, colored white.
11. Go all the way back to the main timeline. Now we need to attach a script to the movie clip. It starts by setting up the *bytesLoaded* and *bytesTotal* variables.

```
onClipEvent(load) {
    // initialize variables
    bytesLoaded = 0;
    bytesTotal = _root.getBytesTotal();
}
```

12. The `enterFrame` handler does most of the work. It monitors *bytesLoaded* and *bytesTotal* every frame. The variable *percentLoaded* is a value from 0 to 100. It is used in the text field but is also used to change the `_xscale` of the bar. Because the registration point is at the left, the left side of the bar stays in the same place, but the right side shrinks or grows according to `_xscale`.

    When the *bytesLoaded* equals *bytesTotal*, the display text is changed to a different message. The `nextFrame` command moves the movie forward to the next frame.

```
onClipEvent(enterFrame) {
    // if there is more to load
    if (bytesLoaded < bytesTotal) {

        // get current amount loaded
        bytesLoaded = _root.getBytesLoaded();

        // calculate percentage
        percentLoaded = Math.round(100*bytesLoaded/bytesTotal);
```

```
            // if there is still more
            if (bytesLoaded < bytesTotal) {

                // display text
                displayText = "Loading: "+percentLoaded+"%";

                // set scale of bar
                barFill._xscale = percentLoaded;

            // no more left
            } else {

                // display complete
                displayText = "Loading Complete.";

                // fill out bar
                barFill._xscale = 100;

                // go to next frame
                _root.nextFrame();
            }
        }
    }
```

13. The main timeline should be broken into three layers. The first layer has the loader bar movie clip that we have built. This stretches across the first two frames.
14. Another layer has two separate key frames in frames 1 and 2. In frame 1 is a `stop()` command, but no other elements.
15. The second frame of this new layer has a button. You can see it in Figure 23.3. The user clicks the simple button script to continue with the rest of the movie.

```
on (release) {
    play();
}
```

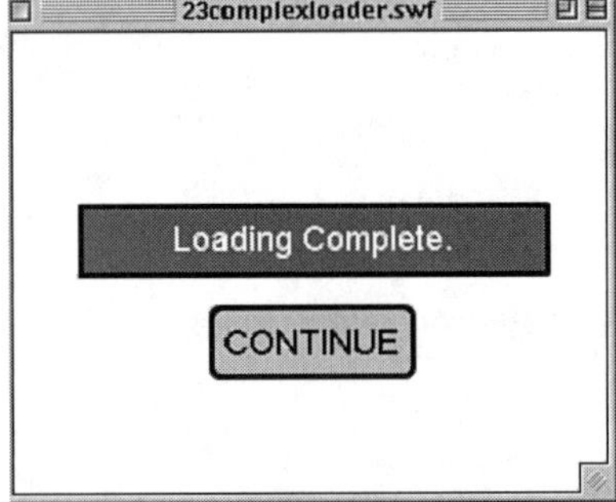

FIGURE 23.3
The second frame of our loading movie allows the user to control when the rest of the movie begins.

16. The third layer of the movie contains the video—the large media piece that causes this movie to need a loading frame in the first place.

Check the movie 23complexloader.fla to see it in action.

Loading External Media

An alternative to streaming one large movie is to create a movie that isn't full of media but loads that media from external files as it is needed. You can build a large presentation that is spread out over several files.

Replacing the Current Movie

The simplest way to do this is to divide the movie into several parts. When one movie ends, you can go to another. All you need to do is issue the `loadMovie` command.

For instance, you can have a frame at the end of a long animation where the movie stops. When the user is ready, he can click a button to go to the next animation, which is in another movie:

```
on (release) {
    loadMovie("animation2.swf");
}
```

Or, you could give the user a choice. At the end of a movie there could be two buttons. The user chooses which animation to see next. In a situation where the user makes a choice like this, keeping content in separate movies is a great choice. After all, the user will probably never see the other content, so why require her to load it over the Internet?

Check out the sample movie 23movie1.fla. When you test it, there are buttons that take you to one of two separate movies. Then the user can go back to the original movie. This is a good but simple example of how you can divide your presentation over several files rather than just one.

Loading a Movie Clip

The `loadMovie` command can also be used to load a movie into a movie clip. Instead of changing movies completely, you can just swap the content in a movie clip.

All you need to do is specify the movie clip that is to be replaced by the external file. For instance, to replace `myMovieClip` with the file othermovie.swf, just do this:

```
myMovieClip.loadMovie("othermovie.swf");
```

When using `loadMovie`, you can use the `getBytesTotal` and `getBytesLoaded` functions to check the progress of the load. This means that you can report the progress to the user with text or even a progress bar like the one used earlier in this hour.

If you want to preload a movie clip to have it ready before the user even gets to a place where it is needed, you can set up the external movie so that nothing is on the first frame but a `stop()` command. Then load the movie into a blank movie clip that is off the stage. When it completes, the movie just sits there on its blank first frame.

However, the movie file will be sitting in the user's browser cache. Now when it comes time to really use the movie clip, do the `loadMovie` command again. The movie will be there quickly because the file has already been downloaded. Then issue a `gotoAndPlay(2)` command to get it past that first frame.

Loading a JPEG

Flash MX has an new capability that developers have been begging Macromedia for since they bought Flash; it can import an external JPEG file.

The way you do this is simple. Just use the a `loadMovie` command like you are planning to replace a movie clip with an external Flash movie. However, give the location of a JPEG file instead:

```
myMovieClip.loadMovie("picture.jpg");
```

The movie clip is now replaced by a movie clip that holds that bitmap image. Check out the movie 23loadjpeg.fla for an example.

Loading a Sound

There are also two ways to play a sound from an external file. They both use the sound object and the `loadSound` command. The sound file needs to be in the popular MP3 format.

Here is an example of the first method, which plays an event sound. This means that the entire sound is loaded into memory first and then played if a `start` command is issued.

```
on (release) {
    mySound = new sound();
    mySound.loadSound("mysound.mp3",false);
    mySound.start();
}
```

Flash remembers that the `start` command was issued, even though the sound has just begun to download. When the sound is finished downloading, it plays immediately.

The second method uses a `true` in the second parameter. This tells Flash to stream the sound in. As soon as some of the sound has been loaded, the sound starts playing. The sound continues as the rest is loaded. If the user's connection is a good one, the user will hear the entire sound as it loads.

```
on (release) {
    mySound = new sound();
    mySound.loadSound("mysound.mp3",true);
}
```


Notice that you don't need the `start` command with a streaming sound. However, you do need to pay careful attention to how you make the MP3 file. For instance, if you use the 128Kbps or 160Kbps setting that is popular for playing MP3 music, it will be too large of a file to stream over the Internet, especially if the user has a modem. 32Kbps or less will give the stream a chance to work successfully.

Summary

Streaming is a great way to ease the user into a large Flash movie. You can use ActionScript to track the loading process. As a movie streams, you can hold the movie on the first frame and then let it continue when the entire movie has loaded.

You can also report to the user the progress of the loading. You can give them straight text feedback, or something a little more visual like a progress bar.

You can also divide your movie into several files and use `loadMovie` to jump from file to file as the user needs the content.

External files can be loaded into your movie using various methods. You can load Flash movies as movie clips. You can load external JPEG files and MP3 sounds too.

Q&A

Q You can load movies into movie clips, but can you unload them too?

A Yes. The `unloadMovie` command removes a loaded movie from a movie clip instance.

Q Can I report the file size of a streaming movie to a user in K?

A A *K* is a kilobyte, which represents 1,024 bytes. So you can use `getBytesTotal` and `getBytesLoaded` to get the number of bytes and then divide that by 1,024 to determine the amount of K that will be loaded. A *meg*, or megabyte, is 1,024K, or 1,048,576 bytes.

Workshop

The quiz questions are designed to test your knowledge of the material covered in this hour. The answers to the questions follow.

Quiz

1. How much of a Flash movie normally needs to load before it starts?
2. What are two ways to determine whether a movie is completely loaded?
3. What file formats must you use for sounds and images to load them dynamically?
4. Using `getBytesTotal` and `getBytesLoaded`, how do you determine the percentage of the movie loaded?

Quiz Answers

1. Only the media for the first frame is needed for the first frame to be displayed and the movie to begin. You'll need to stop the movie there if you want to wait for more before continuing.
2. One way is when the `getBytesLoaded` equals the `getBytesTotal` function. Another method is to check the `_frameLoaded` property and compare it to the `_totalFrames` property.
3. Sounds need to be MP3 files, and images need to be JPEG files. However, another way to do it is that you can load either if it is in an external movie file.
4. If you divide `getBytesTotal` by `getBytesLoaded`, you will get a value from 0.0 to 1.0. If you want to display a percentage, you need to multiply this number by 100. You may also want to use `Math.round()` to convert this to an integer instead of a long floating point number.

HOUR 24

Drawing with ActionScript

A new feature in Flash MX is the capability for ActionScript to draw lines, curves, and fills; create new, empty movie clips; and create new text fields. With this capability, you can start with an empty movie and populate it with elements.

In this hour, you will:

- Learn how to draw lines and curves
- Learn how to draw filled areas
- Let the user draw with the mouse
- Place drawn items into new movie clips
- Create new text fields

Drawing Lines

Flash MX contains a simple set of drawing commands that allow you to create a wide variety of graphics from scratch. You can draw straight lines, curves, and even filled areas.

Drawing Straight Lines

Drawing a line with ActionScript is easy. First, you need to define the line style. The `lineStyle` command takes three parameters: the line thickness, color, and alpha. The color is expressed as an ActionScript hexadecimal number. So 0x000000 is black, 0xFFFFFF is white, and so on. The alpha parameter determines a line's transparency. A value of 100 makes an opaque line, whereas a value of 50 makes a line that is faded 50 percent, and graphics behind it can be seen.

```
lineStyle(3,0x000000,100);
```

If you use the line size of 0, you get a *hairline*. A hairline is a thin line that remains 1 pixel wide even if the line is scaled up. This is in contrast to a 1-pixel line that gets thicker as the scale of the movie increases.

After you have set the line style, you use `lineTo` and `moveTo` to draw. Imagine an invisible pen on the screen. You can direct its tip to move around on the screen. As it moves, you can tell it to draw on the screen, or just move without drawing.

The `moveTo` command moves the tip of the drawing pen to a location on the screen. The `lineTo` command moves the pen from its current location to another location and leaves a trail. Here is some code that draws a line from 275,200 to 300,225:

```
moveTo(275,200);
lineTo(300,225);
```

If you do not use a `moveTo` command before you use a `lineTo` command, the first line will be drawn from point 0,0 to the point specified in the `lineTo` command.

Here is a short program that draws 500 lines from random points on the stage. You can see its result in Figure 24.1.

```
// set line style
lineStyle(2,0x000000,100);

// draw 500 lines
for(var i=0;i<500;i++) {

    // pick random start point
    x1 = Math.random()*550;
```

```
    y1 = Math.random()*400;

    // pick random end point
    x2 = Math.random()*550;
    y2 = Math.random()*400;

    // move to start point
    moveTo(x1,y1);

    // draw to end point
    lineTo(x2,y2);
}
```

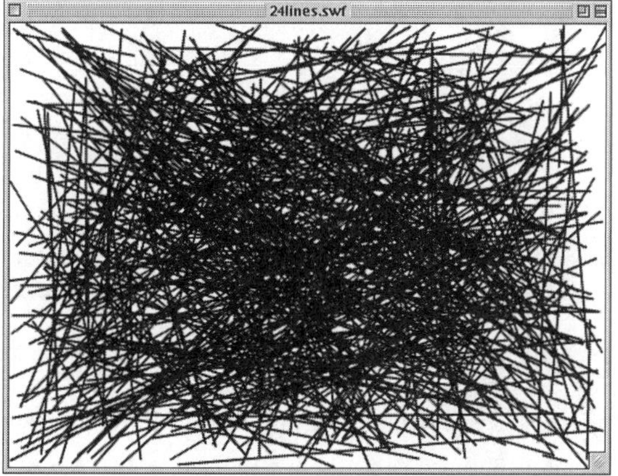

FIGURE 24.1
These random lines were created by ActionScript.

Check out the example movie 24lines.fla. You can play with the line size, color, and alpha. When you set the alpha to 50, it gives the impression that the lines are laying on top of and under each other. Check out 24coloredlines.fla to see a variation where the lines all draw as different colors.

Here is a simple script that draws a crossed pattern on the screen. It creates diagonal lines in each direction all the way across the screen.

```
// set line style
lineStyle(2,0x999999,100);

for(var x=-400;x<550;x+=10) {
    // draw diagonal strip from left to right
    moveTo(x,0);
    lineTo(x+400,400);

    // draw opposite strip
    moveTo(550-x,0);
    lineTo(550-x-400,400);
}
```

Figure 24.2 shows the results of this script. One interesting note is that the movie 24patterns.fla takes up only 186 bytes as an .swf file. However, if you were to create the lines by hand using Flash's drawing tools and make a movie with those lines, the file would be 4,179 bytes. So you can actually save file space by drawing patterns with ActionScript rather than including them in the Flash movie as normal graphics.

FIGURE 24.2
This pattern was created with ActionScript.

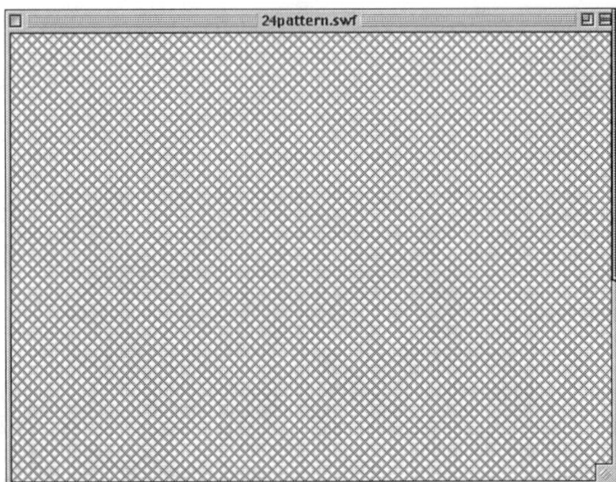

Drawing Curves

Whereas drawing lines is easy and straightforward, drawing curves is more of an art than a science. In addition to giving the destination position where the curved line draws to, you also give a control point. This control point directs the curve of the line.

For instance, the following code draws a curve from 150,200 to 400,200. The second pair of numbers in the `curveTo` command gives the destination. The first pair is the control point. In this case, the control point is at 275,275, which is a little below the center of the line. This causes the line to curve down toward the control point.

```
lineStyle(3,0x000000,100);
moveTo(150,200);
curveTo(275,275,400,200);
```

Figure 24.3 shows the result. There are horizontal grid lines at 200 and 275, and vertical grid lines at 150, 275, and 400. You can see that the line starts at 150,200 and ends at 400,200. In between, it curves out to 275,275 but never reaches that point. The example movie 24curve.fla includes the grid lines that are drawn with `lineTo` commands.

Although you can control exactly where the curve starts and ends, you only have vague control over where the curve goes in between. However, by playing around with different values, you can get close to drawing what you want.

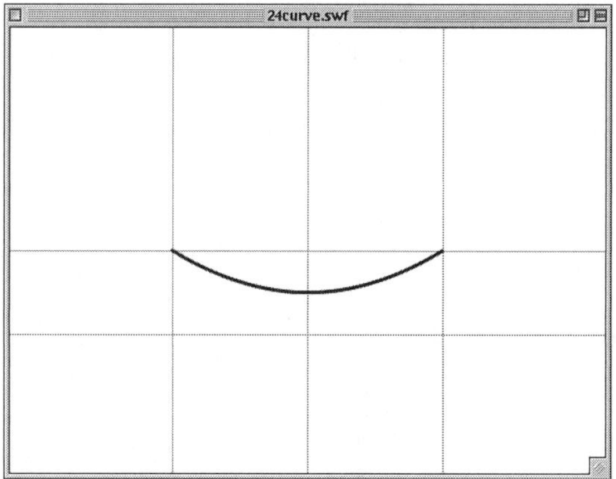

FIGURE 24.3
Ever see ActionScript smile at you?

This code creates a square shape. The lines are drawn with the `curveTo` command, but the control points are placed right between the points so that the lines have no curve to them at all.

```
lineStyle( 1, 0x0000FF, 100 );
moveTo(200,200);
curveTo(250,200,300,200);
curveTo(300,250,300,300);
curveTo(250,300,200,300);
curveTo(200,250,200,200);
```

In Figure 24.4, you can see that the lines have no curve. The larger dots point out where the control points are located.

FIGURE 24.4
These curves form a square with straight sides.

Now, if we move the control points farther away from each side, we can bulge out the sides of the square to make it resemble a circle:

```
var bend = 42;
moveTo(200,200);
curveTo(250,200-bend,300,200);
curveTo(300+bend,250,300,300);
curveTo(250,300+bend,200,300);
curveTo(200-bend,250,200,200);
```

I used the variable *bend* so that the control point would be moved away from each side by the same amount. The top of the square's control point is moved up, the left side's control point is moved to the left, and so on. I can adjust how far the control point is from the original side by just changing the value of *bend* in one place. Doing so, I was able to experiment and determine that 42 is the value that made it look best. Figure 24.5 shows this version of the drawing, complete with marks for the four control points.

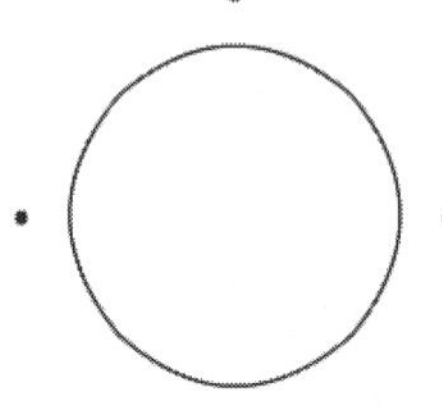

FIGURE 24.5
This circle was drawn with only four curves. The dots show the curve's control points.

The sample movie 24curvedcircle.fla contains both examples from Figures 24.4 and 24.5.

> Although drawing a circle is a great way to start playing with the `curveTo` command, the `curveTo` command is not the best way to draw a circle. Instead, you can get better results by drawing short lines from points along the circumference of a circle using the trigonometry from Hour 11, "Working with Numbers." You can see an example in the file 24bettercircle.fla.

Drawing Filled Areas

To draw a filled area, first you have to plan to draw a series of lines or curves that form a closed shape. Then all you need to do is issue a `beginFill` command before you start drawing and an `endFill` command when you are finished.

The `beginFill` command takes two parameters: the color of the fill and the alpha of the fill. In this example, a box is made out of a 3-pixel thick black line. The fill is red.

```
lineStyle( 3, 0x000000, 100 );
beginFill( 0xFF0000 );
moveTo(175,100);
lineTo(375,100);
lineTo(375,300);
lineTo(175,300);
lineTo(175,100);
endFill();
```

When an area is crossed by the line twice, it remains unfilled instead of being filled. This can create interesting gaps in your filled area. For instance, the following code draws a star with five points. The area at the center of the star remains unfilled. Look at Figure 24.6 to see the result.

```
lineStyle(3,0x000000,100 );
beginFill(0xFF0000);
moveTo(250,50);
lineTo(308,230);
lineTo(155,120);
lineTo(345,120);
lineTo(192,230);
lineTo(250,50);
endFill();
```

FIGURE 24.6
The area double-crossed by the lines is not filled.

There is a better way to make a star. The example movie 24betterstar.fla not only makes stars based on trigonometry but also allows you to set the number of points in the star at the start of the script. Create 5-, 7-, 11-, or 123-pointed stars.

Task: Allowing the User to Draw

You can use the `moveTo` and `lineTo` commands to allow the user to draw on the stage. All you need to do is track the mouse and draw lines from the previous location of the mouse to the current location.

1. Start a new movie.
2. Create a simple shape and convert it to a movie clip by choosing Insert, Convert To Movie Clip. Move this movie clip off the stage.
3. Attach a script to this movie clip. The script starts with a `load` handler that sets the line style:

```
onClipEvent (load) {
    // set line style
    _root.lineStyle(0, 0x000000, 100);
}
```

4. When the user presses the mouse button down at any point in the movie, drawing should begin. A variable *draw* will be set to true. The current location of the mouse will be stored in *startX* and *startY*. The drawing point will be moved to this location with moveTo.

```
onClipEvent(mouseDown) {
    // ok to draw
    draw = true;

    // find start location and move there
    startX = _root._xmouse;
    startY = _root._ymouse;
    _root.moveTo(startX,startY);
}
```

5. When the user lifts up on the mouse button, the *draw* variable will be set to false so that no more drawing takes place.

```
onClipEvent(mouseUp) {
    // don't draw anymore
    draw = false;
}
```

6. The drawing is done by the enterFrame handler. It draws only when the *draw* variable is true.

   The new location of the mouse is placed in *newX* and *newY*. If this is different from *startX* and *startY*, the mouse has moved. In that case, a line is drawn between the two points. The values of *newX* and *newY* are placed in *startX* and *startY* for the next time.

```
onClipEvent (enterFrame) {
    if (draw) {

        // get current location
        newX = _root._xmouse;
        newY = _root._ymouse;

        // see if location has changed
        if ((newX != startX) or (newY != startY)) {

            // draw line to new location
            _root.lineTo(newX,newY);

            // reset location for new time
            startX = newX;
            startY = newY;
        }
    }
}
```

Try your movie or the example movie 24draw.fla. Notice how little there is to this movie before it runs.

Creating New Movie Clips

So far, all the drawing we have done has been on the background of the stage. Everything will appear behind movie clips. All this drawing is also static; it can't be moved or altered, just drawn over.

You don't have to draw onto the stage, however. You can draw into any movie clip. Just use the same drawing commands but with references to the movie clip. For instance:

```
myMoveClip.lineStyle(0,0x000000,100);
myMoveClip.moveTo(100,100);
myMovieClip.lineTo(200,200);
```


You can also use terms such as `_root`, `_parent`, and `this` to define where the line gets drawn. You need to set the `lineStyle` in that movie clip first. You can also place your code on a movie clip, or in a frame inside that movie clip. The `this` prefix or just using the commands by themselves then refers to that movie clip.

Flash MX also lets you create blank movie clips to store your drawings. You can do this with the `createEmptyMovieClip` command. It takes two parameters: the name of the new movie clip and its level. Both should be unique. For instance, to create an empty movie clip and then draw a line in it, you can do something like this:

```
this.createEmptyMovieClip("myMovieClip",1);
myMoveClip.lineStyle(0,0x000000,100);
myMoveClip.moveTo(100,100);
myMovieClip.lineTo(200,200);
```

You can now move that movie clip around by changing its _x and _y properties. You can rotate it, scale it, change its alpha, and do anything that you would normally do with a movie clip. The drawing inside it follows along as if it were created while you were authoring the movie in Flash.

The `createEmptyMovieClip` command can be used for much more than just drawing. You can use `attachMovie` or `duplicateMovieClip` to add other elements inside the new movie clip. Later in this hour, you will see how to create new text fields—these can also be added to the new movie clip.

Task: Dynamic Snowflakes

A simple example would be to create 50 snowflakes with drawing commands. Each snowflake is kept inside its own new movie clip. Each snowflake is also a little different because we will use random numbers to determine the number of spikes and their length.

1. Create a new Flash movie.
2. Edit the script on the first frame. We'll add a bunch of functions there. The first one is a function that creates a snowflake. It accepts the number of this movie clip as the `on` parameter. For instance, snowflake number 1 will be called snowflake1 and be at level 1.

   The function creates a new movie clip. Then it sets the line style for drawing. A random number of spikes and a random length for those spikes are chosen. The function then uses simple trigonometry to draw lines from the center of the snowflake.

```
function createSnowflake(n) {
    // create a new movie clip
    this.createEmptyMovieClip("snowflake"+n,n);
    mc = this["snowflake"+n];

    // set the line syle to hairline, white, semi-transparent
    mc.lineStyle(0,0xFFFFFF,50);

    // pick random number of spikes and their radius
    numSpikes = Math.round(Math.random()*5)+5; // 5 to 9
    spikeRadius = Math.random()*5+5; // 5 to 9

    // create each spike as line from center to point on circle
    for(var i=0;i<numSpikes;i++) {
        mc.moveTo(0,0);
        spikeAngle = 2.0*Math.PI*i/numSpikes;
        x = spikeRadius*Math.cos(spikeAngle);
        y = spikeRadius*Math.sin(spikeAngle);
        mc.lineTo(x,y);
    }

    // return reference to this movie clip
    return(mc);
}
```

3. The last function creates one snowflake, but we want to create many. The `initSnowflakes` function creates a number of snowflakes by calling the `createSnowflakes` function a number of times. It also sets a random location for the snowflake and random values for *`speed`*, *`drift`*, and *`rotate`*. These three variables will be used later to make the snowflake move.

```
function initSnowflakes(n) {
    // remember number of snowflakes
    numSnowflakes = n;

    // create each snowflake
    for(var i=0;i<numSnowflakes;i++) {

        // create snowflae
        mc = createSnowflake(i);

        // set position
        mc._x = Math.random()*550; // 0 to 550
        mc._y = Math.random()*400; // 0 to 400

        // set movie clip variables
        mc.speed = Math.random()*3+3; // 3 to 6
        mc.drift = Math.random()*2-1; // -1 to 1
        mc.rotate = Math.random()*18-9; // -9 to 9
    }
}
```


4. The `moveSnowflakes` function loops through each snowflake and moves it according to its *`speed`*, *`drift`*, and *`rotate`*. If the snowflake moves off the sides or bottom of the stage, it will be reset to the other side or to the top. This keeps all the snowflakes falling constantly.

```
function moveSnowflakes() {
    // loop through snowflakes
    for(var i=0;i<numSnowflakes;i++) {

        // move ad rotate the snowflake
        mc = this["snowflake"+i];
        mc._y += mc.speed;
        mc._x += mc.drift;
        mc._rotation += mc.rotate;

        // bring back to top
        if (mc._y > 400) mc._y = 0;

        // one side to another
        if (mc._x < 0) mc._x = 550;
        if (mc._x > 550) mc._x = 0;
    }
}
```

5. The frame script ends by calling `initSnowflakes` to make 50 snowflakes.

```
// create 50 snowflakes
initSnowflakes(50);
stop();
```

6. There also needs to be regular calls to `moveSnowflakes`. This will be done by a small movie clip. Create a shape and convert it to a movie clip. Move it off the stage. Then attach this script to it:

```
onClipEvent(enterFrame) {
    _root.moveSnowflakes();
}
```

7. The snowflakes will be white. So if you leave the background color of your movie white, you won't be able to see them. Choose Modify, Document and change the color to black or a dark blue.

8. Try your movie or the example movie 24snowflakes.fla. You can also play with the number of snowflakes and the range of values used to make each snowflake. Figure 24.7 shows one possible view of this movie as it runs.

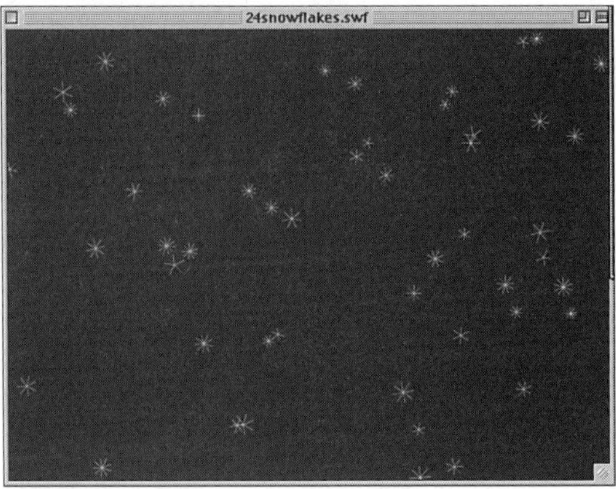

FIGURE 24.7
Fifty dynamically created snowflakes, all a little different from each other.

Creating Text

You can also create text fields from scratch using ActionScript. To do this, the primary command is `createTextField`, but you usually need to do much more to get the text field to look like you want.

The most basic example is to create a simple field and place some text in it. Here is how it looks:

```
createTextField("myTextField",0,0,0,200,40);
myTextField.text = "Hello World.";
```

As you can see, `createTextField` has many parameters. The first is the name of the text field. The second is its level. The third and fourth parameters are the x and y location of the upper-left corner of the field. The last two parameters are the width and height of a field.

The second line of the preceding code sets the `text` property of the field, which changes the text inside it. The result is a simple "Hello World." that appears in the upper-left corner of the movie, using the default font and size. You can test it for yourself with 24simpletext.fla.

You can create a more elaborate text field using some special properties and a text format object. You can read more about the text format object in Hour 10, "Creating and Controlling Text."

Here is a more complex example. The text is displayed in the middle of the screen with a specific font, size, and color.


```
createTextField("myTextField",0,0,170,550,60);
myTextField.text = "Hello World!";

myTextField.embedFonts = true;

myTextFormat = new TextFormat();
myTextFormat.font = "Arial";
myTextFormat.size = 48;
myTextFormat.color = 0x330000;
myTextFormat.align = "center";

myTextField.setTextFormat(myTextFormat);
```

The field property `embedFonts` controls whether device fonts are used to render the text, or whether fonts added to the Library are used.

If you choose to add fonts to the Library and use them in ActionScript-created text fields, you must remember to set the font's Linkage properties so that it exports with the movie.

The text format properties are set so that the font is Arial, the size is 24, the color is a dark red, and the text alignment is centered. You must apply the format with the `setTextFormat` command after you set the `text`.

The movie 24complextext.fla is a great way to test different field and format settings. Consult the ActionScript documentation for the long list of properties of both fields and formats.

You can also create input text fields with the `createTextField` command. You just need to set the `type` of the field to "input." You can set the `variable` of the field to a value so that ActionScript can easily access the information that the user enters.

Task: Flying Words

Creating text with ActionScript can allow you to create some interesting effects with almost nothing on the stage or in the Library. In this example, a whole series of text fields is created inside movie clips. These movie clips fly at the screen and disappear. The result looks something like Figure 24.8.

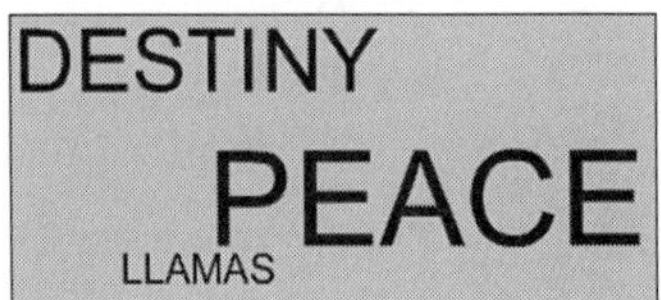

FIGURE 24.8 *Driven by ActionScript, different words fly at the user.*

1. Create a new movie.
2. Open the frame script so that you can add functions. The first function takes a piece of text and creates a new movie clip that contains a dynamic text field with that text.

```
function createText(n,text) {
    // create a new movie clip
    this.createEmptyMovieClip("text"+n,n);
    mc = this["text"+n];

    // set the text format
    myFormat = new TextFormat();
    myFormat.font = "Arial";
    myFormat.color = 0x000000;
    myFormat.size = 24;
    myFormat.align = "center";

    // create a new text field
    mc.createTextField("myTextField",1,-100,-20,200,40);
    mc.myTextField.text = text.toUpperCase();
    mc.myTextField.embedFonts = true;
    mc.myTextField.setTextFormat(myFormat);

    // return reference to this movie clip
    return(mc);
}
```

3. The `createAllText` function loops through an array of text and calls `createText` for each one. It also sets the location of the movie clip to a random place not too close to the edges of the screen.

   The scale properties of the movie clip are set to 0. A *`scale`* variable is set to a number less than 0. For the first movie clip, it is set to -100. The second is set to -200, and so on.

```
function createAllText(textList) {
    // loop through array of text
    for(var i=0;i<textList.length;i++) {

        // create movie clip with this text
        mc = createText(i,textList[i]);

        // set random location
        mc._x = Math.random()*450+50;
        mc._y = Math.random()*350+25;

        // set scale to nothing
        mc._xscale = 0;
        mc._yscale = 0;

        // set scale variable to negative amount
        mc.scale = 0-i*100;
    }
}
```

4. The `init` function creates the array of text from a single text variable, using the `split` command. It then calls `createAllText`. The number of movie clips is stored in `numWords` for later use.

```
function init() {
    // create array of text
    var words = ➥
"Love,Peace,Destiny,Llamas,Fate,History,Cheese,Rainbows,Tiny Rocks";
    var textList = words.split(",");

    // create all text movie clips
    createAllText(textList);

    // remember how many there are
    numWords = textList.length;
}
```

5. The `moveText` function loops through each movie clip and increases its *`scale`* variable. Clips that have a *`scale`* greater than 300 are made invisible. Clips between 0 and 300 are shown at that scale. Clips that have not yet reached 0 are left unchanged.

24

```
function moveText() {
    // loop through words
    for(var i=0;i<numWords;i++) {

        // increase the scale of this movie clip
        mc = this["text"+i];
        mc.scale += 10;

        // hide movie clip when scale is too big
        if (mc.scale > 300) {
            mc._visible = false;

        // set scale of movie clip to scale when it is a positive number
        } else if (mc.scale > 0) {
            mc._xscale = mc.scale;
            mc._yscale = mc.scale;
        }
    }
}
```

6. The frame script ends by calling its own `init` function.

   ```
   init();
   stop();
   ```

7. Back at the root level, use a simple shape to create an Actions movie clip. Move it out of sight and attach this script to it:

   ```
   onClipEvent(enterFrame) {
       _parent.moveText();
   }
   ```

8. Open the Library window and use its own menu to choose New Font. Select the font Arial, or one of your choice. Name it **Arial**.
9. Select the Arial font in the Library and use the Library's menu to choose Linkage. Set this Library element's Linkage properties to Export for ActionScript. Give it the Linkage name **Arial**.

Try the movie. You can compare it to 24flyingtext.fla. Try changing the words, the font, the size, and anything else that you want.

Summary

You can draw straight lines, curves, and filled areas onto the background of the stage. Use `lineStyle` to set the line style and then use `moveTo` and `lineTo` to draw. You can also use `curveTo` to create lines that use a control point to define a curve.

If you don't want to draw on the stage, you can draw on any movie clip's background. You can also create new empty movie clips with the `createEmptyMovieClip` command. These move clips can be used to move around or alter your ActionScript drawings.

You can create dynamic and input text fields with the `createText` command. To change the appearance of the text in the field, create a text format object and assign it to the field with `setTextFormat`.

Q&A

Q Is there any way to draw on top of existing objects?

A Yes. Just draw everything in a movie clip. You can use `swapDepths` to ensure that the movie clip is in front of all other objects.

Q Can I create other common Flash shapes such as boxes with rounded edges and circles?

A Yes, but you will have to do it using the `lineTo` and `curveTo` commands. No other methods of drawing are supported.

Q How do I get rid of movie clips that I have created?

A The `removeMovieClip` command works with movie clips created with the `createMovieClip` command.

Q Do I need to know the width and height of the text field before I place any text in it?

A You need to provide width and height in the `createText` command, but if you set the `autoSize` property of the field to true, the field should size itself to fit your text.

Workshop

The quiz questions are designed to test your knowledge of the material covered in this hour. The answers to the questions follow.

Quiz

1. What one step must be taken before using the `lineTo` command?
2. If a large movie clip covers the stage and you try to draw on the stage with ActionScript, what happens?
3. If you turn on `embedFonts` for a text field, what critical step do you need to do for the text to display correctly?

4. Which should come first: setting the `text` property of a field, or using `setTextFormat`?

Quiz Answers

1. You must issue a `lineStyle` command to set the style of the line.
2. Nothing. The drawing can't be seen because it will be behind the movie clip.
3. The font must be in the Library and set to Export for ActionScript in its Linkage properties.
4. You must set the `text` property of a field first and then use `setTextFormat`. Otherwise, the text format will not change.

INDEX

Symbols and Numbers

A

B

D

E

F

M

Q

R

S

W

X

Y-Z

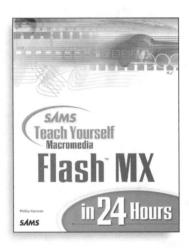